Absender (in lateinischer Schrift angeben)

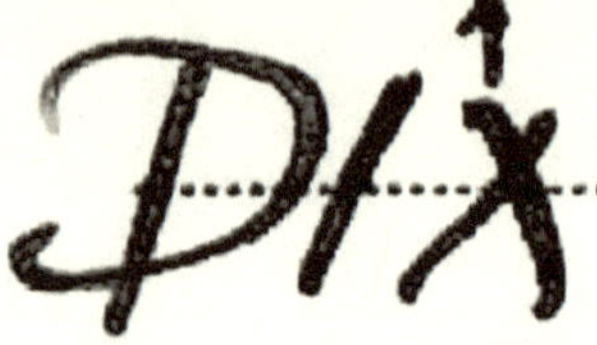

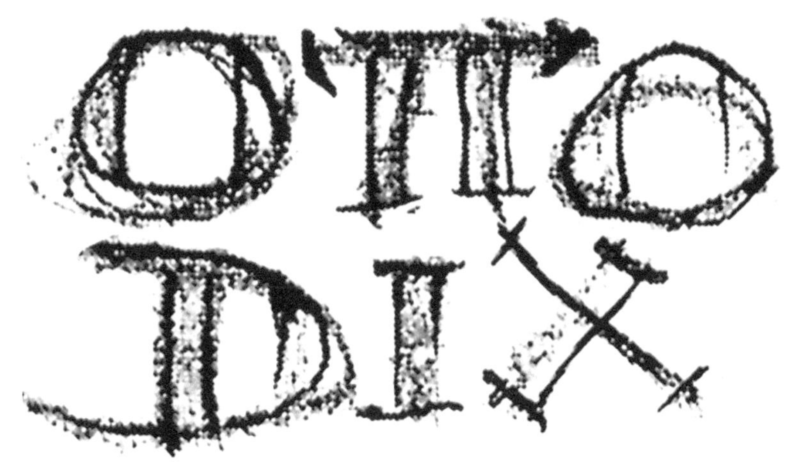
OTTO
DIX

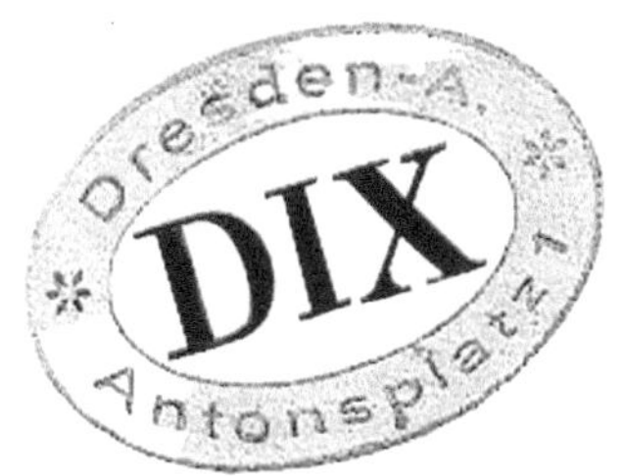
Dresden-A.
DIX
Antonsplatz 1

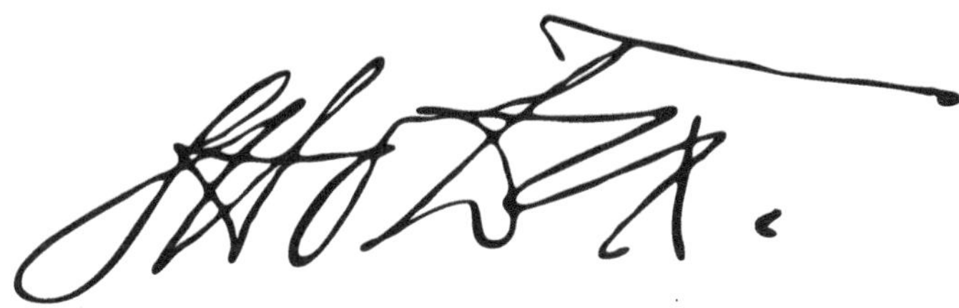

Letters Vol. 1 1904–1927

Translated by

Mark Kanak

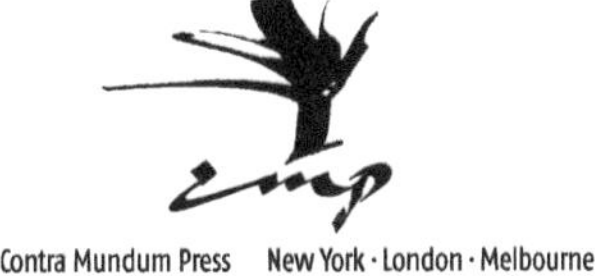

Contra Mundum Press New York · London · Melbourne

First Contra Mundum Press Edition
2016.

Library of Congress
Cataloguing-in-Publication Data

Dix, Otto, 1891–1969

[*Briefe*. English.]

Letters, Vol. 1, 1904–1927 /
Otto Dix; translated from the
original German by Mark Kanak

—1st Contra Mundum Press Edition
290 pp., 6x9 in.

ISBN 9781940625188

I. Dix, Otto.
II. Title.
III. Kanak, Mark.
IV. Translator.
V. Ulrike Lorenz, Gudrun Schmidt.
VI. Introduction.

2016943764

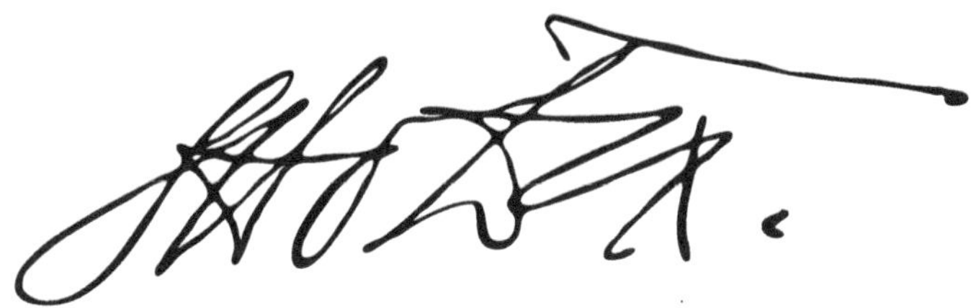

Letters Vol. 1 1904–1927

Translated *by*

Mark Kanak

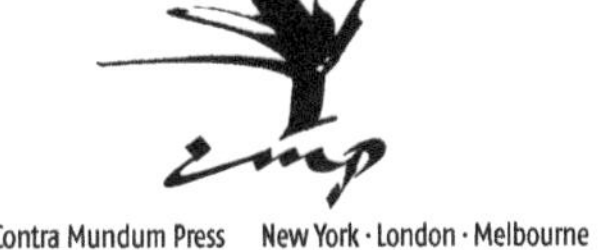

Contra Mundum Press New York · London · Melbourne

First Contra Mundum Press Edition
2016.

Library of Congress
Cataloguing-in-Publication Data

Dix, Otto, 1891–1969

[*Briefe*. English.]

Letters, Vol. 1, 1904–1927 /
Otto Dix; translated from the
original German by Mark Kanak

—1st Contra Mundum Press Edition
290 pp., 6×9 in.

ISBN 9781940625188

I. Dix, Otto.
II. Title.
III. Kanak, Mark.
IV. Translator.
V. Ulrike Lorenz, Gudrun Schmidt.
VI. Introduction.

2016943764

ToC

Introduction

Ulrike Lorenz

An Artist's Life in Letters

"I've never written confessions since, as closer inspection will reveal, my paintings are confessions of the sincerest kind you will find, quite a rare thing in these times."

— Otto Dix to Hans Kinkel (March 29, 1948)

An Artist without Manifestœs

A man of words, this letter writer never was. In response to art critic Hans Kinkel's request to contribute to a collection of self-testimonials of German painters, Dix gruffly rebuked him, surly calling such pieces nothing but "vanity, subjective chatter."[1] And this in the precarious postwar situation, as the 57-year-old — after years of isolation under Nazi dictatorship, prisoner-of-war captivity, and a recent artistic liberation — painfully wrestled once again for recognition and the ability to eke out a living in the German art world, employing critical allegories in an expressive formal language that no one had expected, & no one wanted to see. "Also, I am not willing to reveal the depths or shoals of my soul to astonished citizens and contemporaries. Whoever has eyes to see, look!" Dix further responded to Kinkel. No more than a year earlier the Cultural Office of Dix's East Thuringian hometown Gera had received a similar sharply-worded refusal from the artist to put his paintings and drawings up "for discussion":

> We have now for many years in Germany heard the voice of the people with respect to artistic things [...]. Discussions boil down to the fact that each and every bourgeois type and every blind man wants to voice his little desires. Everyone thinks they know what art should be. Yet few have the sense that belongs to the experience of painting, namely *the sense of sight.* Indeed, a sense of the eye that sees colors and shapes as a living reality in the picture. [...] For what is explicable in artwork is sparse; the essential thing about it cannot be explained, only observed. (July 25, 1947)

In no less than six brief words of gratitude for the honorary GDR citizenship granted in 1966 at his birthplace, Dix succinctly stated his personal vision of the role of the artist in the world: "Painter, do not talk, paint. Dix!"[2]

In living according to this maxim, Otto Dix differed from many of his contemporaries in this respect, hence he had no need to regularly comment on events as most others did throughout the 20th C, so anxious to make declarations about one -ism or another, fighting their culture battles in the process, quite often with the pen. In fact, Dix left neither any sort of manifesto or collected writings after his death in 1969. Apart from some fragmentary lines recorded in a notebook from WWI and some handwritten CVs, one barely finds evidence of any private records and diaries, nor public lectures or articles. Dix consistently and vehemently avoided expressly stated interpretations of his works or systematic self-portraits of any sort throughout his life. He preferred to keep his inspirations and intentions strictly private. Being pigeonholed into one category or another by outsiders is something he steadfastly rejected. He even maintained a cool distance from his two biographers in East and West Germany, Fritz Löffler, an art historian in Dresden, and Otto Conzelmann, a Stuttgart middle school teacher; when writing back and forth with them, he employed, as with practically all letter-writing partners, a reciprocal formal "Sie" in the exchanges.

Conversely, Dix was a painter who imbued his work with his conceptual reflections, as well as artistic speculations, and a secret longing for transformational transcendence in the "magical realism"[3] of his pictures, a resilient, indestructible "lust for grotesques,"[4] and, depending on the piece, sober or sentimental, often boastfully undaunted, sometimes despondently losing touch in means and methods, and certainly occasionally failing, too, in some instances utterly. That says much about the personality of an artist who — repeatedly walking a fine line between the boundaries of the cultural zeitgeist and the political climate — reacted with imagery infused with corrosive sharpness and implacable stubbornness, reflecting Dix's own ebbs and flows in weathering the cæsuras and upheavals of the 20th C. This absolute temerity ultimately also affected the reception of his art, both in Germany and internationally, in both the artistic & academic worlds.

For this son of a principled iron worker and dedicated Social Democrat from the central German provinces, during his own life, only one thing mattered: the image & the work done to realize it. "Set your ass down and paint, even if the Kaiser should happen to come along."[5] This is one of several curt, succinct mottos that accompanied the man, and not only throughout his own early *Sturm und Drang* years. After almost four incessant, brutal years on the frontlines in WWI, Dix was a belated entry but rapid success in the Dresden and Dusseldorf art scenes, full of "dry hemp, sugar, & water,"[6] a dadaist attitude, and actively networking and employing power slogans à la Nietzsche: "In sexual intercourse one finds the highest increase in the world of consciousness, & so it is with art, ecstasy, coitus; the product of highly strained senses and muscles. [...] Art is amoral, anti-Christian, illogical, anti-pacifistic, anti-ethical."[7]

Accordingly, the laconic artist was only ready in the rarest of instances to make fleeting statements about himself, or even public statements. In one of his most important working periods, the era of the Weimar Republic, we have only one single text that has come to posterity. In 1927, under the title "Objekt gestaltet Form" (Object Shapes Form),[8] the Berlin evening paper published a skeptical piece by Dix on the question of what could be considered "New" in the art of the present. In the article, Dix naively labeled himself "a well-known expressionist painter," having long-since advanced from the status of a contemptible personality for the conservative Weimar Republic establishment to a protagonist for New Objectivity. "Anyway, what's new for me in painting lies in the broader use of materials, in an intensification of those forms of expression that existed precisely with the old masters in their forms of expression." Dismissed from his position at the Dresden Academy in 1933 & ostracized as a "degenerate artist" during the Nazi dictatorship, he fled to the extreme southwest, to Hemmenhofen, officially condemned to silence.

It was only in a divided postwar Germany that the media and public urged Dix to make more & more statements about his work & era. As he wrote in a letter to the editorial office of the *Badische Illustrierte Zeitung* in 1948:

"Thanks to the philistines, I've already become unpopular enough through my paintings, and the Nazis' biggest annoyance of all was that my talent could not be denied, so it does not matter if by your publication I happen to become even more unpopular."[9] As skeptical and resistant a contemporary witness as ever, he did however occasionally expound his views on art & the world, both in the GDR and in the Federal Republic, though often through gritted teeth, and in terms of tone and tendency, clearly differently. Whatever he did write was published in the daily press of his old and new homeland: in the West at his home near Lake Constance, and in the East behind the Iron Curtain, in Dresden and Thuringia. A rare exception was the one longer interview in the Cologne *Diplomatischer Kurier* in 1965 with Maria Wetzel,[10] in which he made key statements about his work and techniques, worldviews & life, in vivid retrospect. In the post-war years, however, Dix had really only written three independent texts about art. In 1955, he had penned some thoughts on portrait painting in the *International Bodensee Journal of Literature, Visual Arts and Science*; and in 1958 — quite directly from studio praxis — two longer technical instructions for art students in the publication series "Washington School of Art" about painting and composition and the painting of a figurative composition in tempera and oil.[11] Lastly, in 1966, his hometown Gera finally elicited an endearing memoir about his childhood for the exhibition catalog on the occasion of his 75th birthday.[12]

An Edition of Letters

Apart from the meritorious publication of a colorful, infrequent list of self-examining treatments in journals, letters, conversations & memoirs by Dieter Schmidt in the *Verlag der Kunst* (Dresden), and intermittent, occasional original pieces scattered in print throughout the German-speaking world,[13] with the appearance of this methodically assembled edition of letters, we now have the most extensive collection of original Otto Dix texts ever published. This English edition also includes a translation of the aforementioned "Object Shapes Form." Well over a thousand letters to addressees ranging from friends and family to artists, collectors, colleagues and critics & biographers, cultural administrators and art historians, and academy presidents amongst others, were tracked down by German researchers and Gudrun Schmidt in archives, estates, and museums, supported by the Dix Foundation.

The most comprehensive and intimate collection of letters, spanning 46 years of marriage with Martha Dix, with whom Dix had raised three children, is preserved in the artist's estate. What Dix himself documented & kept (or what survived) — whether professional correspondence or material received from his contemporaries — was left by his widow to the Archive of Fine Arts at the Germanisches Nationalmuseum in Nuremberg in 1977. Dix himself burnt important documents in his first refuge at Schloss Randegg after the National Socialists took over, while another cache of papers were destroyed by Martha Dix in 1938 out of concern for the fate of family and friends after an unexpected house search by the local SS in Hemmenhofen. The letters that were mailed to others, of course, remained in the possession of the respective addressees and ended up, in best-case scenarios, in private estates & public archives. Much of this is being published here in English for the first time. While not a small amount has imaginably been destroyed or lost, or remains undiscovered, other correspondence could not be located, or was unavailable for publication. The greatest and most regrettable gap in the letters is comprised of those from the long-standing close relationship Dix had with Käthe König & their common daughter Katharina, with whom Dix found an existential refuge in postwar divided Germany.

The artist's correspondence is characterized by randomness, depending on its internal structure, the personal attitude to the addressees, and according to external circumstances & events. Some letters strive to overcome distances and speak of the agony of absence from family, working conditions, and related matters. They range the entire spectrum of the present publication — the first of three volumes — and provide a particular, though incomplete panorama of German history & culture. The jagged inner frontiers of a cliffhanging artistic existence become tangible, revealing how Dix braved almost all the fundamental perils in a century of extremes. Growing up as worker's son at the edge of the German Empire, in WWI Dix formulated his individual identity as an artist, "One that has the courage to say yes."[14] Dix's artistic emergence in Dresden, his first successes in Dusseldorf, the peak of his career in Berlin, & his second professorship in Dresden all ran parallel to the rise and fall of the Weimar Republic. Under National Socialist dictatorship he was defamed as an "entartete" Künstler (degenerate artist) & responded physically by retreating into internal exile at Lake Constance. After WWII, the division of Germany became a private burden for him, but also the impetus for a singular East German / West German cross-border existence.

The letters of this edition are divided into three volumes and establish relationships as well as a chronological course of events. In a sense, one might refer to these divisions as in some ways reflecting Dix's "three wars," covering the periods of 1904–1927, 1928–1946, and 1947–1969. The most extensive series of letters are addressed to Dix's wife Martha and to family, including parents, siblings, and children, and we have the artist's friends, art historians, collectors, and brokers, with one of the most important external correspondents being the Ernst Bursche family, who became indispensable to the Dix's survival in the aftermath of the war in the late 1940s. There were vital contacts in Dresden, too, and the two most important interpreters of his work: Otto Conzelmann and Fritz Löffler. Two additional, narrow categories of letters — historically work related, yet still culturally and politically interesting — include Dix's letters to his art dealers, especially to Johanna Ey in Dusseldorf, Karl Nierendorf in Berlin, but also to Israel Ber Neumann in New York, and after WWII, to Florian Karsch and Hans Klihm in Berlin & Munich, and lastly, commercial correspondence with institutions: civic and governmental authorities, cultural offices and art academies and their separate institutions in West & East Berlin, art museums and graphic arts publishers.

Writing Letters in a Century of Extremes

"Secrets should not be spoken aloud."

— Otto Dix to Lotte Simon-Eckener (early 1945)

Whoever expects to read in Dix's letters programmatic confessions and secret messages, or broad statements of artistic beliefs and philosophical reflections, will search in vain for such. Private tendencies reveal themselves at best as declarations of temporary love and rare expressions of friendship. Obsessive extravagances are certainly not disclosed. Even in private letters, the artist seldom or never revealed anything. It is as if his "inner demon" had ordered him not to utter a single thing, to remain silent, where he himself could not hope for a true understanding of his art. "I am delighted that you have guessed something of what lies as the innermost sense in my paintings," he wrote to Lotte Simon-Eckener — the daughter of the much loved Friedrichshafen airship pioneer Hugo Eckener — at the beginning of 1945, shortly before his mobilization in the Volkssturm. "It is that for which the artist himself is neither responsible, nor what he can cause by his own volition. Because in the deepest heart of it all the artist himself is merely a tool of demonic or divine powers that lie entirely outside of his personality."[15] As he only ever rarely did in any other written documents, unusually, Dix expressed himself in a most explicit way in two letters to Lotte Simon-Eckener:

> I have no 'world view' that can somehow be defined. All I know is that I know nothing and that I have a lot of chaos within me. [...] I'm so confused, uncertain, an ignorant man as a thinker, and when I write

> you these things it's already saying too much (because everything goes terribly wrong when one speaks it, or writes it down). Secrets should not be spoken aloud, or only in paradoxes. Anyway, the 'Guardian of the Threshold' warns me with every sentence I write.[16]

Dix wrote letters to his contemporaries mainly by hand, in his sovereign "prole's claw." These were very often difficult to decipher, employing a broad script, with characters and lines flowing between changing pieces of paper. Exceptions can be seen in Dix's early phases when his inner exuberance flowed forth with surprising eloquence, for example, in letters in this first volume, such as the 1911/12 letters to Gera friend Hans Bretschneider, or a decade later in the 1921–22 correspondences with his beloved and future wife, Martha Koch. In the early years, Dix mainly wrote only when absolutely necessary: in times of separation, to gain understanding and information, to maintain connections or clarify business, for settling artistic projects and discussing quotidian affairs. The monosyllabic artist never wrote pointless letters. The illustrated letter comments of the early 1920s to friends and the family of Martha Dix shine a light on Dix as a humorous merrymaker; those in the 1930s reveal a caring father writing out of affectionate kindness for his own children.

Dix had begun writing letters in 1904 — and first attempts at graphic arts work — at the age of twelve, & the first extant correspondence we have from him is a silhouetted postcard to his father. His final letter came 65 years later in 1969 with brief personal & business notes to Fritz Löffler and a graphic arts publishing house. In the decades between, an alternating current of written exchanges flowed freely. Of course, the correspondence of the later years is substantially less full of gaps than those from the period of the Weimar Republic, or even before, which comprise this first volume. Only a few artists or critics of note were sporadic contacts who occasionally received letters: Kurt Günther, Conrad Felixmüller and Arthur Kaufmann from the early years in Dresden and Dusseldorf, later also George Grosz. Franz Lenk, with whom Dix corresponded freely about fears & plans, proved a helpful friend during the Nazi era. At the same time, Dix exchanged letters with collectors who had become friends, and art connoisseurs, especially with pediatrician Otto Kœhler, and margarine producer Fritz Niescher in Chemnitz. The friendship with mill owner Fritz Bienert in Dresden began in 1927 and continued well past WWII. Letters to Niescher became greater in number as the latter fled to the Federal Republic in 1951 and took care to ensure the delicate transfer of an important collection to the West; Niescher later returned the favor with supplies of lithography paper from the Netherlands. Commercial relations with the Old Master collectors in eastern Thuringia, brewery owner Wilhelm Zersch, & especially the royal Reuss family, are available from only one side, or indirectly through third parties.

On the art market, Dix was especially successful with his impressive portraits of celebrities from bohemian life & culture, and then later those from the world of business & politics. Letters join him temporarily with models or their clients, the Jewish lawyers Fritz Glaser & Hugo Simons, and later with Sylvia von Harden, the scandal-journalist who the portraitist famously "gleaned" on the street in 1925, immortalized on the canvas, and who unexpectedly much later called upon Dix again from her exile.

Art and History

Before 1945, museum directors and art historians such as Ludwig Justi and Werner Haftman appear only sporadically in the correspondence. In 1933, both respond in the most insightful manner possible to the Nazis' defamation of Dix.[17] In 1946, Will Grohmann, the agile art dealer and Saxon Minister of Culture, officially reestablishes contact between Dix and Dresden before transforming into an apologist for the abstractionists in West Berlin and the Federal Republic, something for Dix tantamount to a betrayal. In 1947/48, the comparatively extensive correspondence with the later biographers Löffler (who had already been in touch with Dix as early as 1933, informing the escaped painter of cultural-political happenings in Dresden) and Conzelmann begins. Dix only occasionally supplied both with general observations on historical contexts; when it came to spiritual backgrounds and artistic intentions, he said virtually nothing. Only seldom are personal beliefs casually expressed, such as his inveterate dislike of abstract painters, or the demand for emotional empathy in his art, which Dix called "Look" (February 1, 1954). More paper was used — on both sides — in the years of struggle surrounding the monographs. Conzelmann's compact book on Dix was finally published in 1959 in Hannover, one year earlier than the basic Löffler compendium in Dresden,[18] which has since undergone several expansions and improvements. Along with and in addition to Dix's Dresden artist friend Ernst Bursche, Löffler himself developed into a faithful factotum in the GDR art world. He managed not only to sell the lithographs and maintain the corresponding accounts, but was also responsible for exhibition concepts and mediating loans, catalog texts & newspaper reviews, and also for providing reliable information on life and politics in the enigmatic land behind the Iron Curtain. Unlike Conzelmann's eloquent apologetics, Löffler's academic approach proved more enduring, and he himself was a diligent worker in Dix's world; contact with the remote painter intensified in the 1960s. It was also the East German art historian that finally established what to date has proved to be the indispensable catalog of works of a West German publisher.[19]

For the artist's biography, what is of particular interest are those rare documents concerning his desired goals in life, compelled life changes, or plans that might have failed, for whatever reasons, & how those failures were viewed. In these letters, we for example read of the frustrating 1924/25 studio search in Berlin, the 1933 dismissal from his position, the discharge from office and honors in 1947–1950, & the failure (for political reasons) of the Academy calls in Dresden & Dusseldorf, all of which were expressed in different tones to multiple addressees. For the elites in the East, the critical realist's adamant, steadfast indifference to their points of view in his public statements and his late expressive work was deemed politically suspect. Those in the West possessed the opposite ideological mistrust: In his early 1920s work, as well as in his postwar statements, Dix's eastern zone, socialist inclinations were considered highly suspicious. Thus the correspondence with official figures and public institutions in the Federal Republic and the GDR after 1945 provides important insights into the cultural-political & historically relevant personal area(s) of conflict in which Dix was moving. Above all, the various efforts made by the GDR surrounding the artist in the ice age of the formalism debate reveal that the eminent painter from the West was much too valuable as a figurehead for the GDR to ignore, and both officials & friends were all-too-happy to bask in the sun of his growing fame. In 1947, his native town of Gera eagerly discovered the great artist for itself, dedicating regular birthday anniversary exhibitions to him, and even eventually naming him an honorary citizen in 1966. In East Berlin, the Akademie der Künste elected Dix a Corresponding Member, & a year later the first major retrospective was organized and some publishing projects realized. Dresden, the second home, takes center stage in a large amount of the business and private mail. The work stays in the eastern zone and later, the GDR consistently posed travel, passport, and customs difficulties. Currency reform and currency problems were part of everyday life with friends and his second family, as well as the production & sales of lithographs, but the failure to receive a (re)appointment to the newly constituted Hochschule der Bildenden Künste on the Brühlsche Elbterrassen and the complicated acquisition history of the *War* triptych, which took many years, also proved difficult. This edition of letters reveals how profoundly this process affected Dix, which, after all, concerned a key work of his œuvre and at the same time was a model of self-understanding for the GDR.

The signing of the contract in Hemmenhofen in September 1968, as well as the (finally) successful purchase of the antiwar panoramic triptych for the Galerie Neue Meister in Dresden was treated like a state secret until 1990. The painting had been installed in Dresden since the artist permanently loaned it to the museum in 1957. Even then, through Fritz Löffler, Dix had offered the piece for purchase at a price of 50,000 marks. When the sale did not happen, he made repeated attempts to terminate the loan agreement. In negotiations, by the mid-1960s, Dix was insisting on a purchase price of 500,000 marks in foreign currency. (In 1973, Galerie der Stadt Stuttgart would end up acquiring the *Metropolis* triptych for one million German marks.) In this way, valuable portfolio holdings of the state-held art collections had be put up for sale on the Western art market through the East Berlin foreign trade company VEH Antiquäten, which in this case advanced the purchase price as a loan. In return, Dix gave the Dresden Kupferstich-Kabinett (Cabinet of Prints) 44 drawings worth 100,000 German marks.

One of the most important external correspondents is Ernst Bursche, Dix's former master student, who held a fort for him in Dresden during the Nazi years and in the GDR in the rented Dix-studio in the workers' suburb of Löbtau until ultimately fleeing to the West in 1962. The letters to Bursche, which are characterized by great openness and which were conducted employing the informal "Du" starting in 1940, involve especially personal references to current affairs and living conditions, Käthe & Katherina König included, and above all the most substantial statements regarding painting technique, subject matter, and the crucial last turn in his late work to "a new way of seeing, [...] a kind of unleashing" (September 16, 1944).

Focus and Gaps

The greatest correspondence across all three volumes is written by the artist to his future wife, Martha, called "Mutzli" or "Mutzlein" by Dix, beginning in 1921. Martha Dix, born Lindner, daughter of a Rhenish insurance director, was reared in upper middle-class circumstances and had been married since 1914 to the art aficionado Hans Koch, with whom she had two children and lived with in Dusseldorf. When Dix came to prominence in 1921 in the art scene there, he received his first portrait commission to paint Martha's husband Hans Koch; one thing led to another, and it proved the demise of the marriage. Martha followed the artist to Dresden before he permanently moved to the Rhineland in 1922. After divorcing, Koch married Martha's sister, and the children grew up in the new marriage, while Dix and Martha would go on to start their own. The complex family relationships did not diminish the cordiality they continued to share. Mutzli and Otto were married in February 1923 in Dusseldorf. In June of that same year, daughter Nelly was born; in 1927 & 1928 respectively, sons Ursus and Jan followed. The three children softened and somewhat romanticized the sharp eye of the realist, & subsequently their care, upbringing, & education became important letter topics. While the unlikely pair did not remain completely faithful to one another, they did share an inalienable sense of mutual trust, right up until Dix's death in 1969. There were times of separation that compelled a sometimes daily, or regular written exchange: in the 1920s and 1950s, while traveling for commissioned portraits, from 1933–1943, and from 1949–1966, during weeks of working stays in Dresden. In the beginning there are delirious love letters from Dix back to Dusseldorf when he was away on commissions, or in Dresden, simultaneously revealing unexpected facets of gentleness and discombobulation in Dix, the gruff man whom many considered made of granite. The tone naturally oscillates and changes over time, in phases, from loving-buddyish and richly detailed reports, into routine, daily ledger-type expressions of facts. The salutations to Martha changed over the course of his life, from "my most beautiful woman" & "beloved Maud" at first, to "dearest Mutzlein" & "Herzensmutz," then later to simply "dear Mutz" & "dear Mammi." The letters to Martha and the "dear ones" are an ongoing conversation that reflects the private environment of the artist, the everyday life of the traveling painter-servant and print graphic designer, all conveying the accompanying boredom, weariness, and increasing complaints that went along with aging. Among the children, it is primarily daughter Nelly, who Dix referred to as his beloved "Schneckchen" (little snail), who receives little letters from "Pappi" and who developed inclinations for the circus, art, and literature, dying prematurely in 1955, and later to son Ursus, a restorer in distant Munich and abroad, which also stimulated more detailed correspondence.

An edition of letters that is exclusively dedicated to the artist himself naturally has to waive the writer-receiver principle that so satisfies the reader's curiosity and makes more complete narration possible. Given the incomplete archival status, this could not be realized in the present publication. For example, as noted earlier, Martha entirely destroyed all the letters that she had written to Dix. Thus, especially in this important instance, the mirror image of the addressee is absent.

This is even more lamentable when it comes to the extensive, insightful, lively letters of that man who, more than any other, made every effort to promote Dix as an artist: Karl Nierendorf, mockingly referred to (and not without malice) in the Berlin of the 1920s as "Nierendix."[20] His tireless commitment, especially in the crucial years from 1922 to 1927, only ended with his emigration to the United States in 1936. In April 1922, he took up business contacts with Dix; from May 1923, they were writing each other in the informal "Du" (you), a rare thing with Dix, especially in those days. In 1923, he managed the acquisition of the *Schützengraben* [Trench] by the Wallraf-Richartz-Museum in Cologne, in 1924, the distribution of the *Der Krieg* [War] portfolio (in an edition of 50) while bearing all of the accompanying high-marketing expenses. At the beginning of 1926, he organized the first comprehensive Dix retrospective in his Berlin gallery and published a full catalog of Dix's graphic works. In May 1926, he took over all business matters. Dix cancelled his one-year contract prematurely after his Academy appointment in January 1927, but at the beginning of the 1930s, relations with Nierendorf intensified again. In 1935, Nierendorf (together with painter friend Lenk) produced the last Dix exhibition in Nazi Germany Berlin. The Dix-Nierendorf correspondence is marked by the artist's deep-rooted distrust of the world of finance, and his dependence on the commercial success of the art dealer, solutions which often led to emotional derailment and verbal exchanges, which the ever-proper Nierendorf reacted to with equanimity & calm, logical resolve.

The first volume of these Dix letters is comprised of correspondence that reveals much, but certainly not everything. Letter writing, much like complicated, layered painting, demanded a rational conception. No immediate impulse seized Dix, who had intuitively always concerned himself with concealing the sources and traces of his ideas & imagination, beliefs, even secrets. One only ever really comes close to this artist in his painting — or in conversations. "I am a human being that speaks from instinct, speaks from the subconscious, not so much from the mind, you see. But to be precise: what is spoken, is spoken from within me."[21]

Deep in Conversation

"Oh yes, a little brandy and great conversations about art."

— Otto Dix in an interview with Maria Wetzel, 1965[22]

Dix opened up to the greatest extent in discussions and disputes with friends. Although tight-lipped, dry, often grumpy, Dix was equally outspoken, extremely so, challengingly honest, sometimes even aggressive. He could also unexpectedly fly into an effervescent staccato of his very own intellectual promptings, which was striking and concise — such was Dix experienced in personal appearances and encounters. "He follows conversations intently, often without intervening for long periods of time, until leaping in at a certain point with passionate determination," commented a close confidante of the later dada period around 1920/21. "If he is dealing with mentally-trained opponents, he mostly sits quietly for a short time, because as intuitive as his thoughts are, the ability for logical systematization as well as linguistic, expressionistic dexterity is absent. Yet he can, driven by sudden impulses, speak in a lengthy and light manner when it comes to art and life issues amongst intimate friends. His language then has a tinge of pathos and he makes statements of startling originality and conciseness. [...] And he attacks everything, of course, without any systematics. With persistent brooding he intends to approach all things according to their true reasons, which coincidence urges to his restless mind. Violent and impulsive, he lunges at the object [...]."[23]

Nearly four decades later, Giuseppe Marchiori experienced Dix in a similarly exceptional situation — in a violent verbal clash with Will Grohmann, his patron of the postwar era, who had defected to the abstract camp. At a dinner party at the house of publisher Franz Larese in wintry Amriswil, Dix became "more & more aggressive following the meal, all the more so given the rather significant number of emptied bottles [...]. There must have been an old grudge between Dix and Grohmann. The fact is that Dix began an aggressive attack with points & counterpoints, which Grohmann steadfastly rebuked [...]. For two hours, two conceptions of art fought in that old castle in dense cigar smoke, by two figures, representing the eternal antithesis of imagination against reason."[24]

"I have never talked so much. Today was a godsend." Thus did Dix regard himself in rare moments of unreserved flowing thought, as in 1958 at an exhibition opening in a doctor's waiting room.[25] But by far the most extraordinary documentation of this kind — a monologue about art, religion, & war — came involuntarily in 1963 by means of a hidden recorder in his Hemmenhofen studio, and which was subsequently released as a record by Franz Larese's St. Gallen based Erker-Verlag.[26] Here Dix impressively reiterated in inimitable diction the basic principles of his attitude to life and art: "I'm such a realist, you know, that I have to see everything with my own eyes, to confirm that it is so. [...] So, I'm just a man of reality. I need to see everything. All shoals of life, I experience myself. That's why I [went] to war. [...] If you want to be a hero, because you have this mess, you also have to affirm it. Because you have to have been there too. [...] When you have gone to the lowest depths, of lice and filth, of the hunger, the fear, the shitting your pants, then you are a hero. But otherwise, back there, in the storybooks, eh, or in the Bible, the way the Lord Jesus Christ suffered, that's really nothin'. Experience it yourself... be crucified yourself! Existentially! Existence! You have to be everything yourself! [...] Anyway, this is my opinion. But this opinion is a very cautious one, gentlemen. Hidden history, eh? And if these people, now, in film, or on the radio, happen to understand this whole paradox, as human beings, it fills them all with dread too, in this Federal Republic or in this Germany, period. They're downright appalled."[27]

Art as Commitment

"All I have seen is beautiful."

— Otto Dix in conversation, 1960s[28]

Dix, the painter without any written manifestoes, kept close to the reality of the individual and his circumstances all of his life. "One must be able to say 'yes' to the human expressions that are there & will be there, again & again. Extraordinary situations reveal people in all their greatness, but also in all their depravity, yes, as livestock."[29]

The gay science of the affirmation was, for Dix, the fundamental condition of Existence, and the basis of his art. The eternal cycle of Eros & Thanatos, growth and decay (which Nietzsche considered the only realistic philosophy) remained a working & living stimulant for Dix: "The reason is the desire to work: I must do it! I've seen *that*, I *still have it* in my memory, I have to paint it."

"For me, at any rate, the object remains primary, & form is first given shape by the object. And that is why I've always been keenly interested to know whether I can get as close as possible to the thing that I see, because the What is much more important to me than the How! It is from the *What* that the *How* first develops!"[30] — this was Dix in 1927, already one of the most important German artists of post-Expressionism, summing up his views for his growing audience. "I start from what is *seen*," he stated simply in 1958.[31] Or, as Hans Kinkel was able to elicit from him in his studio on Lake Constance at the beginning of the 1960s: "The form starts *from* the experience — it also varies *with* the Experience. Form has never existed in & of itself."[32] In 1951, he wrote his biographer Otto Conzelmann: "The sensuous intuition is, for me, always the most important thing." Anything else would be a literary thought, "because the artist does not evaluate, he looks. My motto is: Trust your eyes."[33] And elsewhere: "I have been called conservative. Maybe I am that, as well, but at any rate, I am primitive & common. I need to connect to the sensible world, the courage to see the ugliness, life without dilution. [...] No, artists should not improve and convert. You are much too low [for all that]. You just have to witness it all."[34]

In his paintings & nowhere else did Dix testify to the "suchness" of the world and his personal view. As a "man of reality," Dix was always both at once: the observed and the observer. His paintings are a reflection and commentary. Art to him was not a guarantor against tragedy, but rather exemplary of witness and daring; something that drove him to the last human abysses, and often well beyond what others might refer to as "good taste." Everything was at stake for him: the man and the eternal existential questions about Eros & Thanatos, violence & passion. For four years in his early twenties, Dix was surrounded, encompassed by the incessant horror of death and his own mortality in the Great War — and some years later he was also present for the beauty of the birth of his own children. He fathomed lure & decay, gleaned pleasure in the brothel & death in the chamber, translated the misery of the petit bourgeois and the discreet charm of the bourgeoisie. His sharp eye was aroused with unerring instinct by fully-formed bodies, wayward physiognomies, and sovereign characters: "No, it was a pleasure for me that life is like this, that's the thing, too, that everything is not just candy-coated colors & beautiful. If it matters, humans can see things in a large — and also a quite small way, even like livestock. That belongs to the completeness of their situation. No, I was not pained in recognizing these things."[35]

Yet programmatic confessions & philosophical speculation were also rather alien to him. "I do paint still lifes," he once said of his war pictures. "It's important to relate things as they are. Indignation cannot be painted."[36] For him, painting was "an attempt at creating order." Art was "banishment."[37] In this way Dix conjured the truths and contradictions inherent in his work, and like no other artist of the epoch, his work spans the attack & defense of the snubbed or exposed zeitgeist. He could never be captured in a phrase. His work was repeatedly viewed and evaluated from opposing points of view: from the left & the right, from East & West, in social & artistic realms, by colleagues and competitors, friends, and the envious. Throughout his entire career his pictures were praised and misunderstood, condemned and destroyed, ignored and admired in surprise. Yet Dix remained true to the harsh decisiveness within, and he himself & his work remain a matter of debate in German art up until the present day: "I don't paint for them, or the others. I'm sorry. I just happen to be such a simple proletarian, eh, that I say: 'That's just what I do!' Because you can say what you want. Why this is good, I don't even know myself. But I'll keep doing it. Because I know it was like this or that, and not otherwise."[38]

1 Dix to Kinkel, reprinted in Diether Schmidt, *Otto Dix im Selbstbildnis*, 2nd ed. (Berlin: Henschelverlag und Kunst, 1981) 14. This letter will be published in Vol. 2 of our edition of Dix's letters.

2 Ulrike Rüdiger, "'Skeptisch. Das ist mein Erbteil aus Thüringen.' Otto Dix und die Heimat," in *Otto Dix. Bestandskatalog der Kunstsammlung Gera* (Munich: 1997) 46 & note 253.

3 The term was first used by Franz Roh as part of the title of his book *Nach-Expressionismus. Magischer Realismus. Probleme der neuesten europäischen Malerei* (Leipzig: 1925).

4 See the remarks Dix made in an interview with Maria Wetzel, "Professor Otto Dix. Ein harter Mann, dieser Maler," *Diplomatischer Kurier*, Vol. 14, № 18 (1965) 731–745. Reprinted in Schmidt, *cit.*, 264–271.

5 A Dix slogan of the 1920s, quoted in Schmidt, *cit.*, 201.

6 Otto Dix, handwritten CV, 1924, private collection, in Rüdiger (1997) *cit.*, 57.

7 Otto Dix, "Vorwort zur Grafik-Mappe 'Werden'," self-published portfolio (Dresden: 1919/1920).

8 Otto Dix, "Objekt gestaltet Form," *Berliner Nachtausgabe* (December 3, 1927). Reprinted in Schmidt, *cit.*, 205 ff. See 218 for an English translation of this text.

9 Appeared as a facsimile in the *Badische Illustrierte Zeitung*, № 12 (August 7, 1948).

10 "Professor Otto Dix. Ein harter Mann, dieser Maler," *cit.*

11 Reprinted in Schmidt, *cit.*, 224 & 229–250 respectively.

12 Otto Dix, *Erinnerungen* (May 4, 1966). Reprinted in Rüdiger (1997) *cit.*, 55.

13 Other publications about Dix's life & works include: Dietrich Schubert, *Otto Dix in Selbstzeugnissen und Bilddokumenten* (Reinbek: 1980; 2008); Lothar Fischer, *Otto Dix. Ein Malerleben in Deutschland* (Berlin: 1981); Ulrike Lorenz (ed.), *Dix avant Dix. Das Jugend- und Früh-werk 1903–1914* (Jena: 2000), as well as *Otto Dix: Welt & Sinnlichkeit* (Regensburg: 2005), & Rüdiger (1997), *cit.*

14 Otto Dix, *Notizbuch aus dem Ersten Weltkrieg, 1915/16* (Albstadt: Städtische Galerie, 2004). Reprinted in Lorenz (2005) *cit.*, 37.

15 As he himself confessed in the recording *Otto Dix spricht über Kunst, Religion, Krieg* (St. Gallen: 1963): *"Also ich muss schon sagen: Ich folge lieber meinem Dämon, der mich irgendwohin führt, ohne dass er mir sagt, welchen Sinn das hat [...]."* Text published in Schmidt, *cit.*, 257.

16 These letters will be published in Vol. 2.

17 Werner Haftmann to Otto Dix, 4/16/1933; Ludwig Justi to Otto Dix, 4/26/1933. In: DKA, GNM, NL Dix, Otto, I, B 12e and I, C 296. The 21-year-old art history student Werner Haftman writes: "The criticism of the individual artistic personality cannot stem from the current situation of a nation but rather from its timeless essence, which to a great extent is reflected in its necessary complement in the European, for the most part. Art serenely goes its way, unaffected by politics, and I think that you, sir, can expect future developments with the same calm and serenity. Art scrutinizes itself; the scrutiny of others is only a matter of the alacrity stemming precisely from this branch. [...] Above all, you should know these officials' attitudes are not the attitude of those always-unofficial people in the vanguard that form part and parcel of art and the conscience." Ludwig Justi, in his capacity as Director of the National Gallery in Berlin, wrote: "It does not surprise me that the current government sees a great deal of umbrage in the attitude that you have displayed publicly. Such pictures were even shocking to me. I saw it as a fanatical treatment of your youthful mind encountering reality, and that would perhaps further retreat from your field of vision, especially if it is possible for the new government to enforce the longed for cleanliness in the life of the German people, in as far as this is humanly possible. I also find your position on the war regrettable, and when I was repeatedly approached from various sides to take your Cologne War Triptych in the National Gallery,

by purchase or even only on loan, I strictly rejected it. My aversion to your depictions of both whores and war has not prevented me from recognizing your unusual talent, and appreciating it [...]. Since the new government and sentiments in Germany are embodied by the National Socialist Workers Party, they would in principle be especially prepared to receive you, having emerged from the 'fourth estate' — and of those among the well-known artists of our time, probably only you — with open arms."

18 Otto Conzelmann, *Otto Dix* (Hannover: 1959); Fritz Löffler, *Otto Dix. Leben und Werk* (Dresden: 1960; 1967; 1972; 1977, 6th improved and expanded edition 1989). In 1982, it was also published in Frankfurt am Main.

19 Fritz Löffler, *Otto Dix 1891–1969. Œuvre der Gemälde* (Recklinghausen: 1981).

20 The letters from Karl Nierendorf to Otto Dix are in DKA, GNM, NL. Dix, Otto, I, C 524. Partially published in Lorenz (2005) *cit.*, 69–71.

21 *Otto Dix spricht* über *Kunst, Religion, Krieg*, *cit.*, 256.

22 "Professor Otto Dix. Ein harter Mann, dieser Maler," in Schmidt, *cit.*, 270.

23 Ilse Fischer, "Der Dadaist (Otto Dix)," in *Das Junge Rheinland*, Heft 9/10 (Düsseldorf: 1922). Reprinted in the Exhibition Catalog *Otto Dix* (Düsseldorf: Galerie Remmert & Barth, 1991) 5–21.

24 Giuseppe Marchiori to his friend Grohmann, in Karl Gutbrod (ed.), *Lieber Freund. Künstler schreiben an Will Grohmann* (Cologne: 1968) 21.

25 Otto Dix, "Gespräch im Wartezimmer," in Schmidt, *cit.*, 226–228.

26 *Otto Dix spricht über Kunst, Religion, Krieg*, *cit.*, *ibid.*, 255–260.

27 Ibid., 255–260.

28 Otto Dix, "Aus Gesprächen bei verschiedenen Gelegenheiten," in Schmidt, *cit.*, 280.

29 Ibid.

30 Otto Dix, "Objekt gestaltet Form," *cit.*, 269.

31 Otto Dix, "Gespräch im Wartezimmer," *cit.*, 226.

32 Otto Dix, "Gespräche mit Hans Kinkel (1961/67)," reprinted in Schmidt, *cit.*, 252.

33 Otto Dix, "Gedanken zum Porträtmalen (March 1955)," reprinted in Schmidt, *cit.*, 224.

34 Otto Dix, "Gespräch im Wartezimmer," *cit.*, 228.

35 Schmidt, *op. cit.*, 269.

36 Otto Dix, "Aus Gesprächen bei verschiedenen Gelegenheiten," *cit.*, 280.

37 See "Professor Dix wieder im Dresden," *Tägliche Rundschau* (16 November 1947). Reprinted in Schmidt, *cit.*, 219.

38 *Otto Dix spricht über Kunst, Religion, Krieg*, cit., 257.

About This Edition

Gudrun Schmidt

"Talent is a vampire."

— Otto Dix to Martha (May 5, 1937)

Otto Dix was a diligent, reliable, & faithful letter writer. He described himself as talentless and realistic, and as "word poor" in a letter to his wife and their talented daughter Nelly. The latter he valued particularly highly for her storytelling ability. "My [spoken] intellectual remarks are a bit too factual & a little too page-filling & actually I'm glad, because one can only imagine how many times in life I would have been embarrassed by what I had written. So I prefer to paint my shortcomings, because no one notices them right away" (Dix to his son Ursus, March 15, 1947). Passages from Nelly's letters, which will be included in the upcoming second volume, differ from her father's letters significantly. On the other hand, examples from Martha are barely extant, because she pointedly destroyed all her letters to her lover and husband (with the exception of a few overlooked exceptions).

Unsurprising, certainly, is the artist's own assessment of himself. Dix was also a taciturn interlocutor, however, making safe & pointed formulations, if called for. This is exactly what we see in his letters.

Quite different, however, are the love letters to his future wife Martha. Dix experienced their 1921 meeting in Dusseldorf as a force of nature, which for him, when back in Dresden, became an almost daily source of inspiration for letters, dictated by a desire for closeness. — Over the years, everyday routines dominated the descriptions, which are filled with great and touching intimacy.

His peculiarity of laconically reporting commonplace events if he happened to be staying in Dresden to work or writing to Hemmenhofen when working on a commission elsewhere or when Martha went away to the spa, mingles with the particularly abrupt jumps between weather, his depiction of artistic problems, and the momentary status of a work, descriptions of film, theater, or concert experiences, encounters, then returning to the weather or a sweater he forgot to bring. A "style," which comprised a foundation steadfastly supporting the family. Precisely because his letters were not written for the public, the modern reader directly experiences the family and atmosphere of the time, and is in turn informed about cultural events in the region and can easily empathize with typical contemporary social structures.

Yet Dix always managed to provide measured formulations in tense situations, as in the year of marital crisis, 1937. In those letters, Dix recognizes his wife Martha as the loser in the matter, who has to cope with the main part of the everyday work beside him, the reclusive artist, without the creative compensation that he himself enjoys. "When I try to visualize and understand all the symptoms that I observe in you, I come to the conclusion that you are just being beaten down due to a lack of happiness. I don't want that, so I wanted to explain everything. I know I'm hard to bear. I also know how unhappiness can degenerate in a woman, namely in illness, taking a philistine attitude to real life and in a hatred of everything that is free in art. All of these things also cause it, and I ask you strictly to think about it. Our life is still short; one should not while it away in distrust [...]. In Love Your Otto" (March 1, 1937). "Be calm and happy. I have only pure and good thoughts for you and your happiness,

I do not associate you with my confused head. Talent is a vampire. One must also take upon oneself the suffering & damage that it causes," he writes on May 5, 1937.

Because of the frequent absences for portraiture work in Dresden, Dix's letters to the family comprise the bulk of his correspondence. With very few exceptions, the Otto Dix Archive possesses all of them.

By contrast, letters to friends, collectors, and personalities are in disparate locations, and many are undoubtedly unknown, in private ownership. Again, there are gaps, too: Fritz Bienert was an important friend & informant for Dix in Dresden. There are only less important Bienert letters to Dix in the Nuremburg archive, and the Dix letters written in return are missing.

The lines between friend and commercial contact are also somewhat blurred in the art trade, and the most obvious example of this is Johanna Ey. She was certainly one of Dix's most familiar and most reliable friends and supporters at the beginning of the 20th C. Equally friendly, the connection to Israel Ber Neumann in New York after he opened his gallery there in 1923. Thanks to the extant letters to him, we have Dix's pointed description after the loss of his Chair and dismissal from his teaching post in Dresden in 1933.

On the other hand, the relationship to the brothers behind Galerie Nierendorf, Karl and Josef, remained tumultuous till the end. In spite of how enthusiastically Karl, referred to by many as "Nierendix" for his loyal commitment to the artist, made the case for him, tensions often arose due to Dix's temperament and obstinate attitude, which was often expressed on the artist's part with a strong degree of crassness. If Dix happened to be angry about a person or a situation, when it came to his letters — no matter to whom they were addressed — he didn't hold his tongue, even when writing to friend and biographer Fritz Löffler in Dresden. More than 600 of Dix's letters are held in the Löffler Estate in Saxon State and University Library in Dresden. The large number is partly the result of the correspondence on the monograph, first published in 1960, as well as the catalog of his works that was also being planned at that time. Questions and answers about titles, dimensions, and dating alternated back and forth and in our edition also justify our selection of letters, because the results of this kind of exchange of letters have long been included in other publications and are no longer relevant. By contrast, some letters to other addressees do help bring some clarity to the dating that Dix often provided Löffler from memory. In this sense, the updating of the catalog of works will benefit from this publication of letters.

The publication of the complete correspondence, meaning everything extant & available at time of original publication of the German edition in late 2013, which comprises more than 2000 letters, would try the patience of most readers. Moreover, this should not, and could not, be strived for in any rudimentary sense. Over time, many letters from Dix to private addressees were inherited and for the foreseeable future will remain inaccessible and/or happened to enter the autograph trade, at which point the trail goes cold.

Letters were selected that in particular provided clarity in connection to the dating of works, sometimes in direct opposition to the dating Dix himself applied to his paintings. He often only dated the works decades later, retrospectively. Likewise, explanations about his working method, tools, and the circumstances of the emergence of a work prove important, and are addressed in the later years as the artist became more conversant in his correspondence about such things. Some letters that characterize relationships, and friends that have subsequently become historically important but at the time were perhaps not so, are also included, which helps augment the list of persons connected to Dix that has become a valuable source over time.

What is referred to in publications as "on the fence" — Dix's artistic position & his circumstances as a "border worker," beginning with the division of Germany after WWII — receives a level of concrete immediacy through the letters selected herein (which will be featured in vol. 2), & casts a light on living conditions on the period that prevailed between the West & the East. It recalls the nagging requirement of having to obtain a residency permit from the GDR for each trip to Dresden as well as the necessary export permits to send his own lithographs from Dresden to Hemmenhofen, which were difficult to obtain from the Berlin Ministry of Culture. This led to the absurd situation of Dix asking his friend in Dresden, Ernst Bursche, to forge his signature on a lithograph because he urgently needed the sheet for a prospective client. In a 1962 letter to Fritz Löffler, which will be included in vol. 3 of our edition, Dix bemoaned all the bureaucratic hurdles to be overcome, including the specific difficulties in printing the lithographs at the Dresden Art Academy: "[...] if I didn't have my friends in Dr. [Dresden], I would have gone to Zurich or Frankfurt to print a long time ago [...]."

After the war, Dix had applied for at least three appointments at art colleges and membership in the German Academy of Arts in East Berlin, which included a monthly salary. None worked out. The documents obtained in archives offer some clarity and destroy legends in the process. Dix was a victim of the Cold War and the impact it had on all spheres of life. This even includes the currency reform of 1948.

Ursus Dix described his father as a man with a pronounced sense of family, who wholeheartedly celebrated Christmas, birthdays, and *Fastnacht* (carnival). He was said to have been an avid dancer. His nickname Jim was derived from the popular '20s jazz dance, the "shimmy." The letters obtained reveal this side of Dix's personality. This was equally the case with his friends in Dresden, as well. By contrast, we have no evidence of the care given to his "second family" there, namely Käthe and Katharina König, nor those sent to Käthe that include erotic/pornographic content. Unfortunately, repeated requests to the family of his daughter Katharina asking for the opportunity to view the extant letters were repeatedly rejected on the grounds that previous representations in publications and films always cast her mother in a negative light. For this reason, the scarce information on the lives of Käthe and Katharina König in the letters to his friends Ernst Bursche and Fritz Löffler in Dresden are especially valuable. The König family also put letters up for auction after the death of Otto Dix. Some of them are still circulating, some are already owned by private individuals, and some were acquired by the Dix family and donated together with the entire written estate of Martha Dix to the German Art Archive at the Germanisches Nationalmuseum in Nuremberg. The present publication acknowledges this (overseeable) deficit.

Additional pornographic content to other addressees is also rumored. Christa Häusler & Lutz Tittel addressed this matter in their essays & notes as part of the Zeppelin Museum Friedrichshafen catalog from 1991; Tittel especially, thanks to the openness on the part of Jan Dix on this topic. When asked about this subsequently, Jan Dix asserted that Tittel's claims were inaccurate. He states that letters that had been offered to him — though he cannot recall precisely — were given directly to Martha Dix, and therefore these form part of the bequest that is also in the German Art Archive in Nuremberg.

While the auction industry has swallowed up hundreds of Dix letters, it also continuously brings old correspondence to light. Many letters from Dix to private addressees have in recent years been inherited & remain unavailable, or were purchased by unknown individuals. Unfortunately, repeated efforts to obtain complete texts of these letters largely remained unsuccessful.

It can be assumed that after the publication of this edition, more Dix letters will continue to emerge. Attempts to reach Hans Kinkel in Berlin for the purpose of obtaining access to letters were also unsuccessful. All mail went unanswered. Dix's letters to Hans Kinkel would have had substantial value, to the extent that this can be assessed through existing publications. This is why the inability to include them comprises a real loss. In his *Frankfurter Allgemeine Zeitung* essay on the occasion of Dix's 100th birthday, published on November 30, 1991, Kinkel quoted Otto Dix, saying he had sarcastically described himself in his last letter as a "dry dog," and on April 4, 1968: "I'm just so inclined that I consider any kind of hedonism, including l'École de Paris, to be a swindle. Now do something about it!" It is hoped that the full texts of letters from Dix to Kinkel will be published one day.

Well beyond proving a kaleidoscope, this selection of letters forms a cultural and historical document; upon reading, it provides a picture of an artist who took a position in his time and suffered from the political circumstances surrounding him, a man that cared for friendships and cared about the value & assessment of his art. In encountering them, we as readers experience far more than a history book can offer, over and above the basic artist's biography, delving into the details of the social circumstances & sensitivities of the 20th C.

Our edition was greatly desired & supported by the Dix family and the Otto Dix Archive.

As a researcher of the letters, the biography, and the directory of persons surrounding Otto Dix (the latter two items will be included in vol. 3 of the English edition), I would firstly like to thank Rainer Pfefferkorn, the Otto Dix Archives, and the Otto Dix Foundation, as well as Andrea and Jan Dix, my colleague Thomas Bauer-Friedrich in the Gunzenhauser Stiftung, the Kunstsammlungen Chemnitz, Ulrike Lorenz, Kunsthalle Mannheim, museums and archive employees with whom we established contact, and many individuals, but especially Stefan Bursche.

Notes

Letters without an indication of source or location are kept as originals or copies in the Dix archive.

Letters to the family are not complete, as can be seen in the answers and events they describe. Generally (& more often than not, understandably so), politically sensitive matters were certainly discussed in person and not sent in written form.

The letters to Sylvia von Harden were discovered by Prof. Marie Gispert, Valence, & presented to the Otto Dix Archive.

All letters from Otto Dix to Fritz Niescher were presented by Ilse Niescher as a donation, by letter, dated February 22, 1977, to the Germanisches Nationalmuseum in Nuremberg, German Art Archives.

After an initially very cautious approach to orthographic and other grammatical corrections and editing, the German editors decided to sometimes alter Dix's punctuation, because it was clear that content without commas & periods or new formatting would cause the reader to have an ambiguous understanding of the intent, & even false correlations in individual cases. Moreover, the reader should not be robbed of the pleasure of reading the letters due to their being obfuscated by presentation issues. However, such intervention only occurred if the content was revealed through the knowledge of the relationships in the texts. This carried over into the translations, and the organization of the correspondence is uniform in order to enable the reader to easily move through the book without interference due to the layout itself. This marks the major difference between the German and English editions — while the German edition is arranged thematically, such as "Letters to the Family," "Letters to Colleagues," etc., the English edition is arranged chronologically, in three volumes.

The spelling in the German was retained after the "Dixian" style, however this rarely carries over into the English, although when instances of vernacular or neologisms occur, they are rendered accordingly. In the German, for example, Dix himself always used the "ß" (sz, today typically written "ss") in his hand-written letters, whereas typewriter keyboards did not have an "ß." He then consistently uses "ss." And when Dix plays with words, adding additional letters at times, such gestures are replicated as accurately as possible in English.

Dix's peculiarity of almost always beginning a letter with "dear," keeping the first letter in lowercase, and continuing the text on the same line, was retained, as all writing mannerisms in the closing salutation.

The special features in the correspondence to the family include the styling "Mam(m)" for Martha & "Pap(p)" for Otto Dix in the greetings. As the Dix family explained, all of the family members used this form of familiar names, including the children, as did the granddaughter Bettina.

In the annotations that follow many letters, all possible evaluation or commentary was avoided so as to allow the reader to reach his or her own conclusions.

Frequently, Dix left his letters undated, and the postmarked envelopes were missing, or were sorted incorrectly. This is why it required a great deal of effort to determine a chronological sequence of the content, and there may exist the odd instance wherein the order of undated letters is possibly misplaced. In particular, the peculiarity of the writer to note the day of the week at the start of the letter, but neither date nor year, resulted to a certain degree in major irritations, because the specified date by another hand often disagreed with the particular week. For the time being, this discrepancy is unfortunately not completely solvable. Letters were arranged and sorted with particular attention to the biography of Dix, meaning according to the year; yet, occasionally, it was difficult to place a particular letter.

It is here that further investigation of Dix's works & details of his biography may hopefully clarify such things in the future.

Abbreviations

AdK, Berlin	Akademie der Künste, Berlin
DLA	Deutsches Literaturarchiv Marbach
GNM	Germanisches Nationalmuseum Nürnberg
DKA	Deutsches Kunstarchiv
HfBK	Hochschule für Bildende Künste Dresden
LAV NRW	Landesarchiv Nordrhein-Westfalen
NL	Nachlass (Dix Estate)
SLUB Dresden	Sächsische Landesbibliothek — Staats- und Universitätsbibliothek Dresden
[PC]	Postcard
[PCF]	Postcard from the Front
[LF]	Letter from the Front
[T]	Telegram
[PM]	Postmark

Letters
Vol. 1
1904–1927

1904

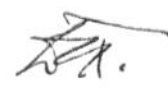

To Franz Dix 7.23.1904 [PM] [PC]

Dear Father!
I should like to visit you once again personally, with a photograph. I would like to show you the bird-shooting. I visited a flea circus, the cinema, and the glass blowing demonstration. I also saw the contortionist and the strong man, along with the smallest horse in the world.
Warm regards Your son Otto

GNM, DKA, NL Dix, Otto II, C 1
Card to his father, Franz Dix ("To Herr Franz Dix c/o Christoph Wehner Salzungen am Mühlberg") who was most likely visiting the spa in Salzungen. Dix was 12 years old at the time.

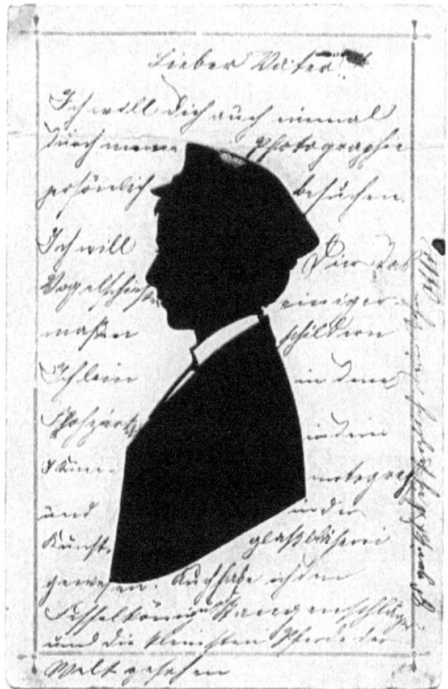

Postcard to his father, 7.23.1904

1911

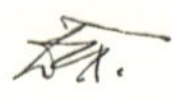

To Franz & Louise Dix [PM '11'] [Dresden] [PC]

dear parents!
Received your package. Many thanks for everything.
Hopefully things are going quite well for all of you.
Regards Otto.
Have gone into the reserves.

Private collection

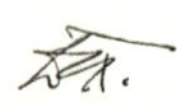

To Hans Bretschneider [early 1911 | Dresden]

Dear Hans! In your letter I truly see a child of our times. I am one, too, with respect to my view of art. What is individual? The involvement of the ego in nature. Our whole time is egoistic. From the lowest pupil to the greatest Master. And you hold my striving for nature, for pure nature without heroic bombastic bragging, for affected? Shouldn't it be considered a thousand times nobler, greater, to master oneself and only see nature rather than bringing the "I" into it all? (I mean only seeing the material side of nature) Of course every nature study I undertake ends up being a personal experience. Yet one ought not experience so much, but rather take it all in, Nature, much like a dilettante. You will no doubt misunderstand, because you yourself are not an artist. What I'm saying is that sometimes you've got to have a firm foundation before you can begin building the house. —

With respect to our lifestyle, you write that "we've been frauds." Are we that no longer, then? It may be the case that, when expressing myself in my letters, one point of view consumes the next. At the moment, I haven't got a single idea in my head. You seem to suffer from the imagined misapprehension that your opinions are set in stone and that you are already a man. Then you accuse me of disgusting myself with some truths. This is absolutely not the case. To the contrary, I am in fact trying to hurt myself somehow in everything I do and am seeking unpleasant truths. I'm now taking care of myself better, more than usual because in a healthy body, I also see the vehicle of healthy knowledge. I'm a vegetarian, even if not completely. I don't enjoy any alcohol, either. I just have to wean myself off smoking. Sports I ought to do more of, dangerous, yet healthy sports. First the body, then the spirit. One should first nourish the body, then the spirit. Oh, what a formidable group the Spartans must have been! What is our art, as compared to that of the Greeks? Diseased, rich in spirit (mine, as well). — Do you think it sinful if one studies the countenances of great men? Or if one wants to be scientific? Nietzsche tells artists "Can you not keep the watch with me just for an hour?" — [1]

1 Friedrich Nietzsche, *Human, All Too Human* II, § 29.

dear Hans! You write that I should come visit you, but unfortunately, I hardly have any time to do so. And only if it weren't so expensive! Your illness has both simultaneously thrown me into amazement and horror. How did you catch it? I advise you to become a vegetarian, too, and to disavow alcohol if you really want to get completely well. For every poison that you put in your body when it comes to meat or other spirits will just cause illness to return. — I'm not much of a writer, so you'll have to technically decrypt my letters yourself. Write again soon. Get well soon, from the bottom of my heart Your Otto.

Private collection

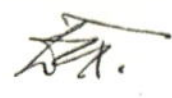

To Hans Bretschneider [early May 1911 | Dresden]

dear Hans!
Finally I've found a way to write you once again. But there really wasn't any helping it. How's it going, old man?! Would love to see you again, but when?

Do come visit me in Dresden. Things are really happening here at the moment. Dresden is fully consumed with the Hygiene Exhibition. A few [days] ago, it was Margerittentag. The whole thing seemed like an exercise in begging to me, "the State goes begging." I had to buy about 10 daisies, couldn't avoid it. Most of the students were buying and you can't opt out. Last night was a lovely night for love.

There is a young girl sharing my place with me. I am really fearful that the whole thing could have consequences.

I'm not going to travel home for Pentecost. The large 1911 watercolor exhibition has opened now in Dresden where one can see a huge range of original art. You have to see this exhibition; there are original pieces by Liebermann, L. Corinth, Weisgerber, and reproductions by the early advocates of impressionism, Monet, Manet, Meunier, etc. Make it happen and come to Dresden. Many greetings   Your loyal friend Otto.

P.S. Please forgive the barren style. I'm not capable of writing a proper letter. More later. Otto

Private collection
The International Hygiene-Exhibition was held in Dresden from May to October 1911, as was the large watercolor exhibition at Brühl's Terrace. – Margerittentag (literally, "daisy day") was a day that was organized by clubs (Vereine) from late 1910 and was especially popular until the beginning of WWI. It took place in many German cities, with the goal of raising money by selling flowers (daisies in this case, but also other kinds of flowers in other German cities) to support local children's hospitals.

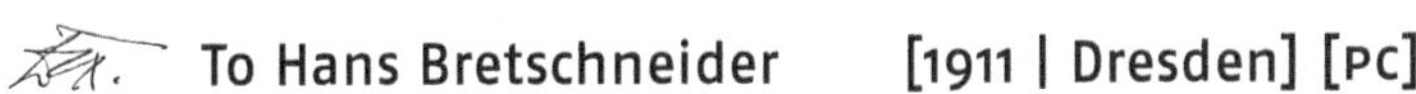

To Hans Bretschneider   [1911 | Dresden] [PC]

Dear Hans!   In the interim I'm sending this postcard. Letter follows right away. On Saturday I'm moving.
Regards
Otto

Private collection

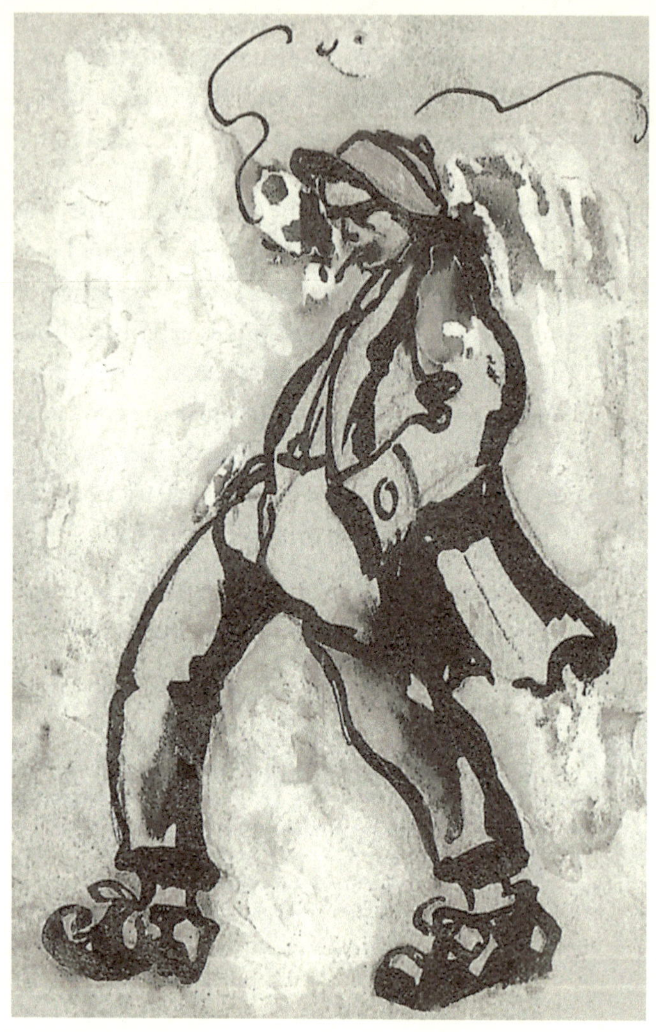

Selbstporträt als Wanderer, 1911

To Hans Bretschneider [summer 1911 | Dresden]

My dear Hans!
Apologies for the long delay in sending you my letter. I moved on the first. I now live at Elisenstraße 45 IV, left, and have a lovely, large place.

During summer vacation, I'll be staying here & working privately. I've received large jobs for portraits from my friend Kroll and am painting them during vacation. I've come up with a whole number of ideas. Here are the themes: "Salome," "Lament," "Regicide," "Captured Knight." How is your "Pegasus" coming along. I never hear the beats of its powerful wings anymore.

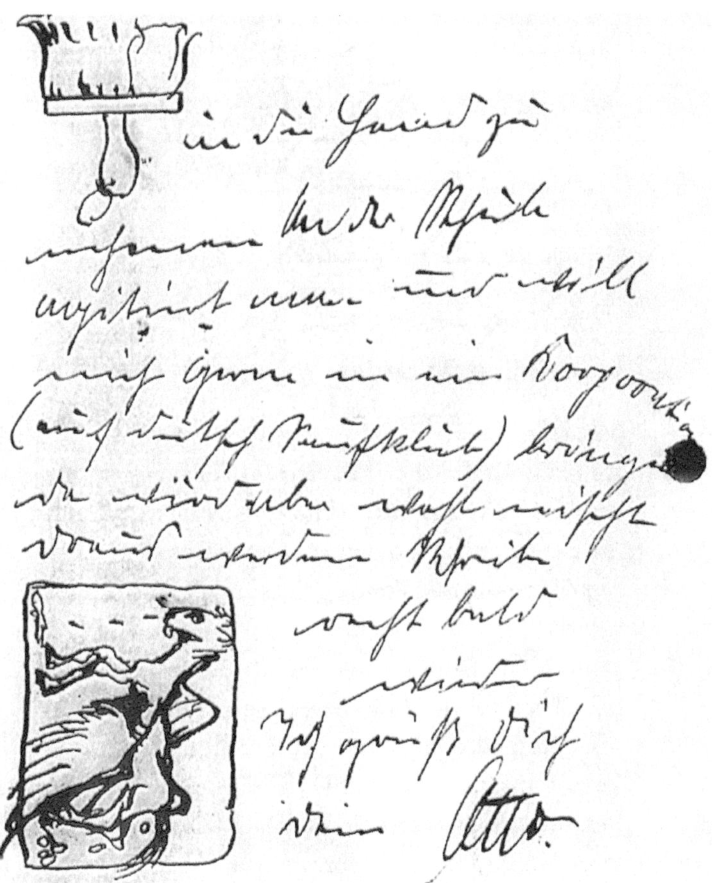

Letter to Hans Bretschneider with the drawings *Pinsel* [Brush] and *Dukatscheißender Pegasus* [Ducat-shitting Pegasus], summer 1911

You ought to be here; then you could study, too. There are people here from all the major countries. — I'm sitting in my place here and writing letters in all directions, all over Germany, to friends, to try to get some jobs. I've sworn to myself that I'd not pick up any large brushes [drawing] in my hand during this break. People are active at school and want to include me in a club (in plain German, a drinking club), but they won't have any luck with that. Write again soon.
[drawing]
Many greetings — Your Otto
How do you like the included sketches?

Private collection
Drawings: Lorenz FW 4.1.4
Friend Kroll: Rudolf Kroll, a fellow student.

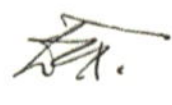

To Hans Bretschneider [late 1911 | Dresden]

My dear Hans!
It's really stupid that I haven't written sooner, but until now I've had little time and also have terribly little time at the moment. Competitions (which I regularly win, of course), private work, and school always keeps me from it. It's exactly 1:30 P.M. I just came home from school and at four I've got to head back to the old hellhole again. I'm attracted, unrestrainedly, constantly, to perishing nature. Thus I always waver between obligation and feeling, the latter nevertheless a thousand times more sacred to me. The work for the Bauernball is already well underway here; I got saddled with a job as a worker in charge of decorating.

I've made a lot of enemies at school because of my incessantly rebellious spirit, but I nevertheless seem to be interesting to people. For a long time I'd noticed that I'm not cut out for applied arts. I simply have much too much respect for nature. I have "private work," but what a load of "kitsch" — You can't believe how much it pains me, if one must deceive oneself & paint kitsch just to make money. But you can't talk anyone into anything; it's as if you're talking to idiots. I have long given up on the point of view that art is for the people & is meant to educate them. Such thoughts are lost on these spiritual fools. Art is only for artists. You could actually come down here; we can help each other out. I've got credit everywhere. With respect to your lines, I'm really not the one to judge, at all. I understand nothing of writing poetry. Seems like a mix of crass naturalism and sentimentality. You write like a fried fish. I also write poems occasionally; I've included one of my latest poems. Please write me your opinion about it, but a wholly honest one. — I find the depiction & mood in the infirmaries of the night better and more artistic; these things are really sensed. You won't be able to impress me with wine and Havana cigars, nor with sausages. I feel much better when eating bread, fruit, & cream. I do have to smoke though, sometimes, to help inspire the spirit. I can, for example, inspire my spirit through special nutrition, so that it can work day and night, without tiring, remaining fresh and at a high level. This, for example.
I have to close for now, for I really lack the concentration to write letters at the moment.

Autumn

1) You call Autumn the
death of nature.
And what a joyful, light dying it is, however!
Not black and clad
in gloomy mourning vestments
No, colorful and diverse,
blue and red
Thus dies nature!

2) You people, linear in
narrow houses
dusty corners of your culture
break free from the product
of your hands
Die happily and joyfully
proud and strong
just as nature does!

Please write me what you think about all this. — Just come down to Dresden when you are capable of working again. (Of course you must adapt yourself to my methods of nutrition) then we'll get along just fine until you are fit again. Write again soon. Get well soon Your Otto. Please excuse my foolish criticism, but I can't really see it any other way.

Private collection
Bauernball: Peasants Ball.
Fried fish (Backfisch): slang for "little girl" or "teenager."

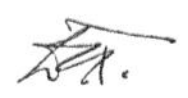 To Hans Bretschneider [1911 | Dresden]

dear Hans!
You know how rarely the need overcomes me to write to you (rather than conversing with Nietzsche, the Dionysian leisure). You, my only true friend (without flattering you). But since today is just such a rare day, I still have to make the most of it, although it's almost 11:15. I've just come from a woman that I previously had before, but who now inspires more horror than respect in me, more loathing than love. You would not believe how much I despise everything now, even the money work that the philistines & socialists consider the only true work. My work is now of idleness, not the clumsy proletarian sort, but a much finer, nobler one. Three books are the treasure trove of my knowledge (i.e., science): the Bible, Goethe, and Nietzsche. But the source, the eternal source of all these products of knowledge, is nature. I've almost become a child again. What an idiot I seem to be as compared to my three holy books, and I stand before nature, like a newborn (oh, if I only possessed the naiveté of a newborn). There's a gaping void in my head. I can sit for hours without thinking. But emptiness is an impossibility in nature. So it could be a maximum of unfinished thoughts that want to develop (I fear too much, these will be premature births). I'm trying with all my strength to render nature as it is, even if it is ugly (that is, nature's rarely ugly, but more so when contributed to by human hands). I am not seeking heroic or romantic motifs anymore, either. I love the sleek, and simple, which to your

eye may sometimes seem naive. Unfortunately, I have an inclination to the Romantic, still. Well, even whipped cream, when enjoyed in moderation, can't hurt anyone. — As for my spiritual, artistic work, I want to paint a Christ figure, indeed, as a warrior for those poor in spirit, with a sword and shield. How do you like that?

You'll have to forgive me the sparseness of the style and the contradictions in thought that may occur, you do know my Janus-head character, which can be forgiven thanks to its immaturity. — You'll have noticed that the teachings of the mind are creeping into the narrative, therefore I have to close for now and not write some tasteless stuff. Do write me again soon, regards, your friend, Otto.

Private collection

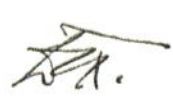

To Hans Bretschneider | Fragment, with poem [around 1911 | Dresden]

Heroic Onomatopœia
From Kypros to Golgotha

From beyond the night rise up
my giant demon wings
and my passions' choir.
Charging forward without reins,
stallions equal, in the morning mist
storming past, with fluttering manes,
mad with lust, neighing,
their nostrils flaring. —

And again the wild scene pulled
me down into the deep valley of sin.
O' my senses flourished.
From the heat of fire in the morning breeze.
This young body's splendor,
white as the brightness of *sumptuous roses*
that do cling close, in the soulful summer's night,
with *moonlight aflame.* —
I was full of young wine,
sparks danced before my eyes and
every *fiber of my being* trembled,
drunk with lust!
And my trembling eagerness blazed,
in wild flames.
They flickered high, and above me,
sizzling, joined together. —
You have burned my heart.
When I left the mounds of Venus,
walking wearily through grey sands,
broken were my wings.
And slowly they ascend, higher & higher,
reaching higher,
penetrating deeper and boldly further —
waves borne, disgusting, sluggish —
and I went so long in that valley of sin,
the giant flowers' sultry vapors
stunned me like an *abyss spoiled*
with purple mirage fantasies.
The bats choir swarmed
'round my weary head
in the great flight and dark poison
my mouth drank drops with every breath. —

And that height I so far,
my dear, would have come
because if not my star,
my lonely star in the pale mist would glow,
if your love had not died
as a wisp of pale light!
O that you never saw the tears
dampening my cheeks each night. —
Perhaps you will feel a shudder
of the hopeless longing power
when the waves gently rinse
my dead body at the shore.
I am so tired, so bitterly tired.
All my castles become ruins,
through my soul resound the songs
of those who die in the spring! —

Write me and give me your opinion. I must close.
It's already 12:30 A.M. Many greetings
Your friend Otto.

P.S. I've underlined those parts that I especially like.

Private collection
Dix here copies verbatim a love poem by Marie Madeleine (Marie von Puttkamer, born Günther) from her book *Auf Kypros* (Berlin: 1910) 117–120. Madeleine (1881–1944) achieved notoriety for her erotic lyric poetry, and the poem quoted here is drawn from a book that was already in its 37th printing. Following her husband's death, Madeleine proceeded to lead a rollicking, lavish lifestyle, travelling extensively, then finally died after 30 years of morphine addiction in 1944.

1912

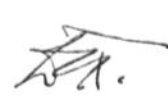

To Hans Bretschneider [early 1912 | Dresden]

Mon cher ami
Your last letter left a truly listless impression. You seem to be becoming more and more sentimental. Must be the effect of your love, eh? Haha. You clearly have the so-called "lovesickness." You should be ashamed. If you don't learn how to renounce this sort of thing, you won't learn how to fight, either. You envy me here in Dresden. Do you perhaps think I am sitting around eating sugar peas? I have to fight, starve, and renounce everything. And this is precisely what makes me steadfast & resistant. You think, perhaps, I am in good standing with the Herr Professors. Some opinions about me.

Ornament-Prof. Hfr. [Hofrat] Rade: Yes, Dix, you can scrawl, and therefore, I can't teach you nothin' more. You are the second coming of Slevogt or Rembrandt, but you simply can't paint.

Flower-Prof. Mebert: There is much that is personal in your work, the color schemes are good, but draw better, draw better. It exhibits fine taste, but don't smear the paint like that. This all means, in other words, "Be good and don't be unusual, yet you are no tradesman and you have to be liked by the people!"

Yet the fact that someone might actually want to achieve something greater in the end, well, none of them think much about that. But I have to.

Our great Master, Böklin, was of no use (in the professors' opinions, with reason) for the Academy. And Menzel had to have a word with Valet in the A.D.B.K [Akademie der Bildenden Künste] sculpture class, "because he couldn't draw." Such nonsense!!! These two Masters could perhaps draw better, second to none, but — they were not good. That's the cause. Everything by the template, tradesmen!!!

That's the mantra. But you see, that's why I'm complaining. Naw, that just strengthens my convictions. Be a man, an artist, and not some sentimental, average guy. You are, by the way, becoming more and more sweet. Regards Otto Dix

Private collection

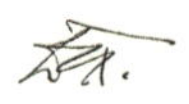

To Hans Bretschneider [after 1.19.1912 |Dresden] Fragment

My dear Hans!

Finally I have found a way to write you once again. 1. Do excuse the fancy stationery (I am starting to take your lead). The Bauernball on January 19 went absolutely splendidly. My decorations for the champagne tent were the best and most original of all the Bauernball. I took biblical events as themes because farmers know nothing but the Bible. An unspoilt rural baroque. In every niche, an image

and indeed
the lost paradise
of the prodigal son
Susanne in the bath

David and Bathsheba
the men of Jericho
Joseph and Potiphar
Samson and Delilah

I'll send you the sketches next time. Then I must confess to you that I'm drop dead in love with a wonderful girl, a student here, her old man is an editor and art critic. She is slender as a pine tree, blond, has as wonderful a profile as I've ever seen, a noble Roman nose like a goddess. Her clothes are as exquisite & tasteful & simple as I've ever seen. But that's not all. She is incredibly intellectual and understands me completely, and my art. When I visited her this week, showed her my work and she asked to pick one out for herself, seeing as how I was indebted to her from the Bauernball, she chose the best of my pieces, that is, what I found best, and you know what acerbic taste I have. I got to know and love her at the Bauernball. I'll have to tell you the whole story in person. My written language fails to express it properly. You cannot imagine how happy I am, finally a woman that understands me, really through and through, and a beauty, too! She is open in thinking & feeling [*continuation missing*]

Business is business, who knows how long it will take before I finally sell something again. I'm sending you another good piece. — I was selected for the committee and submitted my sketches, 3 in number. All 3 and one from Baumgärtl were selected as best, that is, by the committee. Yet this was done without the consent of Wirt, who was standing in for the Director. This fellow found 2 of my pieces offensive, one (the selection of the Israelites from Egypt) because it was against the Jews & the other (the demise of the Egyptians on the Red Sea) was offensive to the politicians. Since the students are celebrating here in Dresden with a grand parade, we had also intended to partake in it. The thing was too red. The third Esperanto Congress or [*continuation missing*]

Private collection
Dix relates above how he met Marga Kummer (1892–1950), his first love, at the Kunstgewerbeschule (school of applied arts) in Dresden where Kummer was studying fashion under Margarete Junge. The letters between the two were passed as "Künstlerpost" [artist's mail] and are very sought after by collectors today.

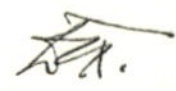

To Hans Bretschneider [early 1912 | Dresden]

My dear friend Hans!

I've had your monstrous letter for some time, but I kept hesitating to answer because I really did not know where to begin. Your love story was sentimental, touching. I'm enthralled at present with a fellow student of ours, a lovely creature! But only clandestinely. This Dix, otherwise so brave, doesn't have the courage in this one. It is Professor Hermann's daughter. My lady from the Bauernball. We all had our pictures taken and will receive the photographs soon. Maybe I will send them to you, i.e., the photographs. But you will have to send them right back to me.

You ask whether or not I believe that you can become a poet, I can't possibly know this; it rests with you. I don't know either whether or not I'll become a painter. But I am "hoping & working" and tell myself, you must become something great. Do you understand, I have to, and even if I lose everything in the process. I presently have all my colleagues in the department under my scepter, i.e., I'm spiritually higher than they are. I am now taking French. When I've learned a bit, I'll write you a letter in French. On Saturday, I'm going to see the opera *Salome*. [*Continuation missing*]

Private collection
Professor Herrmann was the instructor for figure and structural drawing.

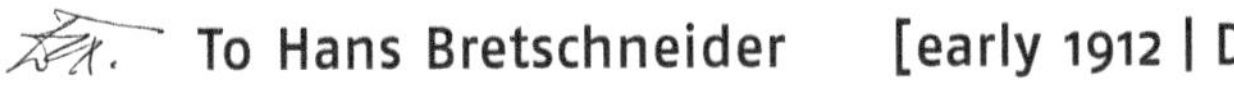

To Hans Bretschneider [early 1912 | Dresden]

My dear Hans!

You've written me a short and long letter about your love story and think I can advise you on it. Well, mon cher, I don't like advising people in such things, it's dangerous. If I were you, I would simply write the girl a cool, polite letter and invite her over one evening to return your books personally. I would then act proud and part ways. If the girl is guilty in the rift and loves you, then she won't be able to find a moment's peace. If it's your fault, then you have to ask her pardon. Incidentally, it's your own fault either way, for you're the one that taught her how to think. In my view, the girl is exceedingly brilliant, is funny, [but] can't keep up with your deep, spiritual sensitivity. I consider the words of our great Nitsche [sic] to hold true:

"women rarely think, and when they do, it's not worth a thing."[2] Despite your greatness you're still a bit petit bourgeois and cannot detach yourself from the "Gretchen affair." If you have the will to be great, then have the will to renounce—. I advise you to put an advertisement in the Dresden *Neueste Nachrichten* and then come to Dresden. You have to get out of Gera! Regarding what Hemann-Jüdemann is looking for, I have to tell you (discretely) that I really have no time for such useless ventures. I'll write to Jüdemann, I haven't located the woman. My friend, do you think you could help me with a job? Hopeless. The man is unpredictable. At the moment, he is in Halle, with his wife. You needn't follow criticism from the likes of him. He's much too stupid for that. What is it you keep writing about my love? I've no idea what you mean. Now follows the "opera singer" story. You are completely, utterly meschugge. I'm quite enthused, for her sake, but relationship! "Don't even think about it."

As for the critique. As you suspected yesterday, I like the psalm best of all, it is great & powerful, I like the "I flame" part as well. But the third, while reading it, I had a taste in my mouth like Anis.

2 This is a close approximation of a line from Nietzsche's *Nachlaß*, hence Dix is probably quoting from memory. As Dix writes: "selten denkt das Frauenzimmer, wenn es denkt, dann taugt es nichts." The original: "'Selten denkt das Frauenzimmer, / Denkt es aber, taugt es nichts!'" (NF-1882, 19[10] — Nachgelassene Fragmente Frühjahr 1882). For one translation in English of the complete poem, see Friedrich Nietzsche, *The Peacock & the Buffalo*, tr. by James Luchte (2010) 110–112.

Terribly sweet! Man, take my advice, give up on the love poetry stuff, that'll do absolutely nothing at all for you! The themes should be powerful, & sublime. In order to give you a sample of what I consider finer modern poetry, I'm sending you a poem by Marie Madeleine.

I really like the poem "Verirrt" [Astray], but it seems to me that you've already cast a sideward glance at Madeleine. You especially don't like the poem. But I do. I understand nothing of writing poetry. In writing a poem, in my view it depends not so much on the external, but rather on the internal worth of a thing. The words simply don't add up if you read them by themselves, but rather in a poem. You say, "I would like to leave Gera, but I can't." That's not true.

Everyone can do so, if he wants to. People do not lack the strength, but rather the will. A firm, unshakeable will is the foundation of happiness. I don't know what else to say, just come to Dresden.
Write again soon. Regards Otto

P.S. I'm sorry I didn't write sooner. I had the time, to be sure, I just didn't take any to do so.

P.S. This nice little lie, I have no time, I hate it, but people always say it "out of habit."

Private collection

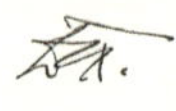

To Hans Bretschneider [possibly Easter 1912, beginning of the semester | Dresden]

dear Hans!
I received your letter. From this I see that you are not only physically ill, but also spiritually not quite healthy. Does vegetarianism have anything in common with dancing and sex? Or do you think that vegetarians are priests that want to deter people from every human need? Do you think these are people that mortify their own bodies through every imaginable self-denial? Do you think that your viewpoint, full of resignation, is correct, arising only from having to deny oneself, not from an overcoming? You pessimists are no better than any priest, not one single bit. You assert that "every kind of sexual intercourse is damaging in our era." That's complete nonsense! — Further, regarding your "strokes of Fate." Do you think that "changing your position" is also a stroke of Fate? — Ascribe everything to Fate (Christians call it God), this unknown Something, so that you all mustn't be compelled to bear the responsibility! Your illness is not even close to being a reason to despair of life and to allow yourself to be cast about by Fate. —

But you still feel well enough to express some divine humor? I don't see any of it. How is this divine humor in harmony with the "insults of your ill compatriots"? Do you think that a divine humor will be victorious there too? — Enough of the spite.

My vegetarianism is not something that is forced where I firstly have to "overcome" myself and fight hard, no; my body quite willingly comes along with my spirit without revolting. That's the first sign of *healthy vegetarianism*. Don't hold it against me, Hans! But you are still terribly pedantic. You want to come to the big city but lack the money for 1 (one) month's living expenses. — What do you think credit is for? Then you want to fall back on burdening your old pals and the guys'll say, "see, he's back there with mommy." — —

It's slowly getting dark in my place & night is emerging from all corners. I'll have to pick this up later. —

So, I ate dinner, lit the lamp, & now I'll continue — —.

I simply wish you would just once be able to come into a circle like the one I'm in so that you can have a chance to think other thoughts. There's a joy, happiness, and levity here. Money worries, food worries, are trivialities to Bohemians; they are well past this idea that only a proper life (as the bourgeois types say), i.e., always having enough to eat, to drink, is the only thing that will make you happy. You'll no doubt assert that "the nation has to sustain that kind of people, they are the cancer of the nation." I assert the opposite. They are the bearers of culture. In all the hustle and bustle of modern life, they maintain the old joy, strength, and steadfastness. This is worth more than all the fat privileges of a good conscience and a full belly. They are people with their own point of view, with them, one cannot say, like Rideamus, "Whoever is nothing, and has nothing, usually becomes a Social Democrat." — —

So you're still seeing "Goscherl"? Man, you really have patience. Committing yourself so soon is really pointless. You'll end up being a homebody. Or do you think that you can still live it up? From the bourgeois point of view, you have to be "solid" as well when she's your woman. Have you really found the "wife"? —— Well, I don't want to harass you about it. I wish you all the best with her. Hopefully you won't be disappointed later. — Today was admission, school begins tomorrow; I have to work and learn a lot this semester. I've had my fill of lazing about over vacation. I submitted to the "Meppendorfer Blätter"; my work was politely returned to me. Do you happen to know a really stupid, naive joke that I can maybe do an illustration for? But it can't be in *demand*. Write again very soon. Your Otto

Private collection
Fritz Oliven, also known as Rideamus (1874–1956), was a German lawyer and writer who was born in Breslau and died in Porto Alegre, Brazil. Under the pseudonym Rideamus, Oliven wrote lyrics, librettos, and other works.

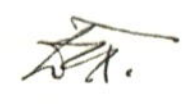

To Hans Bretschneider [1912 | Dresden]

My dear Hans!
Pardon my laziness; I really haven't any excuse for not writing other than there isn't much to say. What should I write every time? You have to write me first and give me something to say. Sometime in the next few weeks I'll be traveling back home, I have some business to attend to there. Are you healthy again or have you at least recovered

somewhat? Does your old man know about the girl? I sent my friend around to see you; maybe he'll come visit you sometime. I went dancing the last 3 days, on Sunday, Monday, and Tuesday I had a very sweet girl. But actually I'm just in love with her body and her little breasts. Too bad. After I've enjoyed her, my "love" disappears in a heartbeat. You'll probably tell me "he's talking to me like Hans Liederjan." It's all the same, for "the woman that isn't loved has failed to make her mark" — "that's all nonsense," eh, but what else can I write, if I don't have anything else to say anyway?
Many greetings Your Otto

Private collection

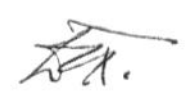

To Hans Bretschneider [mid 1912 | Dresden]

My dear Hans!
Many thanks for your letter. First just let me ask if you need any ink. If so, then I'll send you a bottle. There is so much here, that it has to be sold, just to get rid of it. You seem to be slowly becoming a homebody, a philistine. Necessity has compelled me to become a completely different person.

I no longer play the bohème anymore, running around in modern half-shoes, with bows, multicolored socks, and an ultramodern sports hat. I am, thank God, long since past the time where I need to display my individuality; only blockheads, fatheads, do that. I've given up the long hair, cheap coat, and artist's tie as well. It disgusts me now to have people ſtare at me; in short, *externally* I've become an everyday man, but inside I'm ſtill the same hard-headed guy who, thank God, ſtill has a healthy mind. I have even changed my view of women. Now it's me they're chasing, and so much so that even I find it annoying. I am living well, & happy. As for savings, I'm doing none of that. When my monthly money is gone by the 15th, I know for sure that I'll sell a painting on the 16th. Or get a well-paid job to do. Financial worries only create gloomy thoughts and prevent work getting done. An old ſtudent song goes

> Whatever the world brings tomorrow,
> Whether it brings me pleasure or pain,
> come what may come, rain or shine,
> tomorrow is another day.
> Today is today. —

I have to laugh about your ideal love. Nothing like that happens around here. Wild, I ſtorm out into this roaring life and let people do what they want, to each his own. This one today, that one tomorrow. Being an artiſt means being a man and being a man means having good & bad sides. — Aw, why philosophize when you are much more mature than me and know it all anyhow. I would, however, advise you to seek out a friend who is more mature than you, for I can't be of any help to you on this one —. You wave all sorts of nonsense in my face; I know nothing of that. You're a doomsayer, and to the higheſt degree! If you write me again, write me letters that you've composed in a more sane moment, not a crazy one. Nothing will come of the trip to Gera, of course, what can I do there, anyhow, let myself be browbeaten by these proletarians? I am not longing to see my kin, either. At most I'll travel there on business for a day since I have to go to Schloß Osterstein anyhow. "I love the life of a fella..." Thus begins another Lied. Near the bird meadow lies for many years an old barge in the Elbe. Green are its cabins-walls painted. On the roof of the barge is a garden, red geraniums & yellow cress bloom there. A narrow path leads from the land to the ship. In the warm summer nights, cheerful and fiery songs ring from this boat. Accompanied by a lute. Up & down the Elbe, state steamships or black coal barges move slowly past, northward lies the noisy city with its Florentine lighting — —. Clinking of glasses, merry laughter from below. Dreamily, the lute rings out again, the sounds echoing quickly: "Sons of the Muses, let the rounds be sung happily" etc. Just now comes the verse:

> Sing and joke,
> kiss and embrace.
> For humans, God created wine,
> he has given us women,
> to bless our lives,
> and to gladden us through love. —

At the round table they all sit around, young & old, scholars and tradesmen, the famous and the unknown, all happy, all the brothers amongst themselves, and all looking at life from the bright side. And the next day they're all back fresh at work in the studio or sculptor's rooms or in the sculpture class. That's life; that creates the courage in one to work that goes along with it, so as not to become some sort of animal. So now you know my opinion. I send you my greetings. Otto.

Private collection

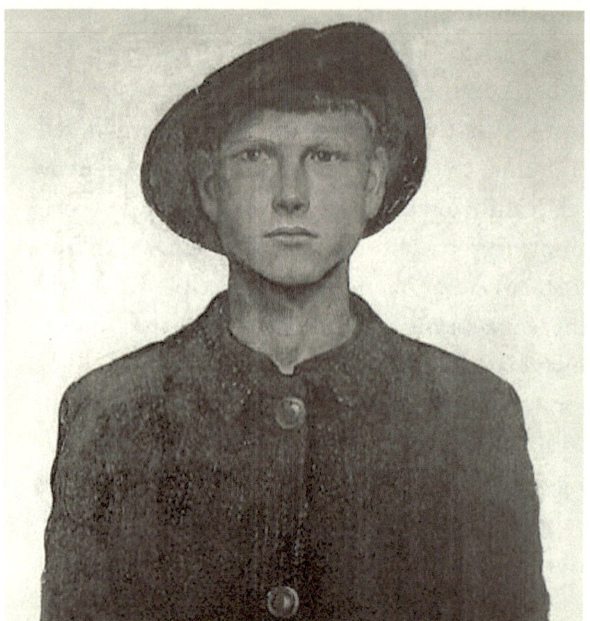

Selbstbildnis mit Wanderhut, 1912, painting

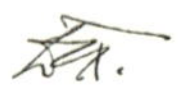

To Marga Kummer 4.10.1912 [PM] [Dresden?]

[Drawing]
I've been sitting now the whole afternoon at home, brooding dully & smoking Vienna ornaments.....
[verso:] Oh, if only I had stylized today! [Drawing]

SLUB Dresden, Mscr. Dresd. App. 2581, 14a and 14b
Drawing: Lorenz FW 4.1.7
Vienna ornaments: Dix is referring to his smoking self-rolled cigarettes with newspaper that had been used to make ornamental designs for a school assignment on ornament and stylization. Thanks to Gudrun Schmidt for this elucidation.

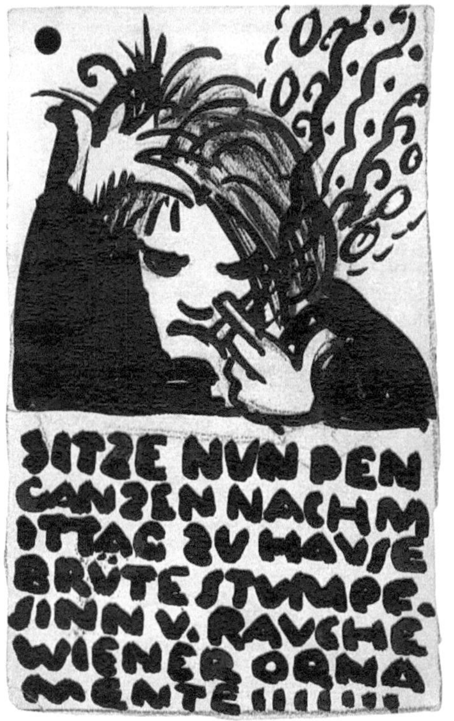

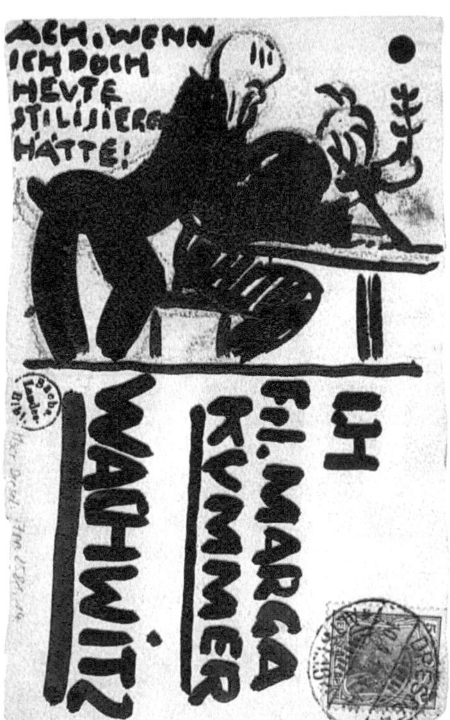

Postcard to Marga Kummer

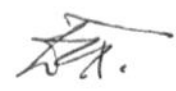

To Otto Baumgärtel 4.11.1912 [PM] [Dresden] [PC]

To Otto
[Drawing]
Elbe landscape on Apr. 10. Morning, 10–11 o'clock.
The man with the jacket in the foreground has
a cold and is continually grumbling to himself:
Goddamn 'tis bad, ah slab, etc. O

Museum Haus Dix, Hemmenhofen, permanent loan from the State of Baden-Württemberg

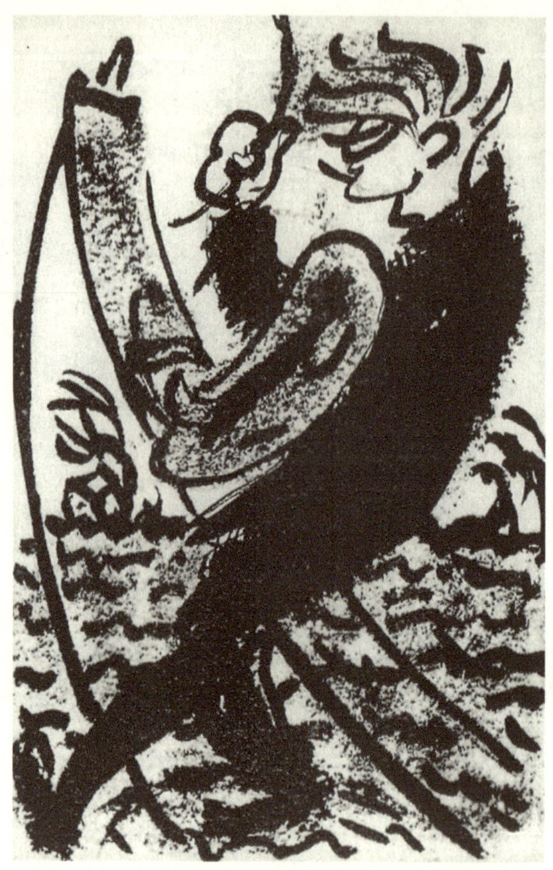

Selbstporträt vor Elblandschaft [Self-portrait in Elbe landscape], drawing, Lorenz FW 4.1.9

To Otto Baumgärtel 9 [?] 1912? [PM | Kamenz] [PC]

dear Otto! Since I've no money here at the moment, I ask you to please go to my landlady and tell her that 3 10 mark notes are in a sock in the wardrobe drawer. She is to give you one. Do you think that on Saturday the stipends [*illegible*] come? Because I still have to pick up mine, too. I feel like going on a hike next month. Do you feel like coming, do you have money? Otto

Private collection

1913

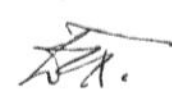

To Otto Baumgärtel 10.21.1913 | Dresden [PC]

Hurrah! Bauernball poster, First Prize Your Dix

Museum Haus Dix, Hemmenhofen, permanent loan from the State of Baden-Württemberg

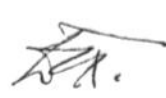

To Otto Baumgärtel 10.21.1913 | Dresden [PC]

My dear Otto!

Hurrah. First Prize. 50 M. So I can claim, according to our agreement, 20% of the prize, i.e., 10 M. When it is done, then you will receive 20% of the money. Of course it is clear that I will sign the poster (also as per the agreement), since the original idea and sketch is from me. Your poster is included, behind. I ask you to please not tell a soul about it. You know that I could not work at the Kunstgewerbeschule. It would be disastrous for you and for me. You needn't tell the secretary anything about it, either. Don't be shy about your work. As soon as I receive the money, I will send it to you. Your Otto

Private collection

On the situation and the possibilities for additional earnings, as well as Dix's participation in contests, see Ulrike Lorenz (ed.), *Dix avant Dix. Das Jugend- und Frühwerk 1903–1914* (Jena: 2000) 57.

– From the 1914 draft, the earliest known color lithographs, *Einladung zum Bauernball* [Invitation to the Peasants Ball] (Karsch 129), and *Plakat zum Bauernball* [Poster for the Peasants Ball] (Karsch 352), the annual student's celebration at the Kunstgewerbeschule at the beginning of the year, served to finance internal school stipends.

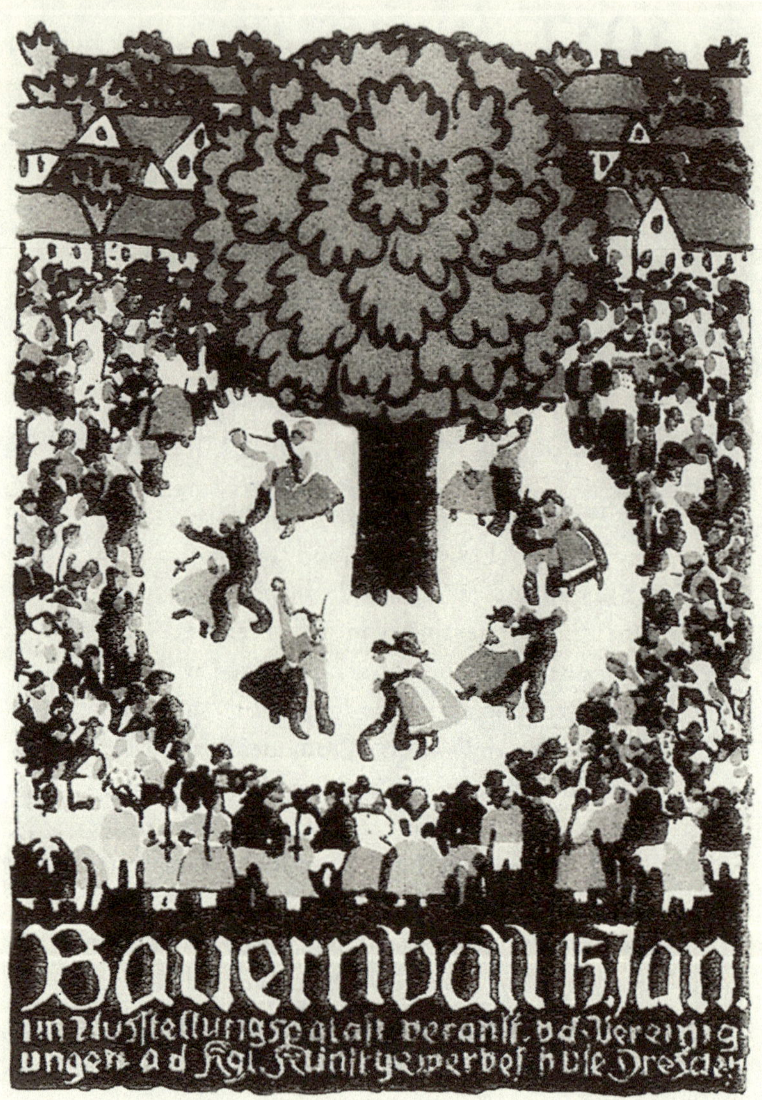

Bauernball poster, color lithograph, 1914

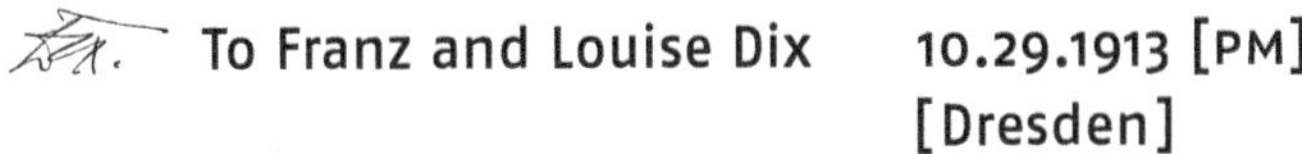

To Franz and Louise Dix 10.29.1913 [PM] [Dresden]

dear parents!
Please send me 50 marks immediately. You will receive my laundry next week; send me back my pictures. Otto
[picture opposite: *The Lovely Cats*]

Kunstsammlung Gera, Dix Archive
During these years, Dix's parents supported him as a student in Dresden whenever possible with produce, laundry, and money.

1914

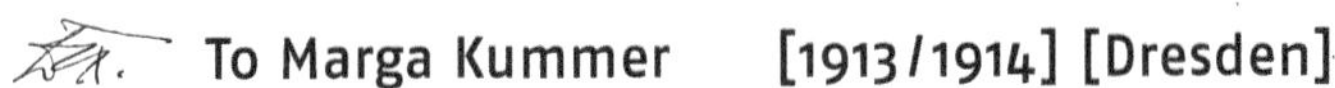

To Marga Kummer [1913/1914] [Dresden]

dear little one! Herewith I send you a number of flowers. They are better thought than drawn. By this, I mean, almost all are physical (three-dimensional), perhaps too difficult to render for you. Please write me again what you think about all this. I received both your letters. If you are making sculptured, three-dimensional flowers, you can allow yourself to use strong color surfaces & spots that can also be deconstructive. In plain German, the colored spots do not need & should not be parallel to the form.
Big kiss
Otto

SLUB Dresden, Mscr. Dresd. App. 2581, 24

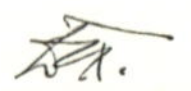

To Otto Baumgärtel 7.3.1914 [PM] [PC]

Is the Nietzsche capable of developing. If yes, then send it to me. If not — — then t[urn] the whole thang pro pro [plus] 75° Your Dix

Museum Haus Dix, Hemmenhofen, permanent loan from the State of Baden-Württemberg
Drawing: *Weiblicher Akt* [Female nude], Lorenz FW 4.1.26

As supported by documents in the Marga Kummer Estate, in the spring of 1914, Dix made a life-size plaster bust of Nietzsche, his only known sculpture. Paul Ferdinand Schmidt purchased the work in 1923 for the Stadtmuseum of Dresden, but in 1937, it was confiscated by the Nazis and offered at an auction of forbidden works in Lucerne on June 30, 1939. Its whereabouts remain unknown, though it may have been destroyed. In a 1939 letter (month unknown, but conjectured to be July) to Otto Köhler, Dix mentions the sculpture being listed in a German art catalog, *Die Kunst*, Bruckmann Heft № 10, for 400 English pounds. Exactly what Dix is referring to in the above letter is however not evident.

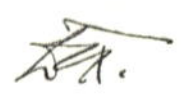

To Otto Baumgärtel October [1914 | Dresden]

dear Baumgärtel! I've been a soldier 5 weeks and haven't heard anything from you for quite a while. Why don't you come to Dresden before we move out. The service is interesting (i.e., even the most interesting thing is boring), but also very difficult, if we have to move 5 cannoneers for example, the heavy artillery are set in motion at the command "battery move out" and must make their way up the grenadier's hill. There's no cause for complaint. That's a "lousy edge." Otherwise, everything is bene, just no money (as ever). I've had a terrible cold since I signed up and the mess hall bread doesn't help either. Interestingly, "something new" was read to us in training yesterday. When fatigued, you are supposed to cross your arms for one minute.

This is refreshing, or one can push upwards forcefully (in the event of leg fatigue) exerting energy against the upper arm, causing one [to work?], thus defeating the tiredness. I'm in my quarters now. It's 9:45, at 10 I have to be back, take care and write soon. Your Dix
4. Field art. Reg. 48 Dresden 1. reserve inf.

1915

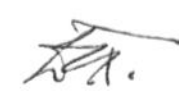

To Marga Kummer — Jan. 26, 1915 [Dresden or Bautzen]

dearest!
In spite of the fact that I'm a soldier now, I still keep to my high-fallootin' plans for art. For example, I intend to immortalize you in sculpture. For this, you absolutely have to sit for me [drawing] or similar [drawing] or the like
I myself am not quite sure as of yet. I painted today.

SLUB Dresden, Mscr. Dresd. App. 2581, 20
Drawings: Lorenz FW 4.1.27 and 28

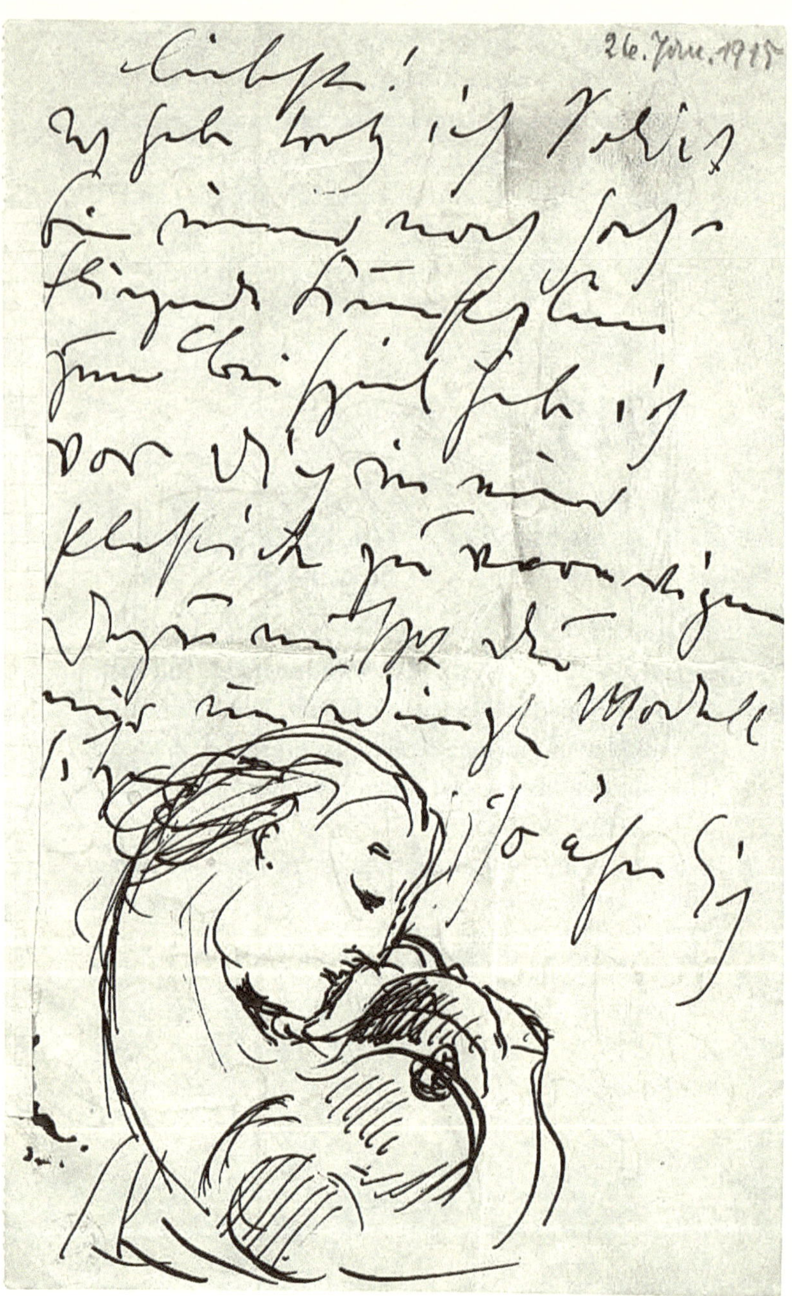

26. Juni. 1915

Marga als Aktmodell [Marga as a nude model], 1915

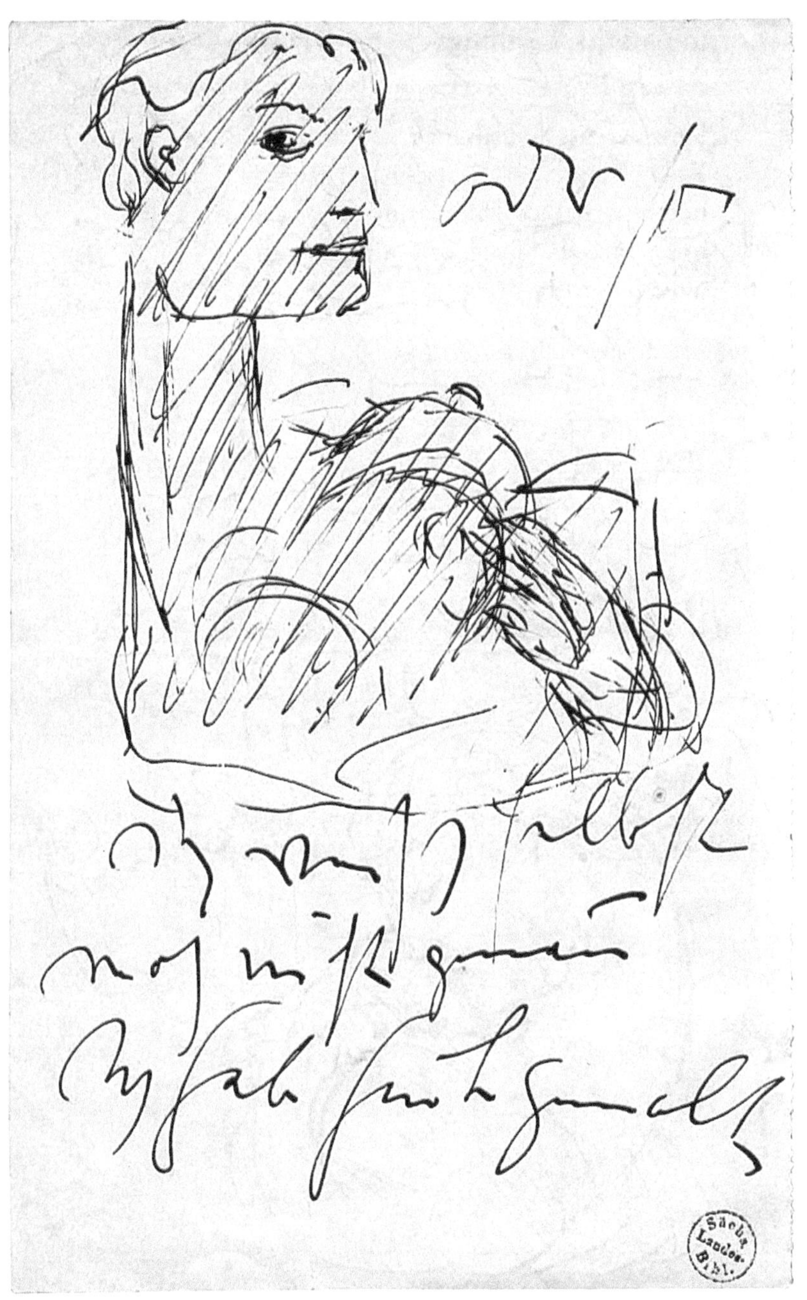
Sächs. Landes. Bibl.

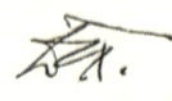

To parents & siblings 6.10[?].1915 [PM | Dresden-Neustadt] [PCF]

Dear parents and siblings
Today, Monday, we're still in the garrison. I believe, however, that we'll be moving out at the end of this week. Here is a picture of our quarters.
Greetings Otto

GNM, DKA, NL Dix, Otto II, C 1
Photo on the front: "Quarters 160"

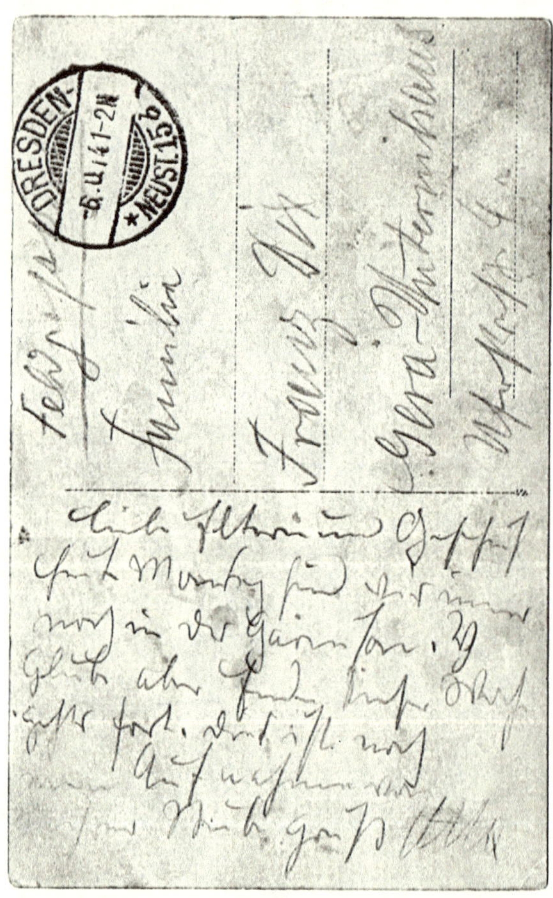

Field postcard to the Franz Dix family in Gera, June 10 [?], 1915

To Lili Schultz 11.11 [1915] [between St. Souplet / Aubérive]

dear Lili!
A thousand thank yous for the package. We are temporarily between St. Souplet & Aubérive, in regimental reserve. The cigarettes are very good! Today, on the 11th, peace? Here we see none of that. Congratulations on your success. Of course I'm "nice" to people, as long as they obey orders.
Many heartfelt regards
Your Dix

Drawing on a separate sheet of paper: Lorenz FW 1.0.64

To Helene Jakob [PCF] attached to a letter from 11.13.1915

[Drawing]
[drawn, verso:] Dugout in the Reg. Reserve, beds are left & right, in the foreground the boots of Sächs.
Corporal Dix
Heartfelt regards

Kunstsammlung Gera, Dix Archive
Drawing: *Unterstand in der Regimentsreserve* [Dugout in the Regimental Reserve], Lorenz WK 1.0.5

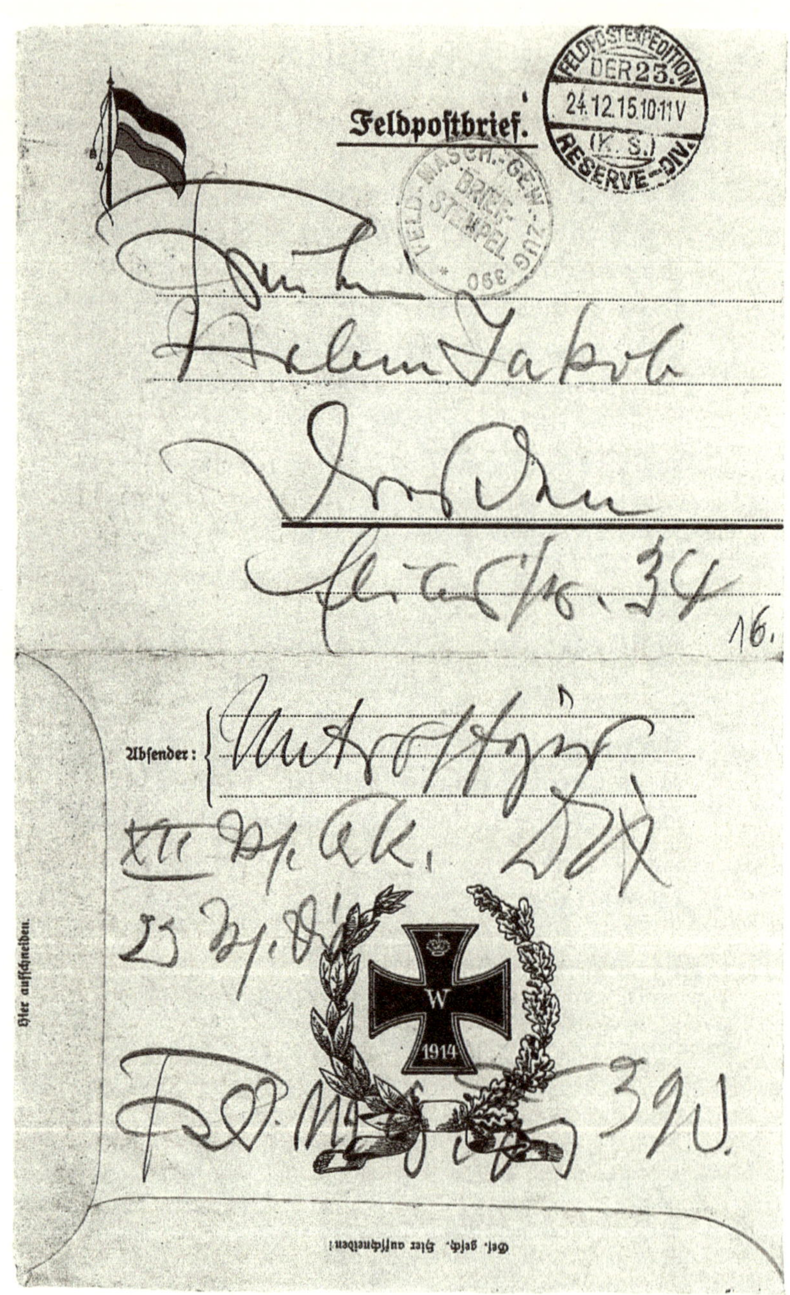

Postcard from the front to Helene Jakob

1916

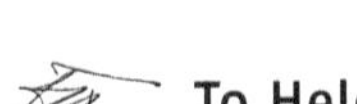

To Helene Jakob [1.1.1916] [LF]

Kara samideanino!
Yesterday, on December 31, I received your Christmas package from the royal K.G. Sch. I was most impressed, of course, by the magnificent graphite pencil, it's splendid! ... Today is January 1. Yesterday aftern. at 12 o'clock the hole suddenly became mobile. The balloon guns (by the way, a very stupidly superfluous contraption because it wastes expensive ammunition and doesn't hit anything) shot firecrackers. The infantry shot like mad and we thought the French were already finished. The 102nd was playing on the chapel square. The Kapelle played "Now Thank We All Our God" not because it was a new year, but because we all happily survived the old one. The streets here have German names, like "Hindenburgstr.," "Bismarck Str.," the filthiest street is always called "Pariser Str." —

We had a mug of beer and the soldiers were completely "fired up." Tomorrow afternoon we're going into position...

Private collection
Kara samideanino: Esperanto for "dear kindred spirit"

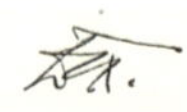

To Franz Dix [Juniville 1916]

dear Father
Many thanks for your letter. I've written you all often enough where I am. Lately, I've almost constantly been in Champagne on a strip of land between Reims and extending in a southeasterly direction to Somme à Prg. [Picardie]. Our division has been moved from its previous position & will probably be moved to the Engl./Fren. front, where Fritz is. We also don't know exactly, anyway, we've now reached Juniville in the Champagne region. Tomorrow we move on. We have relatively good [*the rest is missing*]

GNM, DKA, NL Dix, Otto II, C 1
Fritz: Dix's younger brother.

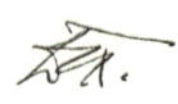

To Helene Jakob [7.1.1916] [LF]

Kara samideanino!
Many thanks for your little package with the pencils & the eraser. It's sad, it angers me that I'm not able to draw much when I'm in position, when I'm in reserves I do more. The weather is grey & inhospitable and if I get cold feet while standing, my stomach immediately feels bad, then I have to keep moving continually.

The French position stands before us like an impregnable map. Dead silence, emptiness, only the labyrinthine trenches and passages arising from the grey-green of the earth. Yesterday afternoon, the enemy artillery entertained us with three full hours of continuous fire. In places, the fire increased to a barrage. We squatted in our dugouts. "On highest alert," an attack expected. On a short section of the front is a dangerous curve; at night, six machine guns are set up there. The French did not attack, however. Success amounted to some wounded, some buried and shot-up trenches.

Directly next to our shelter is a covered artillery observation tower, which is supported by railway tracks with a 30 cm strong iron concrete plate. The tracks were shredded by direct hits and the concrete plate or cover [*illegible*] was blown apart.

The pressure soon forced us down, of course, and the ditch was literally saturated with iron fragments. — The night is dark as pitch and I'm on patrol until 12 o'clock, it goes on and on and it's a relief when the flares ascend into the skies. The infantry goes on shooting, as always. The French bullets whistle over our trenches, otherwise everything is calm. The boredom, the lice, and the fleas, it all secretly consumes you. Otherwise nothing at all is hidden when you're a soldier, except during the ongoing barrage. — I will send 1 mark to you when I get my next wages, please use it to get me a sketchpad, you already know, the kind I had sent to me in Bautzen, with yellowish paper and a red-brown cover and not the large one, but the next smaller one! You know the one I mean.

I send you & your loved ones best regards from my heart   Your Dix

Private collection

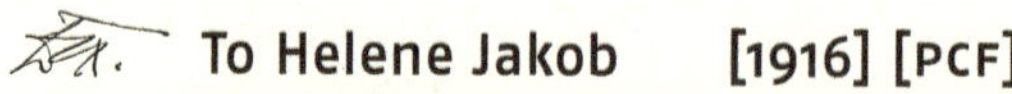

To Helene Jakob [1916] [PCF]

[Drawing]
[reverse, in H. Jakob's handwriting: He writes:]
The battalion's little forest station
The trench winds through a little pine forest. Like waves in the sea the earthen barriers sway, above, over the edge it's flooded — mangled trees, as if the sea had spewed it forth, & beneath it all, animals, living in caves, the rats, mice, men, lice and fleas. The steel roots, deeply sunk in the earth's entrails, but those below not moving an inch.

Kunstsammlung Gera, Dix Archive
Drawing: *Das Bataillonswäldchen* [The battalion's little forest station], Lorenz WK 1.0.17

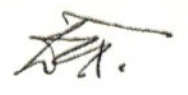

To Helene Jakob [1.17.1916] [LF]

The studies I'm sending you today may perhaps appear somewhat strange to you. Trenches between Aubérive & Jauplet. — 1. Grave of a French soldier. He fell here, in this place. Perhaps no one even knows his name. He was placed into a large 21er grenade crater and covered with earth. The helmet on top! A wooden cross, upon which is written: "Here lies a brave French soldier." This is written on every one of these wooden crosses. It is a lovely grave, some three meters deep. — 2. This is barely a meter deep. Coincidentally, the communication trench was later dug out there, and now the man is stretching his leg out over the trench — ... Yet it would be much less beautiful, however, if he just happened to stick his head out over the trench. At Marie-à-Py and Douarin whole lines of defense consist of dead men whose heads are sticking out ...

Kunstsammlung Gera, Dix Archive

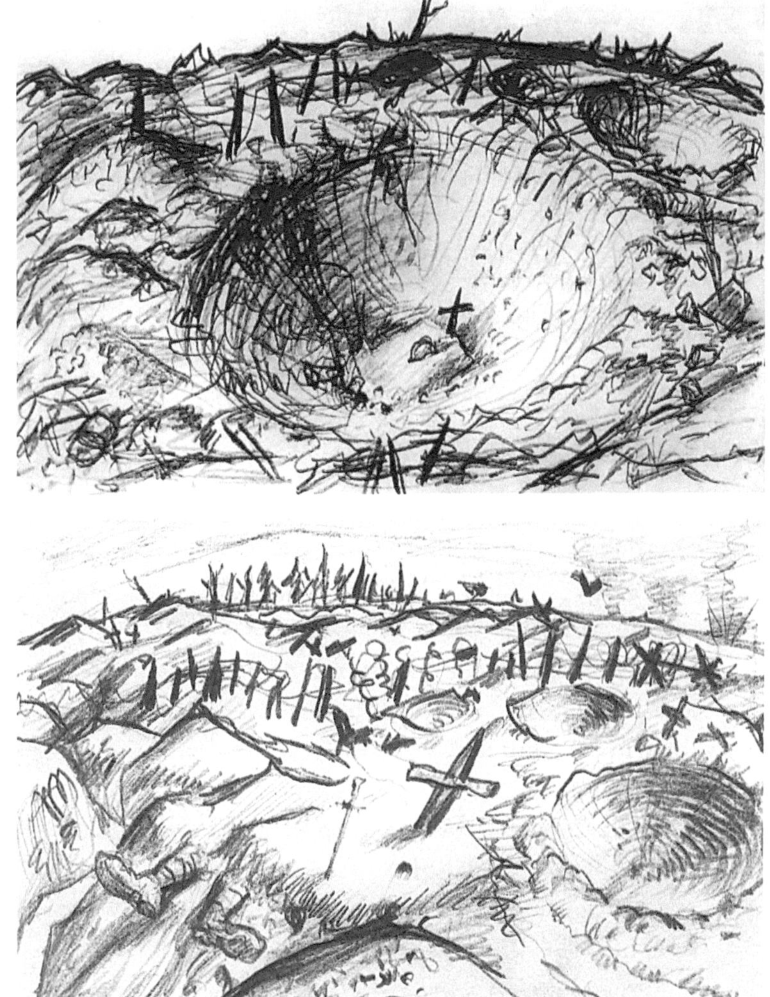

Drawings: *Ein schönes Grab* [A Lovely Grave] and *Ein schlechtes Grab* [A Bad Grave], Lorenz WK 1.0.20 and WK 1.0.19

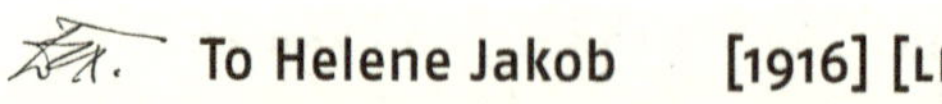

To Helene Jakob [1916] [LF]

[drawing]
[drawn, verso: in H. Jakob's handwriting: He writes:] Decamping in the moonlight. Scattering & clattering, an endless line, armed to the teeth. Around endless curves, everything unfolding silently, because the French are none too shy with the shells. So we scatter, silently — like the Israelites approaching the Red Sea (that was probably much the same) [and] could not have been any quieter than we were.

Kunstsammlung Gera, Dix Archive
Drawing: *Eine Ablösung bei Mondenschein* [Decamping by Moonlight], Lorenz WK 1.0.18

To Helene Jakob [1916] [PCF]

Fräulein Helene Jakob
Dresden
Eliasstr. 34 1916
[drawing]
[opposite, drawn.:] In the rubble of Aubérive — Full impact, shell craters in the villages. / Everything in the area seems to be subject to the dynamics of this enormous sym[m]etrical funnel. They're the eye-sockets of the earth, and spiraling round and round them, these painfully fantastic lines. Those are not houses anymore, nobody actually thinks so either. They are organisms of a special type, with their own laws & living conditions. There are only holes with stones scattered around, or barren skeletons. A strange, rare beauty is speaking here. —

Regards
samideane [kindred spirit]
Dix

Kunstsammlung Gera, Dix Archive
Drawing: *In den Trümmern von Aubérive* [In the rubble of Aubérive], Lorenz WK 1.0.21

To Helene Jakob [2.13.1916] [LF]

[...] I thank you quite cordially for everything and have already begun reading the Schopenhauer. It is written in a very accessible, interesting way. *The Gothic Rooms* is naturally much too fine for the field.[3] I would be interested in some Schleiermacher, too, I've heard quite a lot about the man, but haven't read anything of his yet. — I don't think that I'll be able to exhibit anything before the end of the war; it's so difficult, if one cannot procure the things oneself. On top of that, I can't see any financial advantages at all from it, & as for morally, even less so.

The pupils of Athens had to sit silently seven (or even 10) years and they were certainly chatterboxes. Shouldn't I be able to bear it even longer still, sitting around in the darkness of anonymity? I have the tenacity to endure a slow maturation. For several days now I haven't been able to draw a thing, the weather was nasty, snow & wind. Moreover, I had to lie around in the dugout for 2 days because of gastrointestinal catarrh and nurse myself back to "great form" eating field crispbread and coffee.

3 Strindberg's 1904 novel, *Götiska rummen*.

And on top of that, the French and their blaring racket, it's a real aggravation, the past days in the village, there was no hope to do a thing when it comes to art. One sees such horrible things! [...]

Private collection

To Helene Jakob [2.18.1916] [LF]

[Translated from Esperanto:] Kara samideanino! Many many thanks for your kind letter. It is raining and raining some more here. The artillery fire is very heavy at times. Our quarters are to the right of the village of Aubérive. On this map you can see "rubble." In [the cellars?] of the village there are kitchens with thick cement walls, for protection against fire (better: as fire protection)... Since smoke is generated when cooking, the French think we're encamped in the village and open[ed] heavy "fire" on the village. Very funny! At night it all starts up again even if the firing is in vain, which the French "transmit" terribly. Aside from all that, I am quite well! Again, many thanks, greetings Dix

Kunstsammlung Gera, Dix Archive
Drawing: *Trümmer* [Rubble], Lorenz WK 1.0.24

To Helene Jakob [3.7.1916] [LF]

[...] I have, of course, started the book. Kant uses very complicated language and it requires quiet & concentration in order to read it. Particularly disturbing are the prejudices which one has "drawn" by reading newer philosophers, and it requires a lot of objective intellectual capacity. Does no harm, in such ways the spirit is "fully trained, laced up in Spanish boots."[4] — This morning there was a little snowstorm [...]

Private collection

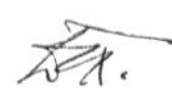

To Helene Jakob [3.8.1916] [PCF]

[Drawing]
[drawn, verso:] 3.8.1916
Dear Fräulein Jakob!
Many thanks for your cake.
These are our quarters. The attic of a house, surrounded by beds, an oven in the center.
Greetings to you,
heartily yours
Your Dix

Kunstsammlung Gera, Dix Archive
Drawing: *Quartier auf dem Dachboden* [Quarters in the Attic], Lorenz WK 1.0.28

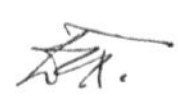

To Helene Jakob [3.19.1916] [LF]

Kara samideanino!
Many thanks for the [*illegible*] *of a Buddha*. It is a splendid book and actually much too nice for the field. But I will make efforts to spare it. — Hopefully you didn't spend all too much on it!

4 The quote is from Goethe's *Faust* (Act 2, scene I). The line is spoken by Mephistopheles.

I won't be able to take leave at Easter, it's been prohibited & isn't conceivable that the ban will be lifted any time soon. So it looks like I'll have to wait a few years. The war won't be ending today or tomorrow.

Included here, I am sending you a study, *Kampfgraben bei A.* [Trench at A.]. Today, I even have a headache from working. It's such fantastic spring weather [...]

Private collection

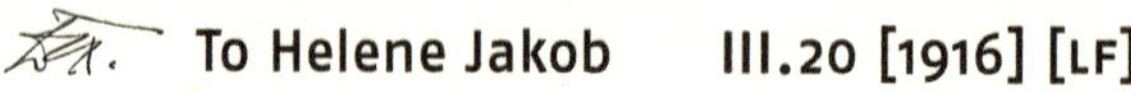

To Helene Jakob III.20 [1916] [LF]

[reverse:] III.20.

Kunstsammlung Gera, Dix Archive

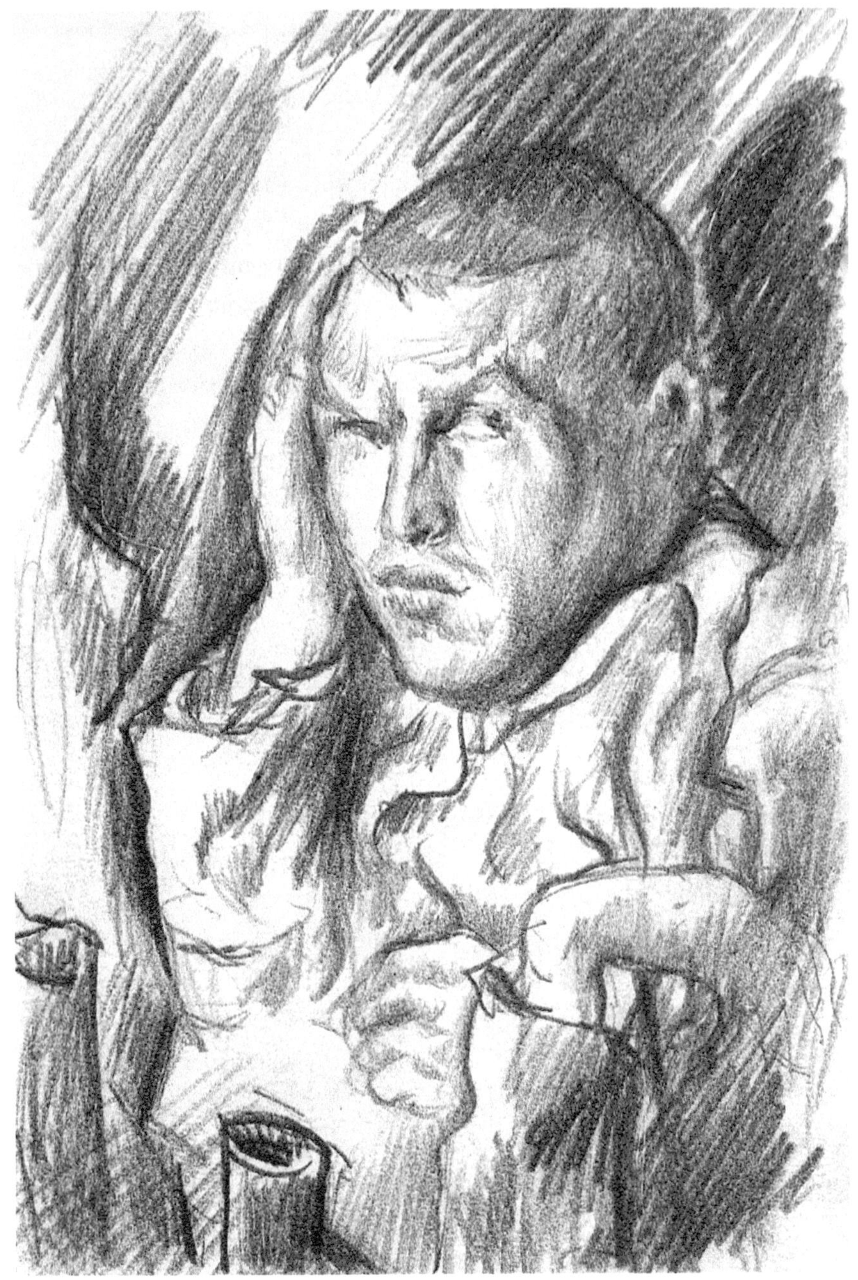

Drawing: *Selbstbildnis im Unterstand* [Self-portrait in the Dugout], Lorenz FW 1.0.30

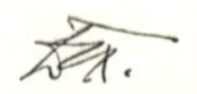

To Helene Jakob March 22 [PCF]

[reverse:] March 22
Kara samideanino!
Many thanks for your package with the oranges! I wrote to your father with the request for 2 sketchpads. Hopefully I'll get this soon since my paper is out. The sketch is a rendering of my communication trench.
Hopefully things are going as well for you as for me. I also received 2 packages from the school again.
Many heartfelt greetings!
Dix

Kunstsammlung Gera, Dix Archive
Drawing: *Laufgraben* [Communication Trench], Lorenz WK 1.0.31

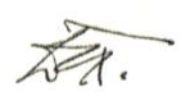

To Helene Jakob 6.4.16 | Fort de la Pombelle in Reims [LF/PCF]

Fort de la Pombelle in Reims 6.4.16
Kara samideanino! This is Fort de la Pombelle in Reims, a fort, still under French control. Our trench is up front. It's nicely cemented and reinforced twice a day. Really German, eh? I thank you kindly for the little package with cigarettes and stationery & your letter. Earlier there was a heavy, but brief, thunderstorm. The thunderstorms are incredibly heavy here, but the thunder is rather ridiculously insignificant compared to a barrage. Now the skies are blue again. We sit all day long in the trenches at our gunner's stations. We've been here 4 days; it's actually quite fresh, like summer.

The cathedrals are illuminated, it is har [?] the same hour tw [?] smoke the food, people are working hard in Reims. I could easily spend the war here, & especially if it takes some years yet, but we probably won't be here very long at all. Then we'll be heading back to the idiotic Läuse-Schlampagne. [On the [PCF] with a drawing of the reinforced machine-gun station]: This is our concrete MG station, you shoot through the slits. Let's hope that there'll soon be peace! Many heartfelt greetings via samideano
Dix

Kunstsammlung Gera, Dix Archive
Drawing: *Betonierter M.G. Stand* [Concrete MG Station], Lorenz FW 1.0.38
– har and tw: The abbreviations are Dix's and could not be deciphered by the editors of the German edition, or by the translator of this one.
– Lause-Schlampagne: A pun. "Lause-Champagne" is the eastern part of the Champagne region of France. The plural of "Laus" (louse) in German is "Läuse," and "Schlampe" is a "slut" or a "bitch."

To Helene Jakob 6.22.1916 [near Souplet] [LF]

[Photo: "Andachtsbild im Laufgraben" (Devotional picture in the communication trench)]
[reverse:] 6.22.1916
[Translation from Esperanto:] Dear Kindred Spirit! For some days I've again been in position / near Souplet. We're shooting at planes with machine guns. But no airplane has been shot down yet; it's not easy. Nothing's changed; the weather is sunny and nice. Today I received cigars from the K.G. Sch. [Kunstgewerbeschule]. But I always have to give them away since I can't smoke myself.

I wish so much that there'd soon be peace, but I don't see it happening.
Many greetings Your Dix

Kunstsammlung Gera, Dix Archive

To Helene Jakob 8.15.1916 [Maurois] [LF]

Cara Samideanino — I received your letters and the cherries and cigarettes and thank you very much for them. Thank God the terrible days of summer have passed. We were detached through Bavaria on the 12th. Our position was to the right of the frequently mentioned farmstead, Monacu. Our company was there three weeks and we detached in 2 days. The first two days with regiment 102 passed relatively quietly. We still had 2 trenches there, one behind the other. Connections through trenches do not exist, naturally. I lay with 5 other MG's in the "brown earth" position. [In] the second position, where Reg. 102 had deepened the trenches as needed at night, the Frogs, who were positioned on a height and can observe everything wonderfully, began drumming away at us on the 3rd day with 28ers, in between with 15s and small caliber guns, too. It was awful! The b. position was so chewed up that one couldn't tell where the trenches were anymore. I sat with my gun [heavy MG] and my people in a mined [?] hole. With each shot, our little enclosure threatened to collapse in on itself. When it got worse, 3 of my people moved out. There I sat, with one other guy.

I was determined to stay. Suddenly a 28er blew so much dirt into the hole that we were standing up to our chests in it. The gun was buried, impossible to dig out in a hurry. So I moved into the next tunnel, further to the left (the shooting had begun from the right). Then it started from the left, too. Soon the big gun of the second tunnel was shot up & the gun commander standing at the entrance had both eardrums perforated. Run! I moved slightly further to the left — the others were racing in a wild flight to the back. I still lay there, alone, in a small hole in the ground 1 mtr high, 2 mtrs long, stuck in the barrage for hours with another infantryman. In the evening, it quieted down, and I went back. The following days were almost even more horrible. In total, we lost 12 machine guns; the Frogs lost 2. On the 10th, I lay with a gun (we had to leave the entrenched position and dig ourselves in 30 mtrs further on a steep slope). There are between gren. Reg. 100 barrages from early, 10:30 a.m., to in the evening at 9 with 28ers. This time went up the steep rock slope — the losses of this regiment are terrible. In the evening the enemy attacked. Due to the fog, an artillery battery fired short of the mark & shot into our steep rock slope. Terrible confusion; terrible losses. The corpses lay about, arms & legs strewn and blown about. From the 6th company of this regiment, 9 men remained. It was a liberating feeling for everyone when the red flares ascended (this means "the enemy is attacking") and we could advance and fire with our rifles. But what good are all these details? You cannot possibly imagine such a thing. Now we are far behind this hell in a place called Maurois. Perhaps soon I [may?] be

furloughed. Many good comrades were left behind out there, too bad for those guys. Many, many greetings
Via samideano
Dix

Cited in Löffler, *Otto Dix und der Krieg* (Leipzig: 1986) 10–11. The place that Löffler read as "Mauvais" was identified by Dix scholar Dietrich Schubert as "Maurois."

1917

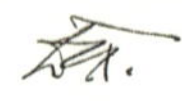

To Otto Baumgärtel 1917 | From the military hospital in Hénin

dear Baumgärtel!
Would you be so kind and (as soon as possible) ask Gerstenberger – Chemnitz if I could exhibit a number of drawings from the field there? The things are drawn, but unframed. You can appoint yourself in charge of my exhibition with Arnold in Dresden and say to him that I was reviewed very favorably by the entire press. It concerns only an inquiry whether and when.

Museum Haus Dix, Hemmenhofen, Dauerleihgabe des Landes Baden-Württemberg
From 9.27–10.29.1916 Galerie Arnold of Dresden had presented the second exhibition (with a catalog) of Dresden artists who were serving with the army. Eleven Dix pieces are mentioned therein.

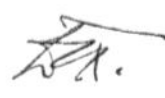

To Helene Jakob 8.14.1917 [near Bruges] [LF]

[photo left, top: My sisters; l. below Dix on vacation] [on the reverse, drawn:] Kara samideanino! I haven't written you in quite a long while and also haven't heard anything from you, either. Hopefully things are going well. We've been waiting quietly for 14 days in close proximity to Bruges, after having to outlast heavy fighting at Y. [Ypres]. I have a request to ask of you: On August 15, an exhibition is opening in Lennestr. in which I will also have drawings on display. Would you send me the newspapers that feature critiques of this exhibition? I thank you in advance! Many greetings, also to your parents and to Herr and Frau Born.
Your Dix
NCO Dix, I. MgK.
R.I.R. 102

Kunstsammlung Gera, Dix Archive

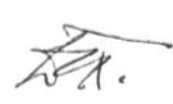

To Helene Jakob [12.12.1917] [LF]

Kara samideanino! Finally, a truce has been declared! Yesterday, our regimental band held a concert at the edge of the trench at the lines. The Russians came right through our barbed wire in droves & shook hands with our men. A historic moment, ready-made for the cinema. I think I'll soon be transferred to the fliers, on the 17th I have to go to Wilna for a final examination before discharge. I'll go on furlough at the beginning of February at the latest. — Today I would like to ask a favor & have a request of you. Please have

the administrator at the K.G.-Sch [Kunstgewerbeschule] put together two simple portfolios, sized 75 cm x 75 cm, with binding straps. I am nearly up to my ears with my work; I hardly know where to put it anymore. Yesterday I received a personal invitation from the Nassau Kunstverein in Wiesbaden with the request to send 5 pictures. I immediately wrote to Arnold, who has all of my work, and asked him to have these framed and to send them there. The exhibition is already opening at the start of January; hopefully I'll be able to get it together by then. My "fame" is already spreading well beyond Dresden!?! There's really nothing specific [for you to do] if these affairs are left to other people.
Regards Your Dix

Private, quoted in: Otto Dix, *Welt und Sinnlichkeit* (Regensburg: 2005) 41.

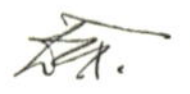

To Franz and Louise Dix [1917] [PCF]

dear parents!
I received your two packages with the eels, etc. Thank you cordially for it. Up until today things are fine & I'm healthy. The exhibition of Dresden artists at the Galerie Arnold in Dresden has opened and I received very positive newspaper reviews from the critics. One piece was even printed in the catalog. If I receive the clipping again, I'll send it to you. Don't be surprised if I don't send money as often now, I need a whole [*remainder missing*]

1918

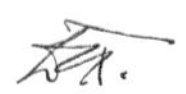

To the Gera City Council 1.4.18 [LF]

To the Gera City Council
His Excellency
I should like to politely inquire whether it might be possible for me, at the end of February, beginning of March of this year, to exhibit 10–15 pieces, a collection of war pictures, in the rooms of the Gera town museum. I am a native of Untermhaus & have studied at the art school in Dresden. I have frequently exhibited at Galerie Arnold in Dresden and at the Kunstverein and my work has been discussed in the press.

My work is in an expressionist vein, and this recent direction would perhaps be of interest for art connoisseurs in Gera.

I look forward to an imminently favorable [?] answer
Faithfully
Otto Dix
Uffz DIX I. M. G. K. R. J. R. 10

City Archives Gera
On 1.14.1918, the resolution of the City Council, Royal Residence, City of Gera was issued: "Approved for 10 days without heating, lighting, & maintenance." After receiving this letter, Dix did not respond further.

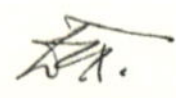

To Helene Jakob [1918] [PCF]

[verso:] RIDer Kara samideanino! I thank y[ou] very much for your letter. Unf[ortunately] I [cou]ld not answer you sooner. I believe I do know Vogler's home village. It is an oval on the cover, with a house and shrubs. Is that right? I'll write you a bit more soon
Cordially
Your Dix
How much money do I still owe you?

Kunstsammlung Gera, Dix Archive
Drawing: *Rider*, Lorenz WK 1.0.48

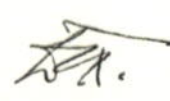

To Helene Jakob 9.24.1918 [PC]

[photo: DIX in uniform]
[on reverse, drawn:] the 24th of Sept.
Kara samideanino! Yesterday, I received your letter of the 12th. I've been released from the infirmary, but will still be here until the 28th of the month, for a course. Herein I am sending you one photo, though not a particularly good one. Cordial greetings
Your Dix

Kunstsammlung Gera, Dix Archive

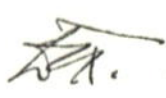

To Otto Baumgärtel [still 1918?] [Dresden?]

de[ar] Baumgärtel, There are no publications about me yet. Now as before, I am controversial.

Enclosed are some photos, years on the back.
With beſt regards
Your Dix

Museum Haus Dix, Hemmenhofen, permanent loan from the State of Baden-Württemberg

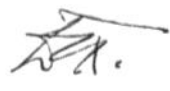

To the Naussau Kunstverein [December 1918] Wiesbaden

To the Naussau Kunſtverein, Wiesbaden
Some days ago I received news from the art dealer Gutbier — Galerie Arnold, Dresden, that he had sent you five pictures, namely:

I. *Sonnenuntergang bei Ypern* [Sunset at Ypres]
II. *Pferdeweide* [Horse Paſture]
III. *Häuser* [?] in *Pœlkapelle* [Houses [?] in Pœlkapelle]
IV. *der Reiter* [the Rider]
V. *Gelände bei Ypern* [Terrain near Ypres]

by express poſt. When I learned of the shipment by normal poſt, the pictures had already been sent. — I would kindly requeſt you send me any potential newſpaper reviews.
Sincerely yours
Otto Dix
NCO, I. M. g. K. R. J. R. 102

Museum Wiesbaden, Archives
See also the [LF] to Helene Jakob of 12.12.1917. The paintings mentioned are not included in Fritz Löffler's list of works.

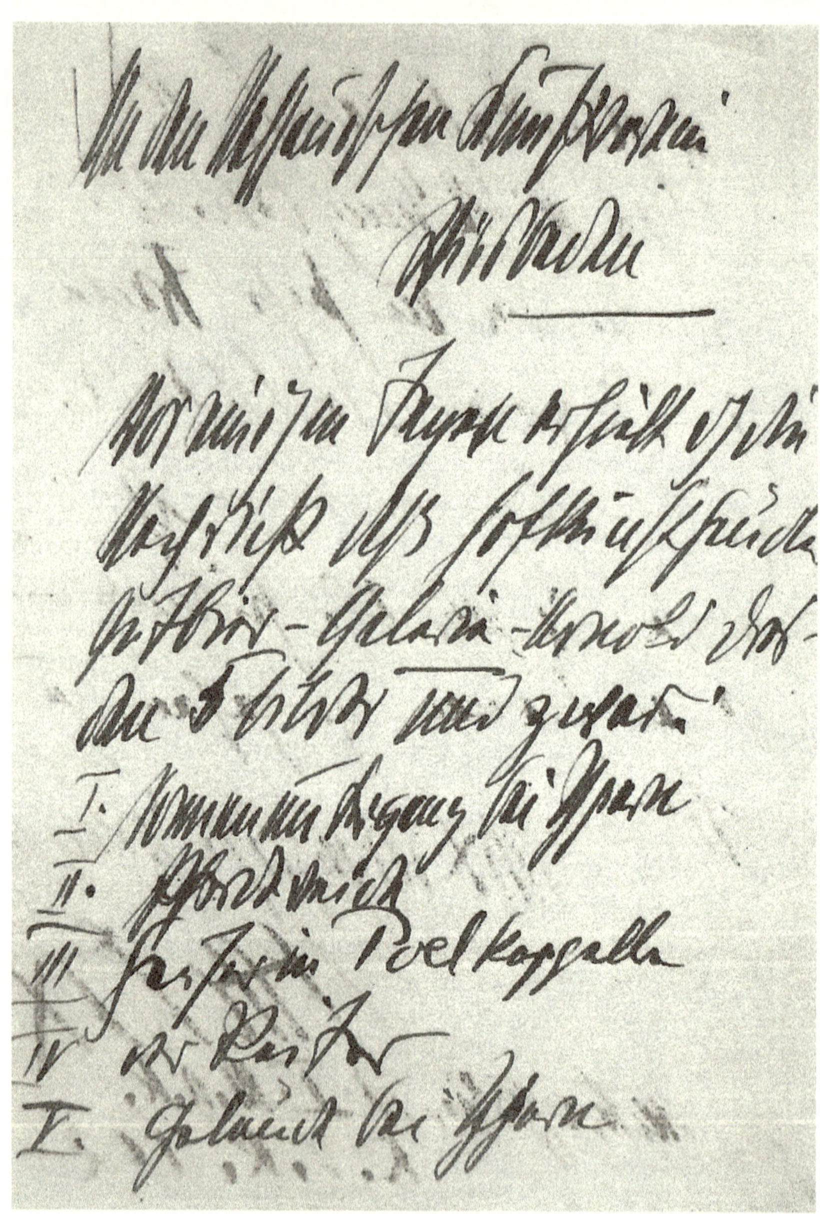

Letter to the Naussau Kunstverein, Wiesbaden, December 1918

1919

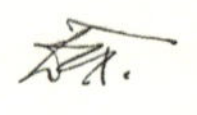

To George Grosz. Attached to a letter from George Grosz to Dix [1919?] [Dresden]

dear Schorsch!
Fräulein Viola Schulhoff, my girlfriend, given that she is a "really serious artist," is against the establishment of a dada university and Dadauniondresden (daduns), however that's sayin' nothin'. Enclosed sending you 2 dadagraphien, and in the next days the manifesto. The *Illuminists,* not just a movement or a dadabranch, but my very own creation.
Greetings Dixtaturdadadix
Inventor of Illuminism
Erwin is completely dadaized Best greetings
Dadabraut

Adk, Berlin, George Grosz Archive
2 dadagraphien / the manifesto: The artworks Dix refers to have not been identified (though it could possibly be the one named "Dada" in the 8.14.1920 letter to Das Ey Gallery), nor to date has the manifesto he names here been located, or its authorship definitively determined.

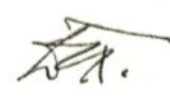

To George Grosz [1919?] [Dresden]

dear George! Herewith sending you the lovely pictures. There are 5. Please pick out 3 for yourself and try to sell the other 2. I need money. I think you must have some connections or other. I will still send the pictures this week. — I hope that you find "pure joy" in the beautiful watercolors.

Say hello to Monteur for me & Wieland Herzfelde
Your
Dixtotur en ALADADADIX
Inventor of Illuminism
Antonsplatz 1

AdK, Berlin, George Grosz Archive, 408
Monteur: refers to John Heartfield, Wieland Herzfelde's brother.

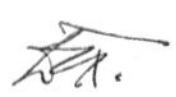

To Kurt Günther [February 1919 | Dresden]

My dear Günther!
Due to the sheer volume of work, I've only been able to get to writing you today in somewhat greater detail. I've begun working on two larger paintings, which I'll exhibit as soon as they're finished. A *Leda & Woman with a Bowl of Fruit*. I've been mulling over these ideas for 5 years or so and have often depicted the themes graphically. — We radical Dresdeners have founded a Secession under the name "*Gruppe 1919*." Next year it will be Gruppe 1920, and so on. All those in Dresden who have anything to say as expressionists are involved. We are getting exhibition rooms at Richter's and are going to have the first big exhibition in April, which will be introduced accompanied with a great deal of bombast (including a double-issue of the *Neue Blätter für Kunst*, newspaper propaganda) and so on. On closing, the exhibition will move on to Hanover. Zehder, the editor of the *Neue Blätter*, is also involved, a very pleasant, passionate chap, who possesses an extraordinary entrepreneurial spirit. I received a commission from the Kunstverein to make the poster for the February exhibition,

in an expressionist vein, of course, although somewhat understated (for my tastes). As of tomorrow it will be glued on all the walls of Dresden. The academics are a bunch of bourgeois types, just like in the books. Thank God Lohse is soon coming to Dresden, so that I have at least one person to converse with. — Greetings from Fräulein Lehnert, by the way. She is actually the first female person who has interested me, and not only just for a few hours. She is very witty, without being pedantic. — How's it going there, can you work there? It's so brutally cold now, we can only really heat the place on Saturdays & Sundays, but can still work intensely. Write me soon.
Your Dix

Kunstsammlung Gera, Dix Archive
Paintings: *Leda mit dem Schwan* [Leda and the Swan], Löffler 1919/4; *Weib mit Fruchtschale* [Woman with a Bowl of Fruit], Lorenz WK 6.3.8. Also see the *Doppelbildnis Dix-Günther* [Dix painted by Kurt Günther, Kurt Günther painted by Otto Dix], Löffler 1920/14, exhibition rooms at Galerie Emil Richter, Prager Straße.
– Kurt Günther (1893–1955) was a close colleague of Dix's. They went to art school together in Dresden, and Günther subsequently served with the air corps until being discharged in 1917 due to severe tuberculosis, ending up in Davos, where he made the acquaintance of Ernst Ludwig Kirchner. The Dresden Secession was a short-lived collaboration of German Expressionism founded by Conrad Felixmüller and Dix in Dresden, during a period of political & social reform in the aftermath of WWI. The group's activity spanned from 1919 until its final collective exhibition in 1925.
– After the war, Günther returned to Dresden, where he undertook artistic experiments with dada, expressionist, and other forms, and was part of the Dresden dada group. While at school, Günther worked closely with Dix, and they shared a studio with fellow student Viola Schulhoff, the sister of composer Erwin Schulhoff. Günther often supported Dix in many ways, including financially. A monument of this time is the now lost (a photo of it exists) painting *Boxkampf* [Boxing Match], in which Dix, Schulhoff, and others were depicted before an audience.
– Carl Lohse (1895–1965) was a painter that Dix had probably become acquainted with through Otto Pankok.
– Lohse participated in the Dresden Secession exhibitions.

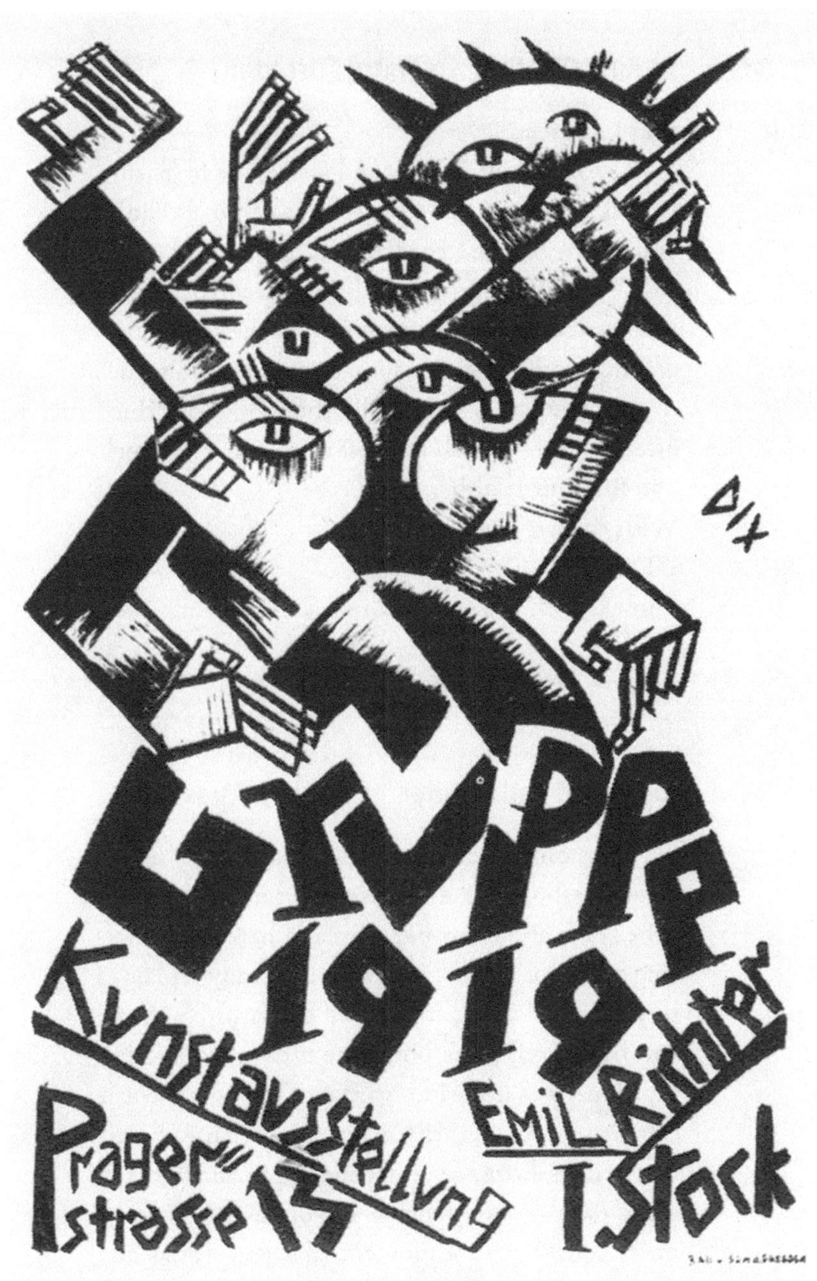

Poster *Gruppe 1919*, lithograph, 1919

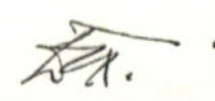

To Kurt Günther [1919] [Dresden]

dear Günther!
I am writing you this second letter, the first will probably be returned because I sealed it. I thank you above all quite cordially for the money (100 Mk.), which I received; I also received your portfolio yesterday. I could imagine that the scribblings coming from the Secession are causing you some degree of upset. I only really thought about this afterwards. — I wish the best to you on your work and for your health.
With cordial greetings
DIX
I now live on Elisenstr. 67 I

Kunstsammlung Gera, Dix Archive

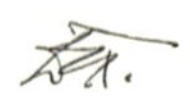

To Conrad Felixmüller [1919?] [Dresden]

[...] It is only afterwards that I really considered what irresponsible nonsense you told those philistine types about my pictures, and here I am referring to the "poster & picture" bit. I already explained to you what I think about it all on Saturday in my flat. But to tell these philistine types that, and in my name, was notorious garbage. Telling the truth can also be temporarily mean; you seem to have resolved to shove me under the rug in an effort to bring even more attention to yourself. Did you never consider for a moment that you would be doing me material harm in the process? I am hardly interested in whether recognition comes from philistines or those who aren't, but first of all, it's mainly about money. — You put yourself first and say the most bombastic things about your paintings. There's little doubt about the effect of all this, but now — I have to suffer the consequences of it all. [...]

GNM, DKA, Conrad Felixmüller Estate
In 1918, Conrad Felixmüller had moved to Dresden, where (as noted above) he became the co-founder & chairman of the Dresden Secession. During his activities in Germany's progressive art and youth movements, Felixmüller, along with Dix and others, worked for various newspapers, including *Die Aktion* in Berlin, *Die Sichel* in Regensburg, and *Rote Erde* in Hamburg. In spite of his colleague's negative assessment, the already successful Felixmüller recommended Dix to the collector & gallery owner Hans Koch in Dusseldorf. Felixmüller wrote to his wife Londa in 1926 (Bielefeld, 7.10.1926): "[...] I am going to continue to express my opinions about art and artists openly and won't spare Dix, either! We are all aware of his hunger for power, and ambition (at all costs!) [...]" (GNM, DKA, NL Felixmüller).

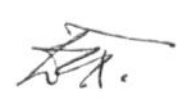

To Artur Schnabel [1919?] [Dresden]

Dear Herr Professor!
Included, your three watercolors and the other for Herr Przemislas. Could you please let me know as soon as possible about the *Schwangeres Weib* [Pregnant Woman] picture. Greetings from me to your spouse & cordial greetings to you from an admiring
Otto Dix
Dresden — Elisenstr. 67 I
Atelier Antonsplatz 1

AdK, Berlin, Music Archive
Painting: *Schwangeres Weib* [Pregnant Woman], Löffler 1919/6

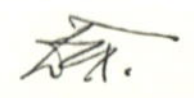

To Paul Westheim December 8, 1919 | Dresden

Dear Mr. Weſtheim!
Mr. Theodor Däubler, with whom I ſpoke, told me today that you have had an essay by him about my work and that you intend to publish it as soon as you have other work from me to reproduce.

Please let me know if I should send you new woodcuts or photographs of paintings. Perhaps you can get plates of the paintings done in one of the art shops here.

I could also send original woodblocks correſponding to the size of the magazine.

I look forward to your imminent answer and am drawing, reſpectfully
Otto Dix.
Dresden-W-
Elisenſtr. 67 I

AdK, Berlin, Paul Westheim Archives 38
Paul Westheim (1886–1963) was a German art historian & publisher of the art magazine *Das Kunstblatt*. Däubler's essay appeared in *Das Kunstblatt* № 4 (1920) 118–120.

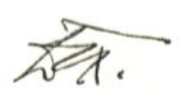

To Artur Schnabel 12.10.19 | Dresden

Dear Herr Professor!
I am sending your picture by express to Charlottenburg today. When opening the crate, unscrew the cover firſt, please; the cover is the side with the signum. The picture is faſtened with 6 screws to the bottom of the crate, which can be loosened

after removing the cover. Please send me the crate back by freight/cargo.

I hope that the work will bring you much joy and would be grateful, if you would further recommend me, occasionally, in Berlin. I hope that you will be so kind & allow me to include the picture in a large special exhibition of my works for a short time.

I thank you very much and greet your dear wife, cordially
Your Otto Dix
Extend my best wishes to the ladies and gentlemen of the Przemilas Quartet for me as well.
Schulhoff is in Prague at the moment. Fräulein Schulhoff sends her best!
Please send the crate to Antonplatz 1, Dresden, Alte K. G. Schule.

AdK, Berlin, Music Archive
Painting: *Schwangeres Weib* [Pregnant Woman], Löffler 1919/6

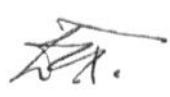

To Artur Schnabel [1919?] [Dresden]

Dear Herr Professor!
Today I received your 2000 marks & thank you very much for it. The picture has been sent and I hope you will soon receive it. Please confirm receipt.
With best greetings to your wife as well, your Dix.

AdK, Berlin, Music Archive
Painting: *Schwangeres Weib* [Pregnant Woman], Löffler 1919/6

1920

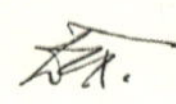

To Artur Schnabel II.17.1920 | Dresden

Dear Herr Professor!
In early December 1919 I sent the *Schwangeres Weib* [Pregnant Woman] picture to you. Perhaps you were quite busy & unable to let me know if you received it. I hope, however, that it arrived well there. Since the picture crate does not belong to me, I cordially ask you to send it back to me immediately. Otherwise, I will have to replace it, and crates are now terribly expensive. Perhaps you could also let me know whether or not the painting arrived there in good shape.
Kind regards to you and your wife
Sincerely yours
Dix
Dresden Antonsplatz 1.

AdK, Berlin, Music Archive

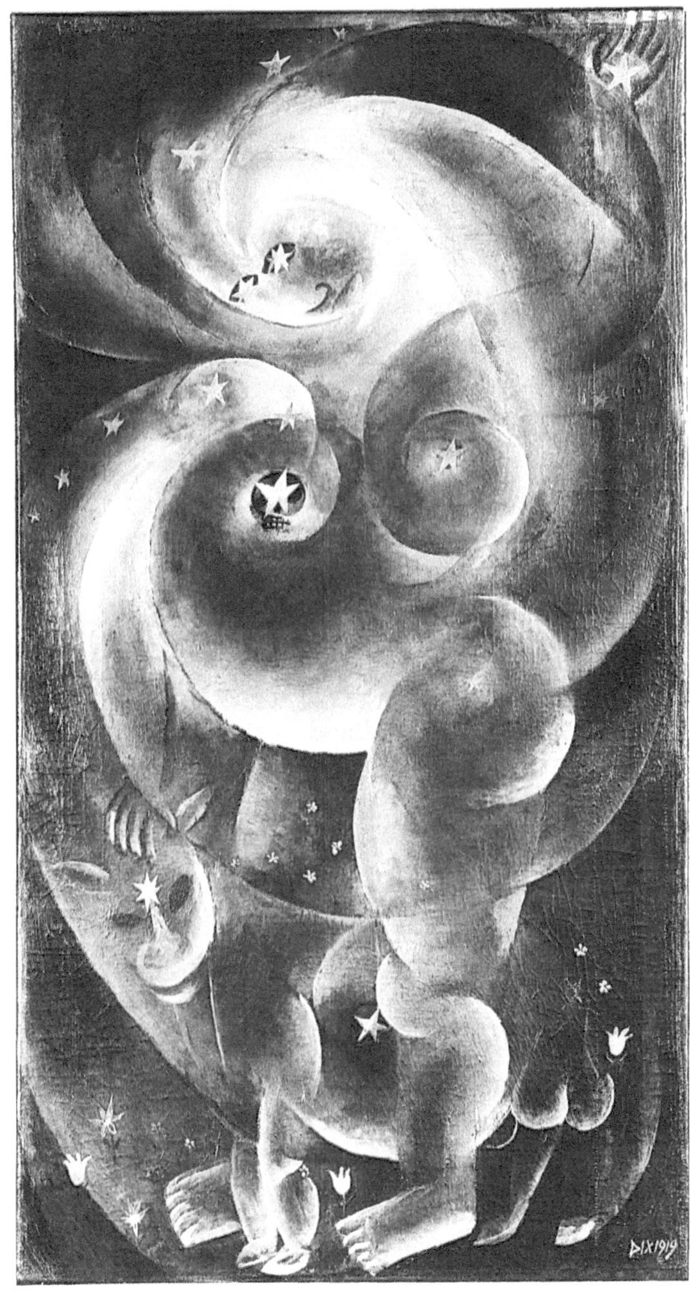

Schwangeres Weib [Pregnant Woman], 1919, painting

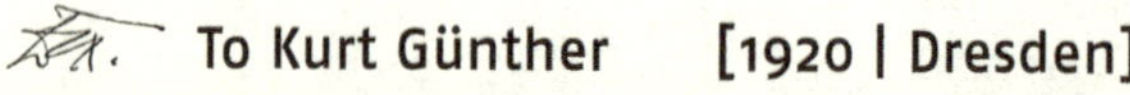

To Kurt Günther [1920 | Dresden]

dear Günther!

Finally, a letter from you! Since Richter has shit his pants and will not show my work, since no art dealer in Dresden has the courage to exhibit me, the whole thing has gone in the tank. I am also none too keen to present myself as a petit-bourgeois lapdog, either. My pictures exist and until further notice will plague the bad consciences of all art dealers, æsthetes, expressionists, and other elderly aunties and geese. "If I did well, let us be silent, if I did badly, then we'd laugh & do it bad again by half."[5]

I didn't attend the artists' festival; I'm glad if I don't have to see these morons. — In the meantime, I've made some new things, which provide an opportunity to shock those with weak nerves; for moralists, the disgusting, and for dancers, jolly tightropes & vaulting horses.

I advise you not to go to Leipzig, it seems completely bourgeois beyond recovery. Your friend Dressler sent me some etchings. I submitted it to the Secession, but they weren't considered radical enough. Too bad the guy is "all graphicked out" in Leipzig. Some people are very hopeful, others are absolutely etching-mad. The man can etch far too well.

5 Dix is quoting from Friedrich Nietzsche's poem, "Among Friends. An Epilogue," which concludes *Human, All Too Human* I (1986; 1996) 205.

I must tell him about it today, as sorry as I am to do it. Write again soon.
Greetings from Schulhoff & his sister [Viola].
Best regards
Dix
Special edition at Pedretti goes off tomorrow.

Kunstsammlung Gera, Dix Archive
Regarding the dating of this letter, see Strobl 1995, 51.
– The reference to Richter concerns Galerie Emil Richter, Prager Str., in Dresden.
– August William Dressler (1876–1970) was a painter and commercial artist.

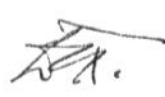

To Miriam Britzel [3.24.1920 | Dresden]

Dear Fräulein Britzel!
I received your letter today and am very pleased that your brother wants to buy the picture. I am of course in agreement with the sum of 500 marks. Herewith, I return you the exhibition paperwork. I introduced the picture as being "not for sale," but you may want to exhibit it. I do hope I'll soon be able to come to lovely Bautzen, perhaps when the exhibition closes I'll pick up the other picture. I'm really looking forward to visiting you there.
With best regards
Otto Dix

SLUB Dresden, App. 2711, 9
The exhibition in Bautzen that included the two paintings mentioned has to date not been documented.

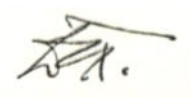

To Miriam Britzel [3.25.1920 | Dresden]

Dear Fräulein Britzel!
Just today I received the 500 marks your brother had sent. Unfortunately I don't have the postal receipt anymore and thus don't have his address either. Please relate to him that I have received the money and thank him kindly.
With best regards Otto Dix

SLUB Dresden, Mscr. App. Dresd. 2711, 10

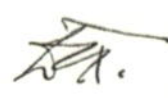

To the Bergh Graphische Kabinett [spring] 1920 [Dresden]

I received your address from Herr Felixmüller. I should like to take the liberty of sending you hereby four of my etchings. The dry point etchings cost 100 marks per piece, the aquatints 75 marks each. Since at the moment I'm facing some financial difficulties, I would request you buy 4 sheets from me. I could offer you the dry point etchings for 75, & the aquatints for 50 each.
Faithfully yours
Otto Dix

Archives of the Remmert and Barth Gallery, Dusseldorf
The Bergh & Co. Graphische Kabinett, run by Hans Koch in Dusseldorf, only existed from 1918–1920. Thereafter it was taken over by I.B. Neumann.

To Hans Koch [1920 | Dresden]

Dear Sir! Some time ago I sent you 4 of my etchings. As of today I still have received no message from you whether you received the same, or whether you want to keep the sheets. Please let me know as soon as possible. Faithfully yours
Otto Dix
Dresden — Antonsplatz 1

Archives of the Remmert and Barth Gallery, Dusseldorf
This is the first extant letter from Dix to Koch, the connection of which was to have unforeseen consequences. Dix was awarded a contract portrait – the first in his career – from the wealthy and well-known Dusseldorf art collector, patron, and doctor Hans Koch. Koch had his own modern art gallery (which he ran with his wife, Martha) and had the best contacts in the Rhenish art scene. While working on the portrait, Dix and Koch's wife, Martha, fell in love. The portrait, completed by Dix in 1921, was not flattering to the client. It shows the urologist with an open coat, sleeves rolled up, syringe and blood-filled catheter in his hands, unshaven, with gnarled fencing scars on his bloated face, irritated & peering through his eyeglasses, surrounded by cool-metallic praxis devices. Whether or not Koch was impressed isn't documented, but conceivably not, because two years later, after his wife had left him for the painter, he divorced her and sold the portrait to Karl Nierendorf, to whom Koch had apparently commented that he found it rather ugly and disfiguring. It was later sold to the Cologne lawyer and art lover Joseph Haubrich for 420 goldmarks. For Haubrich it was the first painting of what would become his magnificent collection of modern art. Koch subsequently married Martha's sister.

To Das Ey Gallery [7.14.1920] [Dresden]

To "Das Ey" Dusseldorf
As per your request, I sent you 10 etchings:

I. *Kriegskrüppel* [War Cripple]
II. *Streichholzhändler* [Match Dealer] (2 pieces)
III. *Lustmörder* [Sex Murder]

IV. *Billardspieler* [Pool players]
V. *Dame im Café* [Lady in the Café]
VI. *Kartenspieler* [Card players]
VII. *Straße* [Street]
VIII. *Matrose und Mädchen* [Sailor and Girl]
VIIII.[6] *Fleischerladen* [Butcher Shop]

in total 10 pieces. Moreover, I've arranged for Bergh (Dusseldorf) to send you 4 additional pieces that I have with them. You would thus have 14 pieces. Could you please confirm receipt of the shipment and receipt of the 4 sheets from Bergh.
Faithfully yours Otto Dix
Dresden — Antonsplatz 1
The sheets cost 75.00 Mk net per piece

Otto Pankok-Museum, Hünxe-Drevenack
Otto Pankok and Gert Wollheim had seen the exhibition of Dix etchings & drawings in the Munich gallery of Hans Goltz and established contact; Otto Pankok had also visited Dix in Dresden.
– Das Ey Gallerie was opened during the First World War by Johanna Ey (1864–1947), who came to Dusseldorf at the age of 17. In 1910 she opened a cafe that became a regular haunt for actors, journalists, musicians, and especially artists. During the war the gallery exhibited pieces from the academic Düsseldorfer Malerschule, but afterwards it became a magnet for modern and experimental artists. Frau Ey, also known as "Mutter Ey," was immortalized in countless portraits, including by Dix.

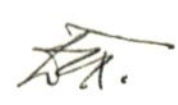

To the "Das Ey Gallery" [8.14.1920 | Dresden]

To the "Das Ey," Dusseldorf, Hindenburgwall 11
To the "Das Ey" art dealers, Dusseldorf!
I am hereby communicating to you that today I have sent 5 woodcuts and 12 drawings to your address.

6 This is Dix's personal version of IX.

Drawings

1.	*Akt* [Nude]	Mk 100
2.	*Minna*	Mk 150
3.	*Anna*	Mk 150
4.	*Schwangere* [Pregnant Woman]	Mk 100
5.	*Der Geiger Carlo von Rust* [The Violinist…]	Mk 150
6.	*Cäcilie*	Mk 150
7.	*Mein Vater* [My Father]	Mk 150
8.	*Mein Bruder* [My Brother]	Mk 100
9.	*Frau in der Stube* [Woman in the Living Room]	Mk 100
10.	*Mein Vater II*	Mk 150
11.	*Meine Mutter*	Mk 150
12.	*Schwangere Frau*	Mk 200

Woodcuts

1. *Die Erde* [The Earth]
2. *Regen* [Rain]
3. *Dada*
4. *Nächtliche Szene* [Nocturnal Scene]
5. *Katzen* [Cats]

Woodcuts are Mk 40 each

The prices are net prices.
Hopefully the collection is in accordance with your wishes.
Please confirm receipt.
Faithfully yours
Otto Dix
Dresden Antonsplatz 1.

Otto Pankok-Museum, Hünxe-Drevenack

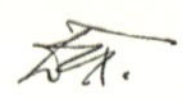

To the "Das Ey Gallery" [9.8.1920 | PM | Dresden]

To "das Ey"
Will gladly make the woodblock available to you for printing free of charge, please let me know which one. If you are doing picture reproductions, I would prefer pictures and would send you good photos, since I'm actually more of a painter than a graphic artist. If you should need an essay about me, then I can tell you that Felixmüller, Dresden, has written a very accurate, still unpublished essay about my work. Happy to hear that you have already bought something and hope that you will purchase even more by the end of the exhibition. Until further notice, I'll leave things to you, in commission. Did you receive my last shipment of drawings, et cetera? Regards Otto Dix
Dresden Antonsplatz 1.
Could you please send me some copies of the book?

Otto Pankok-Museum, Hünxe-Drevenack
The essay Dix here refers to was written by Conrad Felixmüller and appeared in *Das Ey*, № 3 (1921). Wollheim and Pankok had written Dix in Dresden and had invited him to send more drawings.

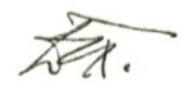

To Otto Pankok [autumn 1920 | Dresden]

Dear Herr Pankok! Since I'm currently also under pressure myself, I request you please send me the amount of the pictures sold. Felixmüller has already offered to provide you the essay [for Das Ey] for free. Please let me know when you need it. I assume my exhibition has already passed, and that it would thus be too late to send the photos.
Cordial regards Otto Dix

Otto Pankok-Museum, Hünxe-Drevenack

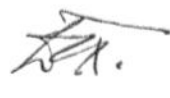

To "Das Ey" [10.10.1920 | Dresden]

To "Das Ey" Dusseldorf
Many thanks for the money. Please let me know right away whether you will reproduce the original woodcut. Please let me know the largest size and the latest date.

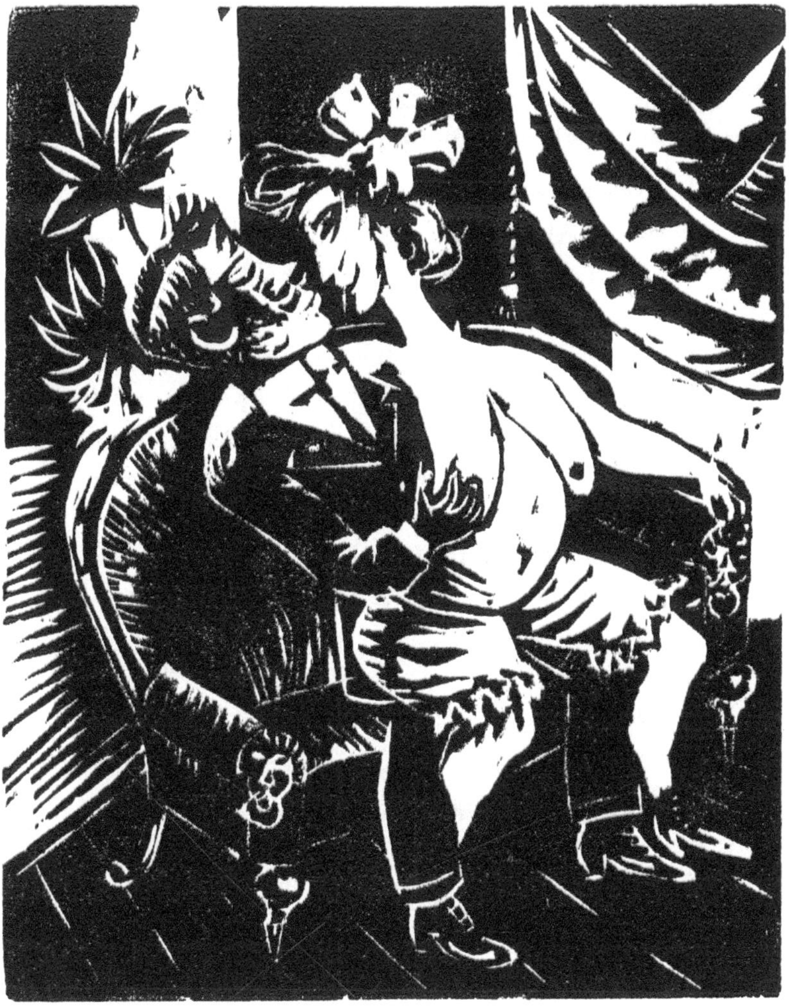

Liebespaar [Lovers], 1920

You can have the essay, as soon as you need it.
With best greetings
Otto Dix
Antonsplatz 1

Archives of the Galerie Remmert and Barth, Dusseldorf
Noted underneath: "answered, Wollheim." An original woodcut, *Liebespaar* [Lovers] (1920), was published in *Das Ey*, № 3 (1921), together with Felixmüller's essay. See Karsch 27c.

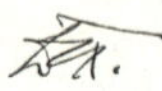

To Israel Ber Neumann [1920 | Dresden]

Dear Herr Neumann
Cordial thanks f[or] t[he] 400 marks, which I received today. I was very happy about the purchase of my picture & thank you very much for it. Quite some time ago I sent etchings to Bergh's Graphische Kabinett in Dusseldorf (the first 4 pieces). However, Herr Bergh wrote me that the sheets are not sufficient for his collection and he would have to send them back to me. As of today I have not received them, however. I would be grateful if you could give me some addresses of collectors.
Your devoted
Otto Dix
Dresden Antonsplatz 1

Private collection
Israel Ber Neumann took over the Graphisches Kabinett of Bergh & Co. from Hans Koch in Dusseldorf in 1920.
– The first four etchings, Karsch 5–8, are from 1920.

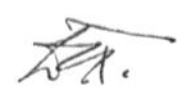

To Herbert Behrens-Hangeler December 11, 1920 [PM] [Dresden] [PC]

Many thanks for your letter. Long live "Kunst für Alle" (1900 collectivism). Tell me, have you heard that there is an anti-military exhibition in Berlin. Could you please inform me about it. Long live this (occasional) tendency in art.
Regards Dix

Staatlich Museen zu Berlin – Zentralarchiv IV / Herbert Behrens-Hangeler Estate 87
Herbert Behrens-Hangeler (1898–1981) was a painter, graphic artist, photographer, and writer. He studied art in Berlin and was a member of the Novembergruppe Berlin from 1921–1933. Categorized as "degenerate" by the Nazis, later as "formalistic" by the GDR authorities, Behrens-Hangeler was driven into internal exile and "exonerated" only shortly before his death. He had one final exhibition at Leipzig Galerie am Sachsenplatz toward the end of his life.

1921

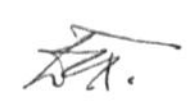

To Otto Pankok January 5, '21 [Dresden]

Dear Herr Pankok Many thanks for your letter. I'm certainly pleased to be part of your circle. If you happen to end up organizing exhibitions, please do send me the [required] paperwork. I hope to be able to personally extend my greetings to the gentlemen colleagues later this year in Dusseldorf & send best regards to you and your friends.
Your Dix
Archives of Galerie Remmert and Barth, Düsseldorf

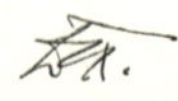

To Otto Pankok 01.15.1921 [PM] [Dresden]

dear Pankok! Thanks for the letter. Relate my thanks to Frau Ey for the 200 Mk. You'll get the *Three Cats* woodcut as soon as possible; there are other drawings & graphics for sale. As far as the etchings I'm sending, please select some for yourself. Would gladly send oils, but transport costs are too high, and I mostly have large-scale things. Maybe you can pick out something if you come to Dresden. Will you please arrange for the woodblock that was printed by Ey to be sent back? — Maybe (in April–May or later) you could even put on an exhibition at Das Ey of a collection of smaller paintings and graphics that I bring in a box, or do they not have space for it? I'll send some photos of paintings soon.
With warm regards
to Frau Ey & Wollheim
Your Dix

Archives of Galerie Remmert and Barth, Dusseldorf.
Woodcut: *Katzen* [Cats], 1920 (Karsch 28). – Regarding the woodcut, see as well the letters above to Ey of 9.8 and 10.10.1920.

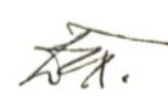

To Otto Pankok [1921 | Dresden]

dear Otto Pankok I always make the excuse that I've no time to write. You must excuse me that I'm only writing you just today. Thank you very much for the sheets. Please do choose 3 of my sheets in exchange. I duly passed on the sheets intended for Felixmüller. — About four weeks ago, I sent "Das Ey" a number of drawings, etchings, & woodcuts.

To date I have not received any acknowledgment of receipt. Would you be so kind as to see to it that these be returned to me soon. In the next few weeks, a friend of mine will come to visit you, the sculptor Otto Krischer, a very clever & talented man, and will deliver you my personal greetings. I hope to hear from you soon. Best regards Otto Dix

Otto Pankok Museum, Hünxe-Drevenack
Otto Krischer (1899–1976) was initially a sculptor and later became a mechanical engineer.

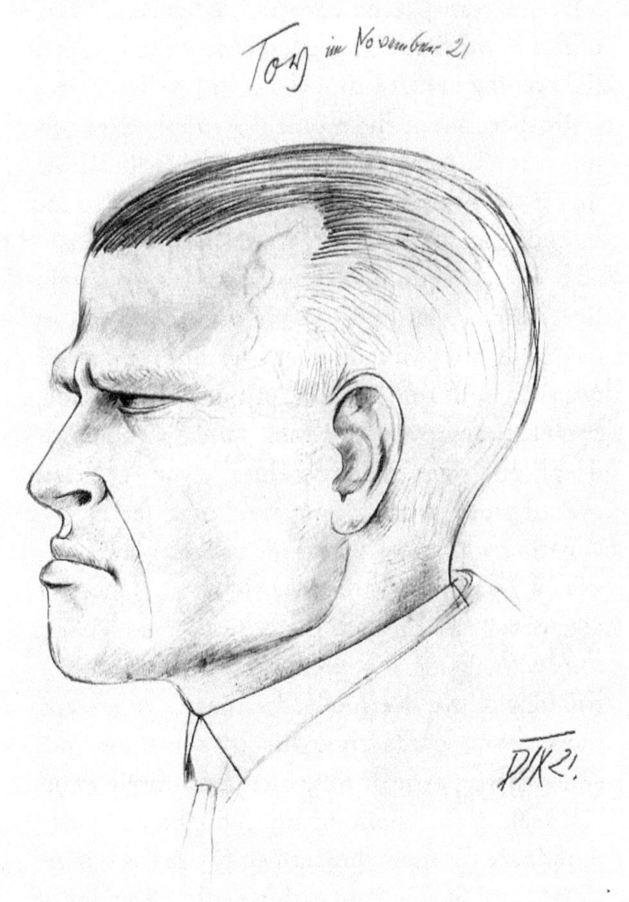

Toy in November 21, drawing, 1921

To Martha [Dresden, after the October visit to Dusseldorf in 1921]

My sweetest, dearest, sweetest love what might you be doing. I'm waiting longingly to hear something from you. Maybe something will come tomorrow. However I might already have had a letter from you, if you had sent it express. — The lamp is casting such a yellow, dim light in my room and the window is a blackened hole with a flaccid, transparent, corpse-like figure in front of it. I know that it's never good to write letters in the evening in a dreadful room with yellowy-grey wallpaper. But at the moment I simply have too much to do during the day. Oh my darling, how nice it shall be when I can be with you. I'm so full of hope that all those who know me are astonished at how I'm running around as if I were drunk. Everything beautiful and good should accompany us on our way; we cannot let trivialities cast a veil over our love. You, most beautiful, I just love you & will always love you; I want to know you more deeply and want to be very close to you. — What are all these words compared to a feeling! Whether you are very near me or are as far away as now — physically removed — the same feeling always courses through me, a nice, grand feeling, the awareness that you exist, that you are alive, thinking of me, the knowledge that all your steps, movements, words, thoughts are somehow and somewhere, partly or fully directed entirely to me. The feeling that none of my thoughts, actions, moods are disappearing into empty space, but are all reflected in you. And within it all, still a tinge of

sadness. It's always like that with me, probably so that the scales balance. For I have never really mastered one feeling totally, some twist of the mind or tiny little nerve also always wants to get a word in, too. — Sweet love, I am with you
Always Your Toy.

To Martha [1921 | Dresden]

Your Toy loves you very much. Toy is a very nice word, better than Jimmy. Always call me Toy. I'm a clumsy guy and a real Biedermeier. I'm so pleased & happy today, the sun is shining and a letter came from you, which has made me so happy. Today I tried to work, it's just not quite right, but I'm not impatient. Actually, in fact I am impatient, namely, to see you. — Something must be working itself out within me, because I don't have the right impulse to get any work done. At the moment I'm obsessed by the idea of [not turning into a] Biedermeier, this really annoys me. All around me, in every direction, all I see are Biedermeiers. Yet again I feel the need to kill off these ideologies once and for all. Often, at times, I have set, fixed ideas that simply will not go away & prevent me from freely working. — Oh you, I believe and am quite certain that everything will be so beautiful, and that you'll kiss away my foggy, grey fantasies. I know that you'll always be able to help me; I know it. The fact that in the future I know I'll think out everything through you, together with you, united, in respect of you, is a voluptuously beautiful thought to me; like a high mast. Bright high skies, distant views, large radius, excitement, longing, intoxicated brightness. O, you, it will be nice! I have such tremendous desire to inhale so much, to see many things, and experience many things, as well. — It's such a shame that your handkerchief no longer bears your scent. — Oh you, it's going to be so incredibly beautiful. — What a miracle, so much so that I often get completely dizzy and can barely believe it. Dearest love, only, fairest you, I want to lay before you and kiss your feet for hours, and thank you. You'll be happy, very happy. I want to feel and sense everything you desire. I want to do everything that you want. You know and have so much of me, and my ways.

O, you, if only too some of your essence were in me! You will awaken so much in me, things I cannot yet see today, I'll experience miracles in myself through you, because I love you, believe in you. Because I know that you are grand & beautiful. — Dearest heart, forgive me, you needn't read what I write; you must read what I cannot write. This is much more. I would rather kiss you, hold you to me, laugh with you, cry with joy and see myself mirrored in your beautiful eyes.
Best fairest I am your Toy

To Martha 1921 [Dresden]

Sweet Maud At first I was annoyed by your letter, then on reading further, laughed happily. I imagine how you must've twisted up your sweet little mouth. No — not like thaaat — sweetest,

you're cute, you stubborn little lass, so you think you've got the whole picture when it comes to me, eh? But the camera, eh, proves that everything is relative (God how mundane), because this apparatus simply records random moods, facial expressions, & lighting, and then — oh, now what you have concocted, you naughty creature, that you have to tell it to me personally, to see what kind of a face I'll make?! You were "unhappy" about the photos, my sweeetest, I kiss you on your little pouty mouth. — I'm waiting for a photograph of you and hope that you'll send me one that looks like I see you (after all, you did promise me you would). My bookbinder always prepares packages clean & cheap — [ok now I'm done] because I've drunk some brandy, actually — a bad tune ringing from the discordant squeezebox, gin over Allasch with a mandarin twist. That's why my handwriting looks somewhat anarchic.
Many thousand sweet kisses Jim.

Since the diminutive "Maud" was already being used by Georg Grosz's wife, "Mutzli" soon became the nickname that Martha inherited, which also happened to be the name Hans Koch had used with her as well. She found her given first name unappealing.

To Martha [1921 | Dresden]

Dearest, I love you, I simply love you. I don't know what else I can say. Sometimes I'm so strange, so pathetic, which then in turn always increases the anger within me. Raging, against myself. Be good to me, when I'm writing such things.

I really won't suppress those things that have hurt me, I want to be humble, not make any demands on you, and will hope that you realize that two people can't grow closer together through selfishness lest those things two people share should grow to some kind of a power struggle.

And that's so boorrring to me. We will not rule or order each other around, or abuse the goodness of the other. We need to love each other and be good to each other. And therefore you must realize that whenever we're together, you have to cast out all strange thoughts.

Herzensmaud, I'm happy about your letters. You see many a thing, I dare to tell you things I've thought of, sentimentalism, because [I know] you've sensed it so deeply, had to notice it; that you should be unhappy about any of this though, even if only for a moment, would however be foolish. For my part, I'm happy when any little sadness in your heart has gone. I also know that all good intentions won't help you and that at the moment we are very foreign to one another, but I'm still very hopeful.

I cannot criticize you; I can only relate my feelings. If we can only have one happy thing, then let it be this: submerge in me completely and be filled, without criticism, without motive, without asking for anything, then you will care!
In love always Your Jimmy

To Martha [1921 | Dresden]

You, my only beloved, fairest sweetheart, how much joy your letter has brought me today!! —— I've been running around like a drunk —— You, you are so good, so soft, you give me so many beautiful things. How much courage, how much strength your words incite within me! My beautiful sun, I want only to worship you! I kiss your hands fervently & long, feel as no one else can feel in this world!

Letter to Martha Koch, 1921

Oh, you — — it's all so beautiful — —

I am definitely coming Friday night, do you want to pick me up at the train station? You know, I'm so thrilled about everything.

It should be something special! And we are alone, oh you, which is nice! I was sad all day yesterday and discouraged. Now, suddenly, everything is beautiful once again. — I'll keep you deep in my heart and won't let you go.

I love you, my beautiful fragrant flower, I love you, You soft velvety cat, I love you, you fine, beautiful woman. I love you Jim.

To Martha [1921?] [Dresden]

Sweetest, it was good that I received a letter from you now. Everything around me immediately became much more beautiful. Freer, happier. I'm trembling with excitement and joy. I'm trembling with joy at our happiness. It's all so humble, what you write; I want to hold your beautiful head between my hands & [*illegible*] maybe I forget with you that I'm a lonely animal on a dark street. Because you're nice and fine and bright and easy. I wish there were also things that you could recognize and discover through me.

Don't take me lightly! Sometimes you write such strange things. What is time, anyway?

I've so much to discuss with you, a lot, to gaze into your eyes so much more. Sometimes I'm miserable. Don't know why. You should always be honest with me, you know that, right?!

It's awful that these letters take four days to be delivered. — So I'll be coming to Dusseldorf next Sunday. I'm not sure what words I can tell you; confess to you, my love, to relate my good luck. I only know that you understand all those things that remain unspoken. Surely you do understand all my vague, indefinable yearnings; maybe you'll even become my partner in loneliness.

One ought not build permanent structures & each permanent condition is a transgression against living an abundant life. What is time; what are these short or long seconds spent with you, happy, completely lost and happy by you, with you, can I not say for certain that I've loved eternally, love, and will love?!!

Dearest, let's not oppress our love with the rut of everyday life. I wish that this time, perhaps, the only time in my life —

I stopped at this point yesterday evening. I was freezing...

Sweet Kisses loonnng kisses   Jimmy

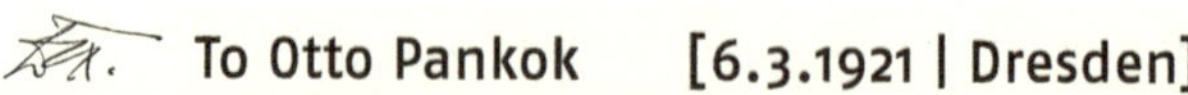

To Otto Pankok [6.3.1921 | Dresden]

dear Pankok When your letter arrived, Mainz had already sent the pictures here. Had I already told you that Mainz would not exhibit the pictures for "moral reasons"? The Nov. [November] Gruppe has now refused a quite harmless picture of mine for reasons of propriety. — I should rather like to put together a number of things for you and a have collective exhibition at your place, maybe, but only in the autumn. Then you will need to communicate the available number of mtrs. As for the studio in the meantime, many thanks. Hopefully it will all work out. Best regards, also to your wife DIX

Otto Pankok Museum, Hünxe-Drevenack

To Martha [Nov. 10, 1921 | Dresden]

My beautiful sweet love Every day that I don't get a message from you is lost and useless. It's so harsh, bitterly cold outside, and the moon is metallic sharp and thin. Any work that I would do now would be pointless. Maybe you are sad! Maybe you are merry. I know that you must always know something about me & that you love me. I know that loneliness and despondency befalls you thousands of times a day and that your eyes shine a thousand times in a day, glowing & slowly dimming; I know that you are physically more unwell than well, that happiness and pain alternate within you as constantly as inhaling

& exhaling do. I wonder whether you are also as unstable as me; if every conversation, every action also seems as meaningless & excruciating to you as me. My Dearest, sweetest, I shall soon be with you! I'm looking forward to you, to your joy, to your happiness. You know, in spite of it all, everything is still so gorgeous, so unreal, I almost did not believe in the reality of my happiness. I sometimes think it might all be a mistake, or that I've had a very nice dream. You, I tremble when I'm fully aware of my happiness.
100,000,000,000 Kisses Jimmy

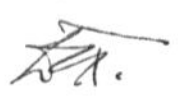

To Martha [11.12.1921 | Dresden]

Most beautiful woman. My only beloved in all the world. Everything I've written to you, any concerns & considerations, are nonsense. For me there is simply no other way forward than to marry you. — How infinitely happy we will be.

For 2 days now I have received nothing from you. I'm running around like a madman; telegraph me. I can't bear it anymore. I'm just going crazy in this situation. Be good to me. Forgive me. Love me.

I'm so unhappy, and yet I know that You love me and that you will turn everything to the good. I'm as happy as a child at all the beauty of what we'll experience together. You'll [no doubt] have a most enhancing & consummating effect upon me. What I can do for you, I do not know; I seem to fall so short compared to you. So insignificant.

Maybe I can make you happy somehow, after all, & serve you. Oh — you, I'm so terribly unhappy and so happy at the same time. I love only you, forever your
Jimmy

To Martha On a Tuesday afternoon in 1921 [Dresden]

Dearest heart I've returned from Berlin at noon today, where I spent 2 days. A telegram from you was waiting for me there, wherein you ask whether or not I've received a telegr. and letter. Maybe in the meantime you also received my 3 letters that I sent to St. Goar. It's unfortunate how everything goes so wrong. During the entire trip from Berlin to Dr. [Dresden] I lived in the sweet hope of finding something from you, a good, kind letter, which makes me happy again & fuller. However, I departed early today, at 8 o'clock, and sat in seat № 78 —

I feel so stupid, so pathetic, and so petty, — oh dearest, I consider myself miserable (because it's me basically), but do not doubt my great, unchanging love & veneration for you, always. Just imagine, in my youth I always lived in poor, meager conditions & [as a result] I consequently lack a freedom, or easy nature, when it comes to material things. — Do you love me? I long for you so much. I'm just a bit sad, yet basically hope to soon be with you and to be happy with you. I mustn't think about the justification for this hope! Your always melancholy-happy
Jimmy

To Martha 1921 [Dresden]

My only Beloved, sweet, dearest good, dearest You You, are you happy? I know that you're always waiting eagerly for something from me. I couldn't come at once, so, you're not angry with me. If you think it wise, I'll come to you next week and we can discuss things somewhere. I do hope you can understand that I just need to collect myself first in order to make a decision (whereby I find all decisions in matters of practical life difficult). Also, I didn't want to discuss the matter with Hans because I just don't understand what interest Hans has in our matter. — I'm so excited, sometimes racked with terrible doubt, partly full of courage and partly full of joy, excited about all new things, feelings, and experiences that I'll experience with you. Dearest, dearest, it's impossible not to think of you, constantly. It's terrifying to think that you were displeased with my previous letter and that you think I'm ugly and petty.

Oh, dearest, it would be so nice if all these things weren't all in play, to be weighed, did not exist. For I love you like no one else in this world. I'm tired and sick now. I feel as if I'd run 50 km. My legs are worn out & I feel a terrible pressure in my chest. I would just love to shout something out, if only I had the strength to do so. It's hot and humid in this room, & outside the wind is howling. If I go outside, my condition will not improve, but worsen; there I feel my whole homelessness. I long for you, for your warm smile that is sometimes cruel, as your soft red mouth, long for your scent, for your so dangerously clever brow, for everything. Love, dear, sweet, soft, proud, beautiful, beloved — if I were with you now, I would cry like a fool for joy, cry in yearning pain, cry in anger, with love. I'm writing stupid nonsense.

To Martha [1921 | Dresden]

My sweetheart
Now it's just about a week 'til I'll be with you. Oh my dear, it's going to be so beautiful. For the time being I'm still working like a madman. Rushed, as the time quickly passes. It's so nice to think of you. With a silent lasting joy I think of you. My rock, my life, my love, my beautiful joy, I will always be good and loving & kind to you; our love is, our lives shall always be beautiful, always happy. Long, endless yearning — I want to put my head in your lap, not think of doing anything without desire, without violent desire, I want to hear your heart beating as it keeps time with my same clock; want to hear your blood circulating as if it were my own; would like to know your good loving thoughts that are mine, too, and no longer want to be [only] *me* and feel You as only you. I know that there are such moments. I would want so much that they last endlessly, nothing interfering or coming between. — Harmony? I don't know what I should call it. Ultimate trust perhaps, security, a sense of home. I don't know if you know what I mean, if you sometimes have this great longing for sweet tranquility. Rushed, I run around, rushed, even when entwined in sexual embrace, so I am. —

It's so nice to talk to you. — Have patience with me. — Be human & be my comrade. — I talked a long time with you; it is good that we will soon be together; I act and speak continuously of my idea that I have of you, not with you.
Always your Toy.

To Martha [1921 | Dresden]

My sweet darling! So I come Sunday afternoon. How beautiful it shall all be; I am thrilled. I'm actually already en route to D. [Dusseldorf]. On the street, & when I'm sitting together with friends, and in the evening before I fall asleep, I think of you again. I am happy & fulfilled when I think of you. And I'm also proud sometimes when I think of you. Proud that I love such a beautiful, great, perfect, sweet woman, proud that this woman loves me back; that's all a lot more than the greatest works a person can create. — — —

Instead of making myself bad again, I've drawn this line. — I sometimes find myself imagining everything at once: Your movements, your face, your eyes, your hairline, your mouth. I'd love to hear you sing again. Huh, you'll often here me singing out loud. It's going to be so incredibly wonderful. We'll be the happiest people, and things can only get better & better.
Your lucky longing
Jimtoy

To Martha [December 1921?] [Dresden]

Mutzlimaud many soft, sweet kisses! Today I'm happy, full of joy and light. I [*illegible*] wrapped, i.e. a box, tomorrow I pack the 2nd & 3rd. Probably I'll stay until Dec 15, here in Dresden. I've received a portrait commission (Mk 3000), I still want to do it. Tomorrow I start. I will then travel home to finish the portrait there already because you'll surely go back to St. Goar on the 17th (or not?), and I just can't work particularly well in this little shack in Dusseldorf. However, if you stay in D. [Dusseldorf], I'll postpone my trip home & travel a bit later. — Tomorrow I'm going to sell some sketches for 1500 Mk; the shop is moving. After a certain amount of time one should leave behind a city where one is sufficiently well known, since people get worried & buy fast. What are you up to all this time in your castle on the Rhine? Are people giving you a hard time? Dearest, I am so thrilled about our happiness. Sometimes I flatter myself, drawing parallels between Rembrandt and myself (*Selbstbildnis mit Saskia*) [Self-Portrait with Saskia], you know? I mean the same blustering joy, the frothy cups, feathered beret, silk, still life with fowl, abundance, earthly joy. And the beggars, Port of Amsterdam, prostitutes, peasants, erotica. I am happy, even if not quite so so engulfed by happiness as Mynher van Ryn. — but this is a strange letter: I'm happy, I love you very much, I want to kiss you long, long, feel your warmth & softness and laugh with you
Your Jimmy.

Portrait commission: possibly *Bildnis Dr. Paul Ferdinand Schmidt* [Portrait of Dr. Paul Ferdinand Schmidt] (Löffler 1921/14) or *Bildnis Rechtsanwalt Dr. Fritz Glaser* [Portrait of the Attorney Dr. Fritz Glaser] (Löffler 1921/15).
– The Schloß am Rhein [Castle on the Rhine] Dix refers to is Villa Rheinfels in St. Goar, the family home of Martha's parents, surnamed Lindner.

To Martha [1921? | Dresden]

My sweetest I love you, endlessly!
I've received such a sad letter from you. You good, dearest beloved, don't be upset & let my negative thoughts come and frighten you! I love You over everything, forever, always! I was very depressed at the thought that I might have saddened you. Dearest, my only one, I'm always honest with you! I always want to be. You cannot doubt me, my love for you is greater than ever and you're the only creature in the world I love. I kiss your fragrant hands and beg your pardon, because somehow I must really be to blame. You are my only desire, sweetness, I worship you as a goddess. Oh — I've made you so sad, I want to be with you & my kisses should tell you that you, only you exist for me. Most beautiful dearest, best, You are a [*illegible*] everything, everything is empty and dreary without you. I think of you fervently in sleepless nights! Yesterday I couldn't sleep half the night and thought only of you — when I'm working you're with me, everything I do and think, I'm doing it all with you in mind. Oh — believe me, you're everything to me and I want to be everything to you. I'm coming on the 16th, certainly in the evening. My work has been completed here. I lie at your feet, kiss them, & am always Your Toy.

To Martha [1921 | Dresden]

Sweetest love many beautiful sweet kisses on your sweet eyes, on your sweet little mouth, on your beautiful little white teeth with the small pale red tongue between, on your little forehead & on your defiant Mutzli-neck. I love you, and I love you more and more. I feel a little bit guilty because I've taken no further action concerning our apartment. Glaser has again printed an advertisement in the newspaper and I can pick up the offers there tomorrow or the next day. — Why can't I get any work done? Well, maybe because I just have too much imagination and arrive at the goal before the material is there. My way of working requires too strict a construction that must be completed to precise, clean execution, too much discipline. Today I've constructed a parquet in a cumbersome way & it is just unsatisfying. But all will be well. — In the meantime, I do have some plans to do some pictures — work is there. Often, some instances of the critical mind come to the fore, but soon enough, stupidity sets in — which is also part of painting — and the desire to conquer again.

Don't worry yourself about any of this rubbish, that's just me. I'm freezing, and going to bed. Before I fall asleep, I still think of you Ever your Jimmy.

At first, a life together in Dresden was intended, since Dix had a studio at the Akademie until Easter 1922 and was continuing to use it.

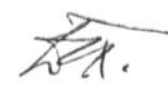

To Martha [1921 | Dresden] [single sheet]

To Martha
I send you a lot of soft sweet longing kisses on your beautiful girly mouth! I've already sent out feelers for an apartment on the Weißen Hirsch. The director of the spa knows an acquaintance of mine. You'll surely come soon, you'll see, we live here much cheaper than in D. [Düsseldorf]. Everyone here is talking about the fact that I might have a fabulous, beautiful, elegant (and consequently rich) woman. I'm again lodged in the Lustmord apartment, the gas is burning dim & it's cold...

At the end of this letter, Dix refers to the apartment where he had created the Lustmörder drawings in 1920. The term "Lustmord" can alternately be translated as "sex killer," "sexual murder," "lust murder," or the like. Generally speaking, paintings and drawings of naked, murdered, or butchered women were common in German art galleries and avant-garde publications in the 1920s especially, the two major proponents of which were Dix and Grosz. Dix addressed the theme of Lustmörder (a sex murder[er]) on several occasions and in various formats, including in etchings & in watercolors, perhaps most famously in the painting rendered as a self-portrait. Aside from the 1920 self-portrait *Der Lustmörder*, Martha later recalled an additional Lustmord painting, which Dix had included on one of the panels of the 1920 *Altar für Kavaliere*, which was later destroyed by the Nazis as degenerate art. See Eva Karcher, *Eros und Tode im Werk von Otto Dix: Studien zur Geschichte des Körpers in den zwanziger Jahren* (Berlin: 1984) 49.

To Martha [winter 1921 | Dresden]

Most loved one A sweet, long kiss for you. — There's a little snow outside and I feel my fateful loneliness & homelessness deeply, and profoundly. — I have a longing for the warmth of your eyes, your mouth, and your sweet body. —

But I'm no longer so depressed; I received your letter and see everything so easily, so beautifully, and hopefully and auspiciously. Sweetest, everything is bound to be alright! — Even my distrust for Hans has subsided; he cannot still be so very despicable, or that's how I've imagined him sometimes throughout the dull dark hours of the last days. Perhaps he means well with us. I'm writing you about everything — my concerns, in material terms, and the matters, in purist terms, that are so foreign and hostile to me, but still remain like a threatening cloud, hanging above me. I still can't get any work done. How I spend my time, even I don't know. I'm like undulating water that cannot rest. I must have clarification; You must give it to me; You need to dispel doubts, otherwise I won't find my footing here; otherwise I cannot work, either. Either you'll push me completely into despair wherein you realize what I wrote, and see no way out, or You'll make me happy, erase my concerns — both will be strong stimulants for my work, while I still hang in the air, I can't breathe, can't concentrate, and had pain in the spine, am always tired & always restless & inattentive. — I don't believe that You should worry about the thing with Hans and your sister — etc. Hans has loved your sister for some time. — I even hinted in a letter, namely, that Hans wants to remarry immediately and has been thinking of your sister. — For everyone seems to say she's even more beautiful than you. — I have much to discuss with you. I'll come as soon as you like. But I have to talk about everything with you, alone, before I talk to Hans.

Sweetest love, don't feel lonely, I'm with you always, I don't want to leave, cannot leave you. All cold considerations are painful to me, but I have to think of all to cause myself pain, to find a counterweight to my drunkenness.

I think of you every hour, over & over. My most lovely, sweetest love! — Fairest, sweetest, finest, cleverest woman of my life. I have only loved you, always believe me, for so long, in all that I have left behind, and from which I run away again, I've wanted only you, loved only you. I can hardly believe that I've only known you 5 weeks. I so long to caress your *Christzeichen*; it awakens such a strange pleasure & lust in me, I don't know how to express it. You, soft you you you you hot, sweet, scented velvet, you're with me, I know, what is distance for us!? I feel you — sometimes your beautiful defiant forehead furrows curiously; sometimes your mouth is so soft, and sometimes you look inward and breathe, and sometimes you are shivering too. I send you thousands upon thousands of longing greetings
Jimmy.

Christzeichen: A play on "Kreuzzeichen," meaning sign of the cross. Exactly what Dix means, as what he is referring to, is not clear.

To Martha [12.7.1921 | Dresden]

Mutzlimaud sweet Maud Herzensmaudmaud! So — I was ashamed at having written you the birthday story, etc., I immediately took note of how stupid I was. — So — I am to prove myself — "as a man" — so, how am I to do that? Today was the 7th, I had imagined that I could work well on this day and see —! It went well. — I didn't spend much time at all thinking of you. I've only been able to read your sweet letter once due to sheer running around, and work. But tomorrow I want to read it several times. Just imagine — I've already received money from Goltz, 1920 Mk. Goltz wants to put on an exhibition of my graphics with Ensor in February, probably wants to make a contract with me, publish a nice catalog, and makes me eulogies. — There's only one obstacle there — I have no graphics. — A hundred thousand sweet kisses, on your feet, your knees, your thighs and lips Jim.

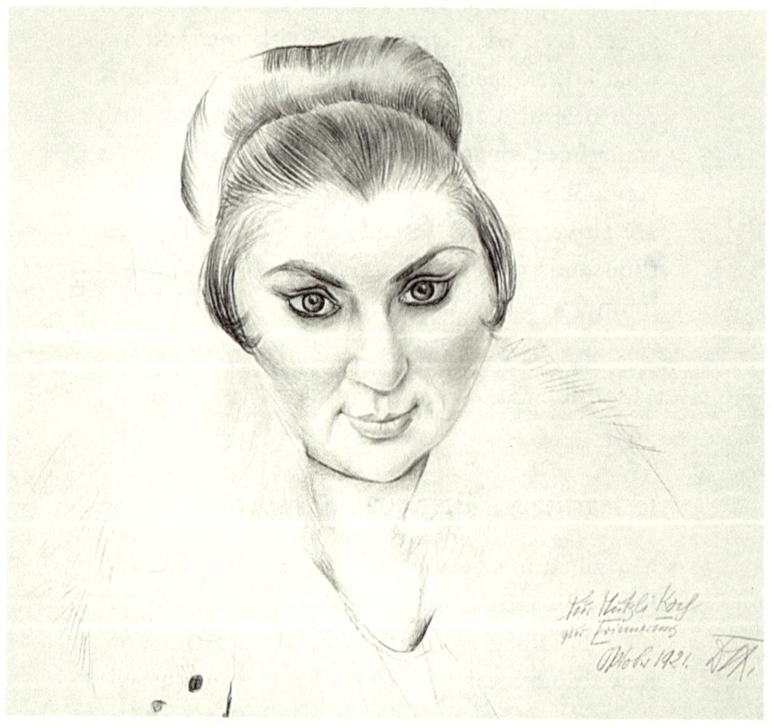

Portrait of Mutzli Koch, 1921, drawing

On December 5, 1921, Hans Goltz sent incidentals on sold etchings and wrote to Dix: "I see in your art such opportunities, which are so significant, that I even want to dare to attempt to put the entire prestige of my company on the line for you. I therefore intend to stage an entire exhibition in February next year, together with Ensor, of your graphics [...]." After Dix included paintings in the exhibition, and Goltz had agreed, Goltz changed his tune. In January 1922, Dix received a rejection: "[...] I am absolutely disappointed in most of the things. What caused me to want to contact you for an exhibition were your etchings. I did not believe at that time that I would mainly have to show, with the exception of some good portraits, brothel scenes and brothel-madams in the exhibition [...]. Unfortunately my opinion on the drawings is still unrestricted in its denial. [...] and it goes without saying that I now have had my complete fill of the brothels, the prostitutes, the murdered communists, and road grime to last me a lifetime." Dix responded with an "arrogant answer," to which Goltz responded: "The tone and content of your letter unfortunately makes it impossible for me to deal with you personally in any correspondence or other communication forthwith" (GNM, DKA, NL Dix, Otto I, C 199).

To Martha [1921 | Dresden]

[*The 1st page is missing*] [...] studio, which is available to me until Easter 1922. I definitely have to work now. I simply can't stand it anymore. As long as we do not yet have the apartment, you will still go on living in St. Goar, no doubt, & so I'm just as lonely there as here. — For I have 3 large boxes full of pictures & drawings. If I bring them into the small attic, where the furniture is stowed already, and my bed will go, too, there is barely room to work.

When I come home at night & enter my icy gaslit room, the writing pad on the table, I start to write, and though usually I don't know what to write, I write anyway (for example, I really have nothing new to relate today). I saw *Richard II* at the Schauspielhaus today, new production, new staging, sat in the first level [*illegible*] of course, among so many very proper people. In front of me sat a perverse delicate lady who smelled terribly, of lilies. So I associated the lily smell with the play and thought continually of "noble corpses," theater corpses & necrophilia, the stage cardboard, semi-Reinhardish, semi-Stage-illusion (the stuff had been mortised by Hettner).

In the first act the king sat on his throne, which stood on a 2½ mtr high chest, and since no ladder led up there, I kept asking myself, how did the man actually get up there? He also looked like a green king in a card game, which I found very good; everything was probably intended that way. — Most of all, I shudder to think of the terrible room that I have to work in, in Dusseldorf. I wish winter were over. I must have a studio as soon as possible. If the matter with our apartment has not been solved by February, and I still haven't found a studio in D. [Dusseldorf] yet, then I'll keep working until then in my Dresden studio. What are you doing, how are you, dearest! You are probably "waawking" hard. In the meantime midnight has come, I am going to bed, I'm still going to think of you for quite a while and kiss the pillow. I look forward to tomorrow morning, there'll be a letter from you, or even 2, because today was Sunday, and I wasn't able to go into the studio. I love you with all my heart, I am always with you, I kiss you, intently, & embrace you, fully Your Toy.

1922

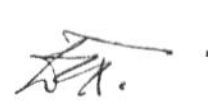

To Martha [1922 | Dresden]

My sweetest, dearest, good & only Herzensmutzli, I have read all night and shortly before Dresden finished *Madame Bovary* — oh you, poor Mutz, you had to go back home alone like this! Today I worried about all kinds of things and tomorrow I'll actually start working. You Sweet Girl, I've you to thank, oh how beauuuutiful [you are]. You've packed my bags again. It's funny, when I unpacked it but, I was so very happy about it & felt the tender care provided was a lovely gift. You, my sweet, beautiful woman, I adore you; I always think of you; I love you very much. — Keep me always, always loving, as I'll keep loving you always in my heart. — You mustn't misinterpret my occasional fantastically dully rapt moods. Sometimes I think that I'm making you sad with such things — but I won't spout my madness any further about it.
I am always Your Toy

Kisses to Hanali & Muggeli from me.

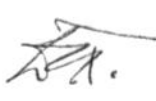

To Martha [1922 | Dresden]

My only dearest one Today I worked with real momentum. I have drawn out the three sketches for the *Marientriptychon*, but in the evening of each day, I then feel that I have done too little; I'm also insanely hungry, starving. Sunday I want to leave early to Berlin. Tonight I've spent the whole evening with my friends at the café; it was hot & uninspiring, old habits returning — to drive off the evenings, to drive them away, literally expel them, then go home, sleep, be happy without too much fatigue and look forward to the next day, happy when the night is over. I'm being very remiss; too lazy to shave, even lazy to dress nicely, actually am really only interested in working. It is quite good that you're not here, at least provisionally, as much as I on the other hand want to be with you, for later I will be in Dusseldorf, that is, when I return, unrestrained, with complete abandon, oh, do you somehow feel somewhat neglected? In D. [Dusseldorf] I've come to see that I simply cannot work if I sense or believe I have some sort of obligation toward others. These sorts of concerns make me a bit lethargic. I know that you're smart, and so everything will be fine! The clock is ticking madly; this monotonous noise is driving me crazy.

Dearest, be "peaceful," namely because this letter is boring. But how can you think up better ideas at night when you're exhausted, sitting in a gas-lit room with frozen feet?

I love you; I always think of you in my lonely hours; it all comes back to me, in my mind, your sweet girliness, your full, proud womanhood, I think of my whole, sweet Mutz Your Jim.

To Martha [1922 | Dresden]

Sweetest, dearest What are you doing! Are you cheerful and gay? For me, one day is almost like the other. I work — badly, convulsively, and had given myself the illusion that I could work easily. — Today I went to the circus, beautiful aerial acts, high-wire acts on the tower. 48 lions, bears, monkeys, horses, a very nice springboard group, lots of light, color shirts, equipment, ropes, harnesses and rope ladders, then I sat & yawned at the cafe and we all talked about constructive perspectives — because I have just begun putting together my jazz band picture. —

My beautiful, good, sweet smelling girl, I long for you so much, for your sweetness, for Your goodness, for your sweet mouth and your sweet little breasts, I am very lonely — it's no good without you, without your physical closeness — I again start denying myself, & my actions — apparently this is a disease with me! —

You, my only, I need you; I need the person who is lighter than I am, to help me, and affirm me —!

It'll be spring again soon, then my state of mind will improve, & then I'll be happy. — I'm so happy that I have you. We're going to see beautiful things together. We will always want to be very happy. — My most beautiful sweet woman, I seem so miserable when I think of you, your beauty and your wealth and your flexibility. I've always some dark thought or other — namely, that you could

find me boring, stubborn, surly & selfish. — You cannot be angry with me. — The light is so dim & so yellow — outside the wind is howling — my serious state of mind emergent, from darkened corners, I *long* for you so much!
Jim.

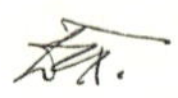

To Martha [1922 | Dresden]

Dear heart, You dearest, dearest sweetest many sweet kisses for your pink letter. I am happy and long for you, deeply.

Write to me like this, always — won't you!? Your letters make me so happy and so airy, I've done a good job today, though not much, but I've thought and I've prepared. I could work day and night — if I had the strength to do it, because by 4 in the afternoon I'm usually already exhausted — mentally I'm always fresh and working out many things, thinking intently. I'm going to Berlin on Sunday morning and hope that I get the commissions. Try to concentrate on it with me, too. I want to set high prices. For the 4 pictures, 30,000, but that is actually pretty low. Today I was at Dr. Glaser's, he is going to publish an ad about our apartment. However, I have no money for the time being. Glaser laments that he can't pay. It's more Schmidt that can't pay until he has presented the picture to the commission and that will not work before March because the picture is in Munich. That leaves my Fritze-etching — that is, if it sells, and it's a pretty rotten head. But if we are somewhat reasonable, it'll be enough. I think that I'm going to rent an apartment for the beginning of February. Then you can come whenever you can, or want. You'll see, it'll all work out, and we want to be very happy!

I'm looking forward to it, especially to paint you. Poor Mutz! How bored she'll be, seated as a model! But you'll do it gladly, because you'll become an immortal, [drawing — laurel wreath] Mutzli, just think of it! You sweet, loving, soft cat, dearest beloved heart.
I love you always love
Jimmy

Drawing: Lorenz EDV 01.13.51
Paintings: *Bildnis Rechtsanwalt Dr. Fritz Glaser* [Portrait, Attorney Dr. Fritz Glaser], Löffler 1921/15, and *Bildnis Dr. Paul Ferdinand Schmidt* [Portrait of Dr. Paul Ferdinand Schmidt], Löffler 1921/14. Schmidt had lobbied for the acquisition of the picture *Kriegskrüppel* [War Cripple] (Löffler 1920/8) for the Dresden City Museum. In 1937, the painting was among those confiscated, and it is likely that it was destroyed as "degenerate art."

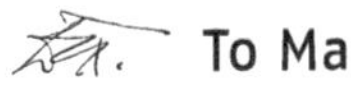

To Martha [1922 | Dusseldorf]

My Dearest
I didn't get a little letter from you today, & haven't earned one, either, because I wrote such rotten things to you. Serves me right! — I was at the Kochs' this morning and evening and Koch and I played ball with Hanali, then they did not want to let me go since the Kochs' had not yet arrived. In the evening Ndf [Nierendorf] had me dropped off. Kielmann was also there, and I discussed the coal thing with him.

I have to buy him the same amount of coal and deliver it to his house. Mutz, I paid Preyer. Today I received 9,000 Mk from Ndf, which I will use to pay Schneider in Dresden. Maybe I'm going back through Berlin to see some exhibitions. — Hanali was so sweet & quite wanted to seduce me into playing the piano. When I was there in the evening, Kahsen had just come, prosecutor or whatever he is, and announced the Muggelis' arrival. — What's wrong, my dearest, I put your picture on the bedside table, you're gazing at me in such a melancholy, sad way that I myself am very sad about it. — It's so empty and desolate around me, if you're not here. — I am ever so sad and just don't know why.

Why must we always experience so many awful things, so much fighting, why do we need to make our lives so hard for each other. I am turning fearful and shrinking in the face of it. — Be *good &* dear to me. Your Toy

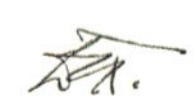

To Max Grünbaum 1.19.1922 [PM | Dresden] [PC]

Dear Herr Grünbaum!
The sketches for the Triptych are done, for the other picture, not yet. Maybe I'll come to Berlin on Sunday & present the things to you, because I think it's better if we discuss the matter personally. Also, I'll retouch the damaged picture at the same time. I'll write to you again.
With best regards
Your Dix
I'm back, for a while, at Dresden Antonplatz I

AdK, Berlin, Visual Arts Autograph Collection № 43
No *Marientriptychon* is included in the catalog of Dix's works.

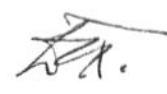

To Johanna Ey [spring 1922 | Dresden]

Dear mother Ey! How are you? What's [drawing — Wollheim] up to?

I have a request

I want to make a series of 6 etchings, but did not bring enough plates along. Now I'm running around to buy zinc today, but this type is only available in whole sheets. Since my etching plates are still there, I ask you kindly, please immediately send me 5 pieces, namely: [*The rest is missing*]
[Back:] since. — I hope that my wife is still coming to Dresden this week. —
Drillhase [Trillhaase] wanted to try to help us with an apartment, do you know anything about that?
Greet everyone from me
With thanks in advance

Your Dix

Antonplatz I

Dresden

[drawing — *Dix küsst Mutter Ey die Hand*
[Dix Kissing Mother Ey's hand]

Archives of Remmert and Barth Gallery, Dusseldorf
Drawings: Lorenz EDV 01.13.27 and 28
Gert Wollheim's painting *Lenkbares Stück Festland passiert unter wehender Flagge den Raum von Omega* [A steerable piece of land passing Omega under a flapping flag] had been confiscated by the authorities and there was an ongoing trial against the artist.
– Dix had located a studio in the meantime that he quickly found unsatisfactory.

Liebe Mutter Ey! Wie geht's?

Was macht

Ich habe eine Bitte

Ich will eine Reihe von 6 Radierungen machen habe aber nicht genug Platten mitgenommen. Nun bin ich heute schon herumgelaufen um Zink zu kaufen aber diese Stärke gibt man nur in ganzen Tafeln ab. Da ich nun meine Radierplatten noch dort stehen habe bitte ich Dich herzlich, sende mir doch umgehend 5 Stück davon und zwar:

Letter to Johanna Ey, with drawing *Porträtskizze Wollheim* [Portrait sketch of Wollheim] & *Otto Dix küsst Johanna Ey die Hand* [Otto Dix kissing the hand of Johanna Ey], spring 1922

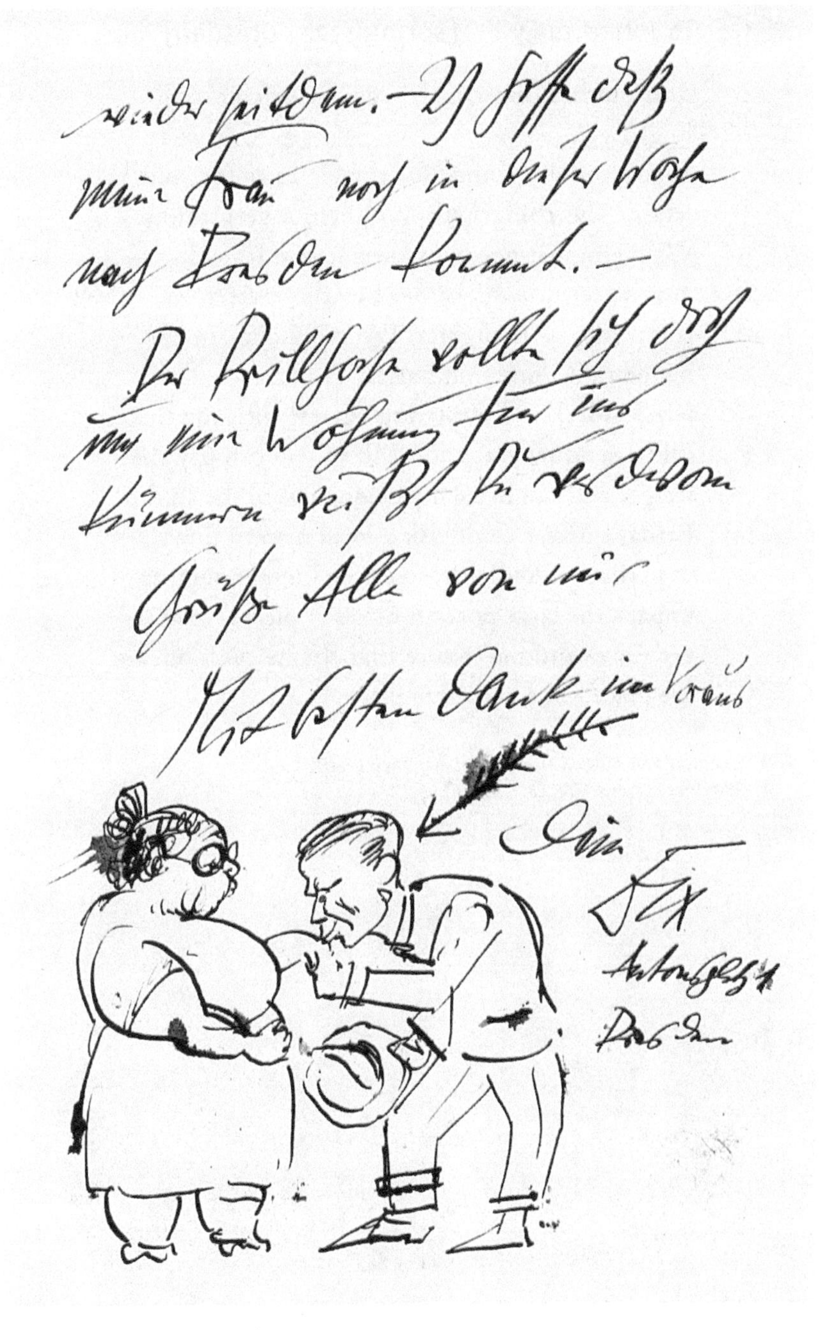

wieder seitdem. – Ich hoffe daß
meine Frau noch in dieser Woche
nach Dresden kommt. –

Der [illegible] sollte sich doch
um eine Wohnung für uns
kümmern [illegible]

Grüße Alle von mir

Mit besten Dank im Voraus

Dein
Dix
[illegible]
Dresden

To Johanna Ey [spring 1922 | Dresden]

dear mother [drawing — egg-laying chicken]
Egg! Egg!
Thank you very much for the plates & for your letter. The thing with Wollheim's very funny. Wollheim just needs to keep strong [drawing — gun battery], *battle-strong*! in the matter. [Drawing — firefighter, Ey, Wollheim; in the balloon: "I don't mind at all"]
[Back side:] So I wanted to [share] with you that I'll be sending you 2000 Mk so you can pay the freight and can bring my belongings to the studio. Perhaps Meier could ask a local man to unpack & perhaps Wollheim would be kind enough to unpack the large portrait boxes (3 pieces) to oversee times and make sure that the heaviest ones are placed in a rain-free place.

Remmert and Barth Gallery Archives, Dusseldorf
Drawings: Lorenz EDV 13.1.29

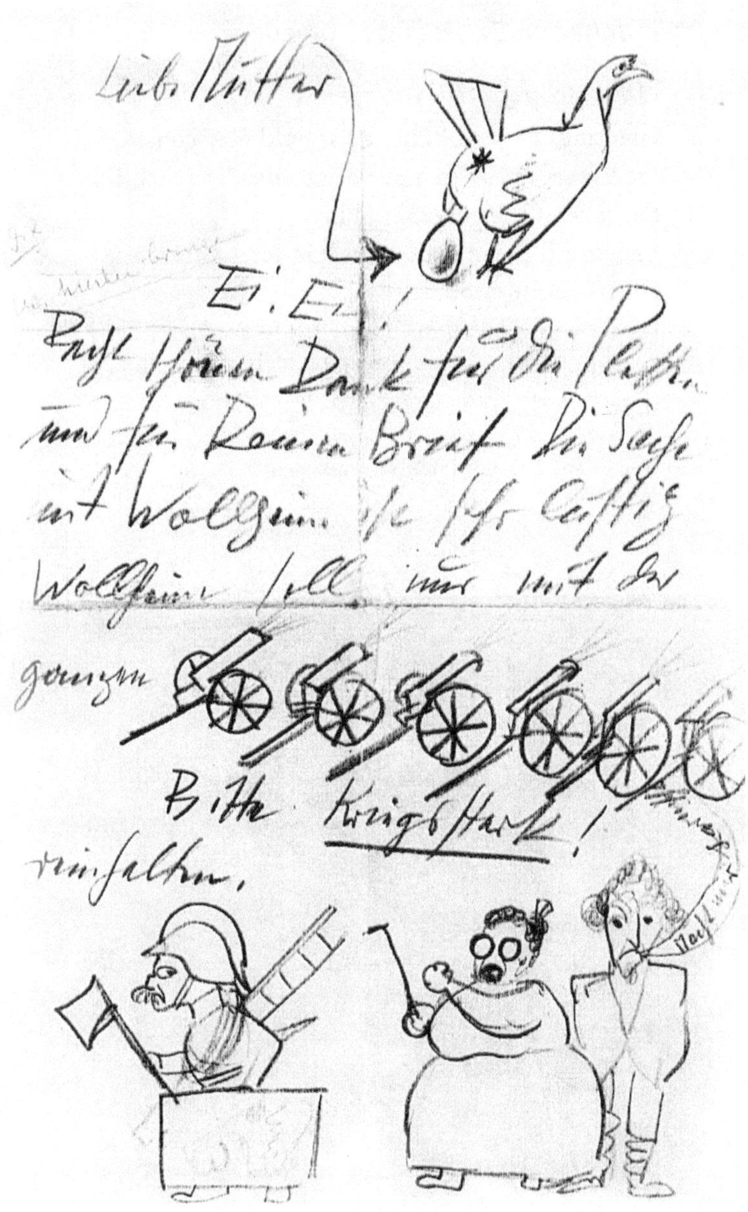

Liebe Mutter

Ei, Ei!

Besten Dank für die Platten und für Deinen Brief. Die Sache mit Wollheim ist sehr lustig. Wollheim soll nur mit der ganzen

Bitte Kriegsstark! einfahren.

Letter to Johanna Ey, with drawings on Gert Wollheim's picture *Lenkbares Stück Festland passiert unter wehender Flagge den Raum von Omega*, spring 1922

To Johanna Ey [1922 | Dresden]

[The beginning of the letter is missing]

Greetings to Wollheim, he should also consider the times we live in and not sacrifice so much for the sake of the general public.
Maybe I'll come to Dusseldorf later this week.
This time for good.
I greet you with all my [drawing — soul] & all my [drawing — heart] & with all my [drawing — mind]
Your Dix.

Archives of Galerie Remmert and Barth, Dusseldorf
Drawings: Lorenz EDV 13.1.25

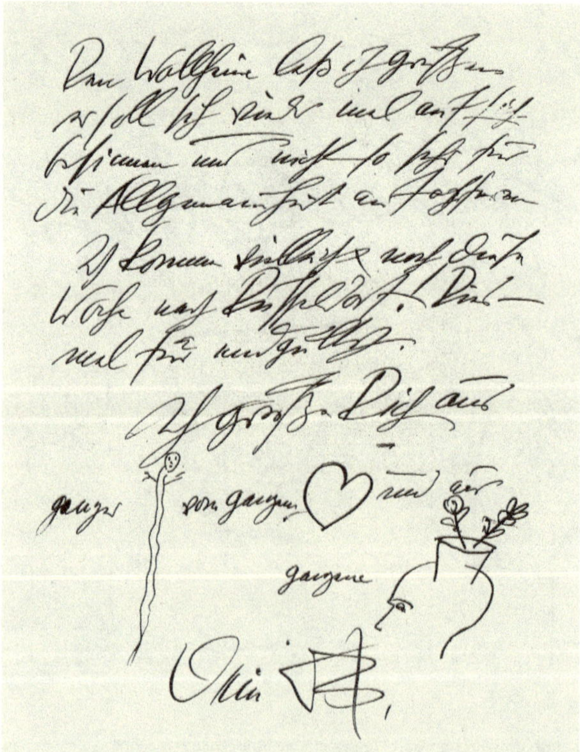

Ich grüße Dich aus
ganzer
von ganzem
und aus
ganzem
Otto Dix

Letter to Johann Ey, with drawings "Seele, Herz, Verstand" [Soul, heart, mind], 1922

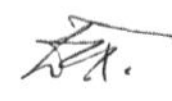

To Max Grünbaum [1.20.1922 | Dresden]

Dear Herr Grünbaum
Enclosed are 3 new sketches for the center image of the triptych. Hopefully one will prove to be in accordance with your desires.
The big picture will be finished later this month. Along with it, I am sending you an invoice for my paint dealer and kindly request, because I have no more money and the man is no longer willing to grant me any credit, to settle this for me. I ask for a quick reply & greet you sincerely
Your Dix.

AdK, Berlin, Visual Arts Autograph Collection № 43
See the previous letter dated 01.19.1922.

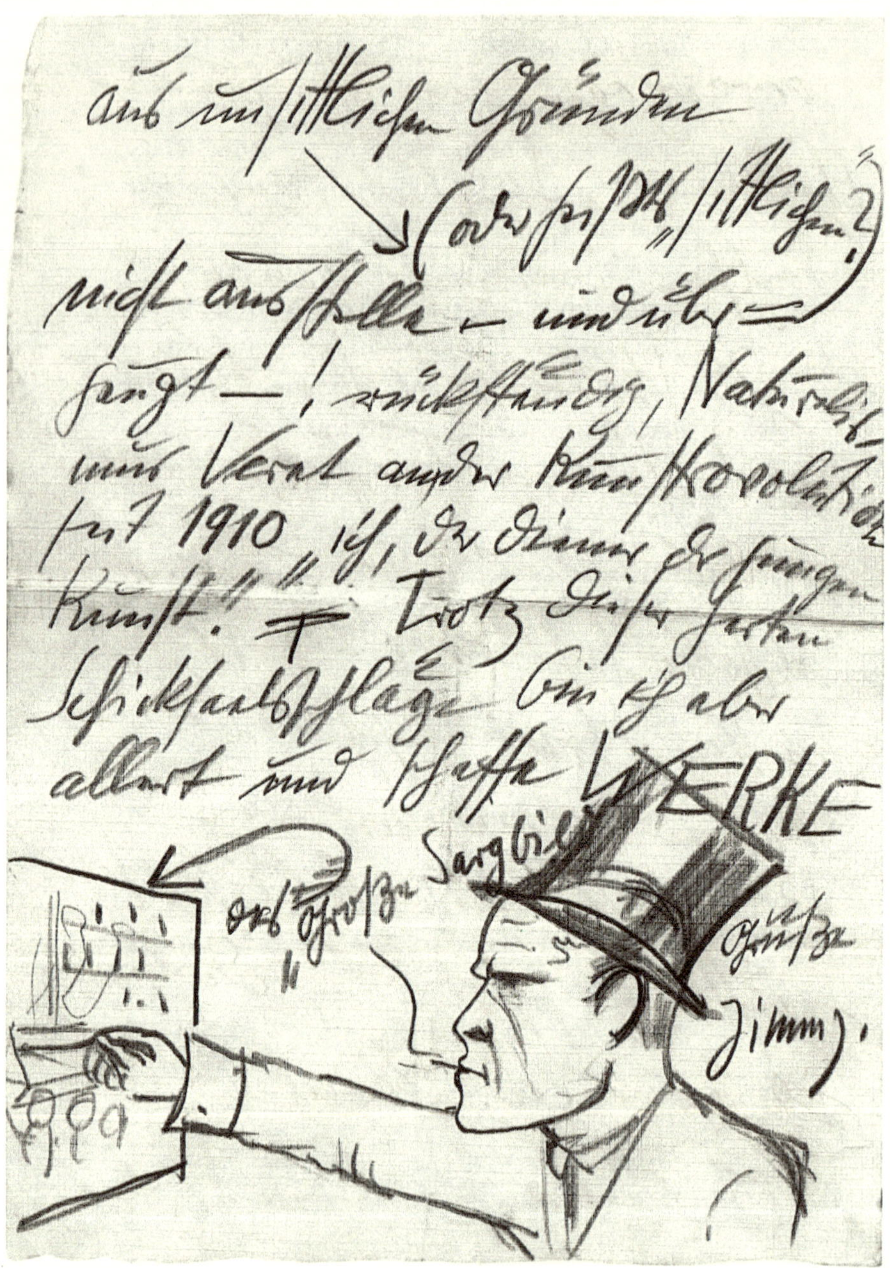

Letter to Hans Koch and Maria Lindner, with drawing *Dix am Sargbild arbeitend* [Dix working on coffin picture], 03.17.1922

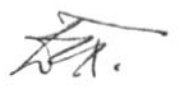

To Hans Koch & Maria Lindner 3.17.1922 [PM | Dresden]

dear Hans & Tamolli
So — the thing was so: I have, after I received the summons, i.e., on the 14th, I asked the lawyer if I could receive the thing in writing, as your lawyer had suggested. Here I was told that it could not be in writing; I had to make the statement orally (or not make any statement at all). At that, I went to the District Court, where I there received the news that it would be impossible to settle the matter in writing, etc., especially because it involved a refusal to testify, and lastly Hinz & Kunz could certify the document, probably even the complainant himself could do so. No, [I] did not go. When I was talking to the man, saying that I had to leave on the 15th so, could not be there on the 18th, he said that the date would be postponed (and when it comes to these people, that is — [drawing — Paragraphenmännchen [Little paragraph man] — always 4 weeks) and I was responsible for the costs of postponement.

So at that, I instead just decided to appear on the 18th. — "See here in Saxony it's always the same." The Dusseldorf lawyer is a fool if he did not know that. — Goltz wrote me a very nice letter wherein he writes me with great bombast & honest indignation that he and others will not exhibit both pictures (except the portrait) for immoral reasons (or is it better said "moral"?) — ever — ! backward, naturalism, betrayal of the Art Revolution of 1910,

"I, the servant of young art." — Despite these harsh blows of fate I am alert and creating WORKS — the "Große Sargbild" [Large Coffin Painting]. [drawing — *Dix am Sargbild arbeitend* [Dix working on the coffin painting]
Greetings Jimmy

To Martha:
Now you're still getting a little Mutz letter:
Are you happy? As it is with Jimmy now?
Pure innocence!
Among us lives of all things the man who interrogated Jim

Remmert and Barth Gallery Archives, Dusseldorf
Drawings: Lorenz EDV 13.1.9
The summons was related to the divorce of Hans and Martha Koch. Only after this could the new constellations of Hans Koch and Maria (Tamolly) Lindner – Otto Dix and Martha Koch – be made possible. – The rejection letter, here mockingly referred to as "nice" by Dix, is from February 4, 1922 (GNM, DKA, Dix, Otto I, C 268). See also Dix's letter to Martha from December 1921, which refers to the development of *Tod und Auferstehung* [Death and Resurrection], Löffler 1922/4.

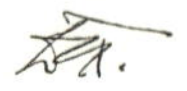

To Hans Koch April 6, 1922 [Dresden]

New merchandise is continually being completed. The court photographer S. M. of the King of Saxony has taken magnificent pictures of Mutz & the Dix couple. These are to be exhibited in the cases alongside Graf Kaiserlingk and Kokoschka. As far as this side goes, there is no slacking off!

Quoted in: Lothar Fischer, *Otto Dix: Ein Malerleben in Deutschland* (Berta: 1981) 45. – Otto Dix and Martha Koch were married in February 1923. The photographer was Hugo Erfurth.

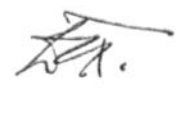

To Maria Lindner & Hans Koch, letter, with drawing 4.12.1922 [Dresden]

Itta — Itta — Itta — sand color. Art is basically complete sh[it]. Money — Contract — Art is hard. While Jimmy wrestles the deepest problems in life with furrowed, tormented brow, Mutz sits in a chair, reclining, munching chocolates & Easter eggs and dealing with the equally serious question of the ITTAS. Such is life!!!!!!!

Remmert and Barth Gallery Archives
Drawing: Lorenz EDV 13.1.12
ITTAS: Dix referred to hats as "Ittas."

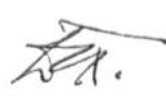

To Hans Koch [early May] 1922 [Dresden]

dear Hans!
At the end of this month the Dresden publisher is publishing a folder with 6 etchings by me, the topic being *Tod und Auferstehung* [Death and Resurrection]. Some time ago you told me that you would like to write something about me. The time is right (says the poet), so if you like, here is the famous winged steed seeking praise
[drawing]
Dixian ride, climb aboard, and please share this with me as soon as possible, the reward will be forthcoming.
[drawing]
Material rewards shall also be thine. The Dresden publisher will give you a signed numbered portfolio as compensation (edition of 50). If you like, I'll send you the proofs, once you are done.

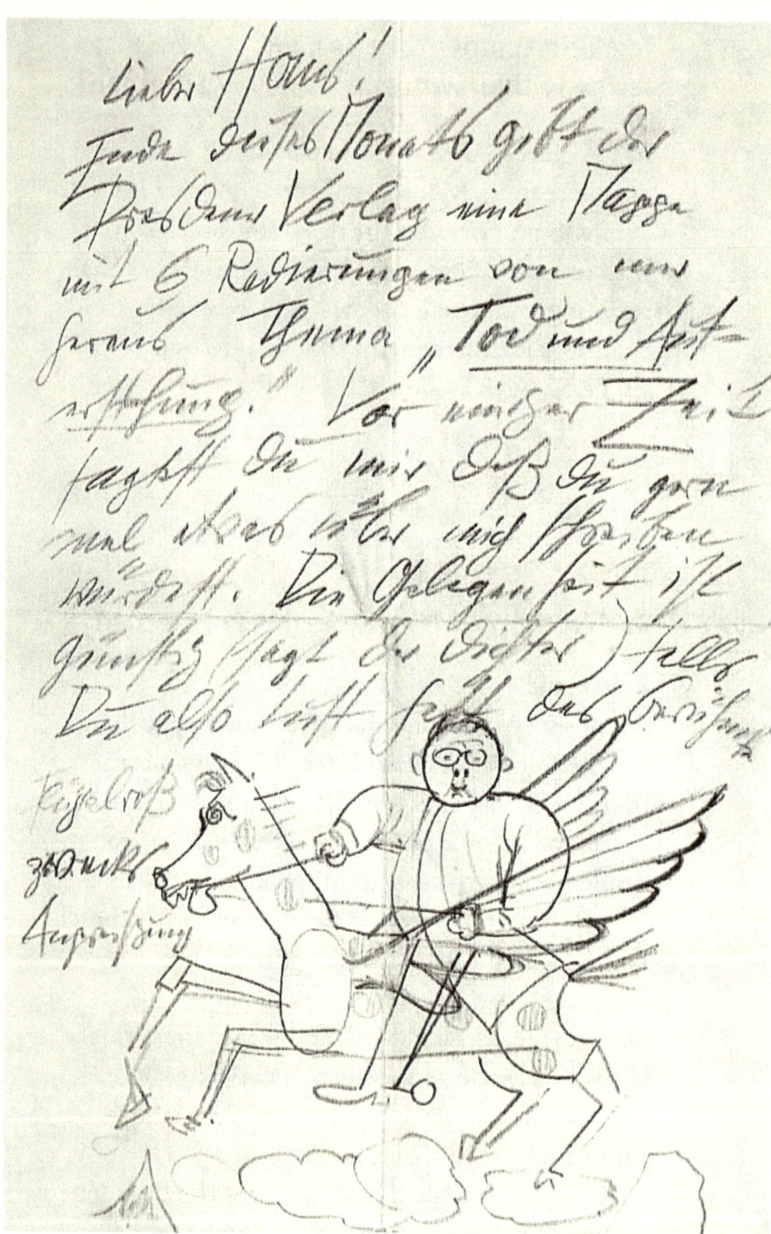

Lieber Hans!
Ende dieses Monats gibt der
Dresdner Verlag eine Mappe
mit 6 Radierungen von einem
Thema „Tod und Auf-
erstehung." Vor einiger Zeit
sagtest Du mir daß Du gern
mal etwas über mich schreiben
würdest. Die Gelegenheit ist
günstig (sagt der Dichter)

Letter to Hans Koch, with drawings *Hans Koch auf dem Flügelross* [Hans Koch on the Winged Steed] and *Hans Koch mit Lorbeerkranz* [Hans Koch with Laurel Wreath], early May 1922

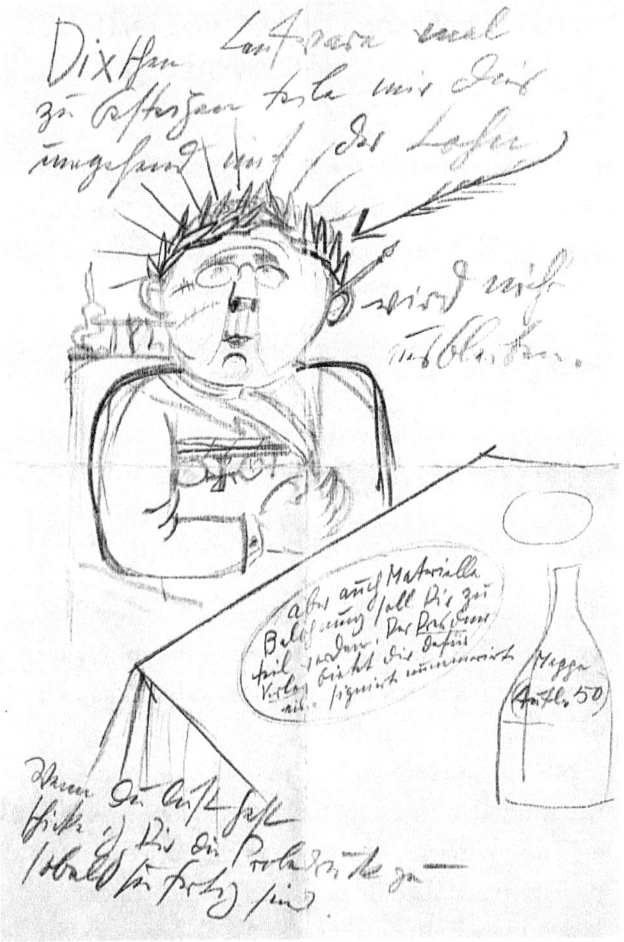

Nevertheless I must once again emphasize that this is not about storage material but materials to be moved, & I ask you to please let me know if you have time to take care of the issue as soon as possible.

Remmert and Barth Gallery Archives, Dusseldorf
Drawings: Lorenz EDV 1.13.16 and 18
The portfolio *Tod und Auferstehung* appeared as a self-published project in 1922, in Dresden, in the aforementioned edition of 50 (Karsch 43–48), with accompanying text by Hans Koch.

To Max Grünbaum May 6, 1922 [PM] [Dresden] [PC]

Dear Herr Grünbaum!
I should like to take the liberty of inquiring as to whether the painting has come or not. Sent in early April, it should long since have arrived in B. [Berlin]. Perhaps one would have to inquire to the shipper.
With best regards Otto Dix

Adk, Berlin, Visual Arts Autograph Collection

To Hans Koch 5.17.1922 [Dresden]

dear Hans! Today a roll with 6 etchings has been sent to you. The A1 proofs of the things are together in a portfolio and this is called *Tod und Auferstehung*. I cordially ask you to write the thing, if possible, before your trip. — (I am to ask if the rhododendrons are blooming in the garden!) — The etchings sent you are to be received gratis, postage paid, also the portfolio, form, etc., once it is completed. The text is to fill a printed page in the size of the etching. Please send the manuscript to me. It would be very nice if I could have it quite soon, because the printer is already going to delay the thing. With kind regards — also to Tamolly, Muggeli, & HANA from Uncle Jimy from america.

Galerie Remmert and Barth Archives, Dusseldorf

To Martha [summer of 1922?] [Dresden]

My sweetest, dearest, nicest, best!
Today is Friday, and you'll surely be traveling over Fkf [Frankfurt] to go back to St. G. [Saint Goar].

It would be so nice if we could meet and spend time somewhere before October. Maybe you'll come to Dresden again.

Yesterday I was at the lawyer's, Schilling was also there. The court hearing was already scheduled. Now, however, an agreement has been concluded whereby the contract was amended in some important points, and in my favor. The 2nd point: Schilling is to pay me the 3200 Mk that he owes me by the 26th of the month. 3. he must bear the court and attorney costs. You, You Sweet Schönstes, I love you beyond all possible meaasure (is that spelled correctly). Today I was a bit unlucky, went home 2 x in the morning and in the afternoon only because of your little letter, but it wasn't there, & now it is here, and I'm happy again. All day today I have been so confident and excited. I have done *so* much today: Copper printer, banking, medical bill, painted frames, bathroom, & picked up prints in Hellerau, purchased bookbinding ribbon for portfolios, Galerie Arnold. I am always *just* running around. Then I bought another beautiful book for Mutzlein. At Bender's, I happened to read the following about *Hofer* in the June edition of the Kunstblatt: Hofer hasn't got the makings of a popular painter, but he hasn't the makings of one as unpopular as Grosz, and as for Dix, well, he's beyond contemptible!

[Drawing]
I'm eating now! It's not nice to eat alone; I never again want to have to spend the money in life that I earn alone, I always want to spend it together with my Mutzlein and always give it to my beautiful, beautiful Mutzlein. It's all so pointless alone! Alone, one is much poorer. Today I talked with Keil. She could not do enough to praise you and what great luck I have to have such a hardworking & neat and simple yet elegant woman. Even if it's Keil that's saying it, nevertheless, she's still right.

The portfolios look very chic and serious. I had imagined they'd be more gaudy, but the business is already done, Monday, it all gets shipped out. You'll have a lot of difficulty getting the right letterhead. The rose petals in your blue letter smell so sweet and delicate, the color is gorgeous against the paper. Shek händs! Mutzlein we shouldn't tarry too long.

I'll give you a lot a lot of [kisses drawing]
I am and remain
Your Toy who always loves and adores you.

Drawing: Lorenz EDV 13.1.6
Dix painted a portrait of Schilling in 1922 (Löffler 1922/10).
Heinar Schilling published the first Dix graphics portfolios in Dresden. Since *Etchings I* (Karsch 5–10) and *Etchings II* (Karsch 11–15) were both published there, exactly which portfolio Dix is referring to cannot be determined.

To Martha   Tuesday night [1922 | Dresden]

Sweetest   It hurts me so that I have put you in a bad mood & clouded your hours with my whining. I'm just a kid sometimes. When I come to D. [Düsseldorf], I want to fix everything with you with kisses and make everything all right again. I'm so looking forward to it! On Friday night I'll come to D. and, if it's alright with you, come & pick you up on Saturday afternoon at the station. If that's not alright, write or telegraph me (I'll leave here early on Friday morning, at 7 A.M.). Dearest, sweetest, I know that I've left all the difficulties to you, and I'm whining even more now. I'm really a very ungrateful man! Did you actually think it possible that I want to stay in Dresden? I'd much rather leave this city sooner than later. I have only one desire, & that is to be where you are. Reg. the studio, I've already commissioned Wollheim, but if I come back now, I will manage the thing by myself. Things just have to get much easier, and as soon as possible. —

I'm such a terrible grumpy fellow, sometimes unworthy of being loved, to the most extreme degree! Every time I act like this, you should rap me on the knuckles or give me a happy kiss. I know you will, too, because you care about me. And I don't want to be grumpy because I love you dearly, so dearly.

So very much, so deeply. I'm looking forward to you, even to have a discussion with Hans together, for now I am so secure & self-confident & am sure

Hans thinks it just fine with us. My most lovely, sweetest love! I'll love you, no matter how you are. Cheerful, or sad, or serious, or otherwise. Everything, I love everything in you, because everything is lovely about you. I am, always, Your Toy

I love you in my heart of hearts. You are so good, you wonderful, dear, person. I only ever want to be your Jimtoy

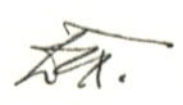

To Franz Dix [1922 | Dresden]

dear Father I received your letter and am very inclined to act according to Your will. I hope you are well. We are going to move to Dusseldorf this year in Sept. I implore you to consider that my mail is being opened, and to write carefully.
With best regards to all
Otto
Don't worry about the money I lent you. I don't need it for the moment.

Kunstsammlung Gera, Dix Archive

1923

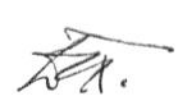

To Adolf Behne Jan. 1, 1923 [Dusseldorf]

Dear Mr. Behne!
Herr Stössinger forwarded me your commitment to represent me as an expert at my trial.
Thank you very much for that. I hope that we will be able to make the court understand that my painting is not a matter of an immoral act, but an ethical one, and that it is impossible to induce the injurious "normal feeling of shame" as people refer to it.
I'll be coming to Berlin a few days before the trial & I hope that I can discuss the matter with you beforehand.
Best regards
Yours sincerely
Otto Dix
Dusseldorf, Hindenburgwall. 3

AdK, Berlin, Adolf Behne Archive
Max Liebermann had written to the art dealer Alfred Flechtheim before the trial regarding the painting *Mädchen vor dem Spiegel* [Girl at the Mirror] (Löffler 1921/8 – destroyed): "Dear Mr. Flechtheim / I already received the invitation from my lawyer in Dusseldorf 14 days ago to stand as an expert in the Dix matter. *I had to cancel*, however, because *at my age* I cannot come to the court hearing all the way from Wannsee. Also, Slevogt and a lot of other artists have been called; otherwise I would naturally stand and speak for him. / With best regards, Sincerely, very truly yrs. M Liebermann" (handwr. GNM, DKA, NL Dix, Otto, I, B 23). On Dix's immediate reaction to the trial, see the postcard to Martha from 4.18.1923. Experts and evaluators for Dix included Max Osborn, Karl Hofer, Adolf Behne, Karl Nierendorf, and Carl Einstein (GNM, DKA, NL Dix, Otto, I, C 191).

verletzt werden kann. Ich komme
einige Tage vor dem Prozeß
nach Berlin und hoffe daß
ich Sie vorher die Sache mal
mit Ihnen besprechen kann.

Mit besten Grüßen

Ihr ergebener

Otto Dix

Düsseldorf, Hindenburgwall 3.

am 1 Jan 23.

Dix?

Sehr geehrter Herr Bene!

Herr Höfinger übermittelte mir Ihre
Zusage meine Prozeßsache als
Sachverständiger zu vertreten.
Ich danke Ihnen herzlichst dafür.
Ich hoffe daß es uns gelingen wird
dem Gericht begreiflich zu machen
daß es sich bei meinem Bild
nicht um eine unsittliche Hand-
lung sondern um eine ethische Tat
handelt und daß mit dem Bild
unmöglich das „normale Scham-
gefühl" wie das die Leute nennen

Letter to Adolf Bene, 1.1.1923

To Martha [1923 | Dresden]

My dearest, most cherished one I am in Dresden and am staying with Griebel. I slept quite well on the chaise lounge, even if I did freeze a bit. Today I went to the copper engraver's, Klein's, and the tailors', leaving money behind everywhere I went. The suit will be precisely "fixed" so to speak, [drawing — breast, without a Lorenz Nr.] will get made, padded, & the shoulders widened. I had no idea that everything is so terribly expensive. This morning I picked up some butter, cheese, & bread for breakfast — 200 marks, and we ate it all. —

It just occurred to me, Wollheim bought a little house in the Eifel & wants to farm the land there. He asserts that within a year every man will have to make a decision to be a farmer or a worker. I would rather prefer the latter and be a gardener in St. Goar. Maybe one has to cozy up to the governor in the event that one should need him at some point. I am looking forward to when we can go dancing in Dusseldorf. Mutzlein in a red ITTA, Jimlein in a Jimmysuit. What else is going on with you, my dear? I am so looking forward to seeing you! I so long for you my dearest, soft sweetie. How is the little Mutztoybaby? It's going to be a sweet little child.

Dearest, you shouldn't think badly of me if sometimes I am a bit mean.

I am looking forward to starting my large *Kriegsbild* [war picture] in Dusseldorf.

I've already thought it all through; it is going to happen! You will help me with it. You will always help me. I would like to suck into me all the things as you see them and paint it all out. I care for you from the bottom of my heart.

You are ALWAYS the most beautiful, dearest, & best in the world — Your Jimmy.

The painting *Der Schützengraben* [The Trench] was mostly painted in Dusseldorf in 1923. At the invitation of Max Liebermann, who was the president of the Prussian Akademie der Künste, Dix's painting was included in the 1924 spring exhibition. The piece was also depicted in the show's catalog, and there is only one contemporary reproduction of it, which was later destroyed by the Nazis. During the show, Dix and his wife were travelling in Italy, and Karl Nierendorf wrote in May 1924: "The war painting is now on display at the Akademie [...] hanging in the front main room to the right, on the main wall. Yesterday we took care that adequate space was provided to the left and the right. [...] Liebermann told me that he thought the painting very good. You ought to do a portrait of the old man." Dix in fact did meet Liebermann at least once before his death.
– "Dear Colleague, your visit will be very welcome at 3 o'clock on Nov. 26, Saturday. Yours very truly, Max Liebermann" (GNM, DKA, NL Dix, Otto, I, C 461).

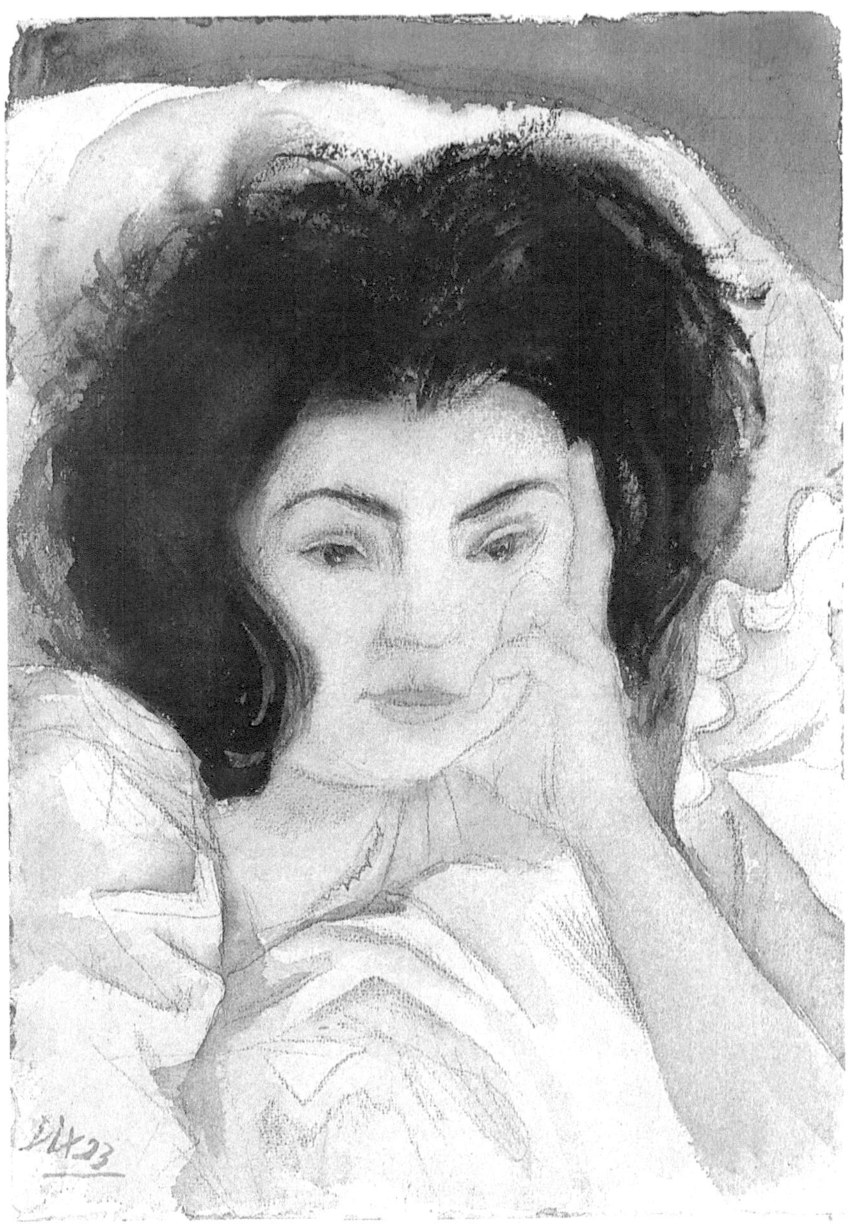

Bildnis M. Dix (Dem Mutz) [Portrait of M. Dix (Mutz)], watercolor, 1923

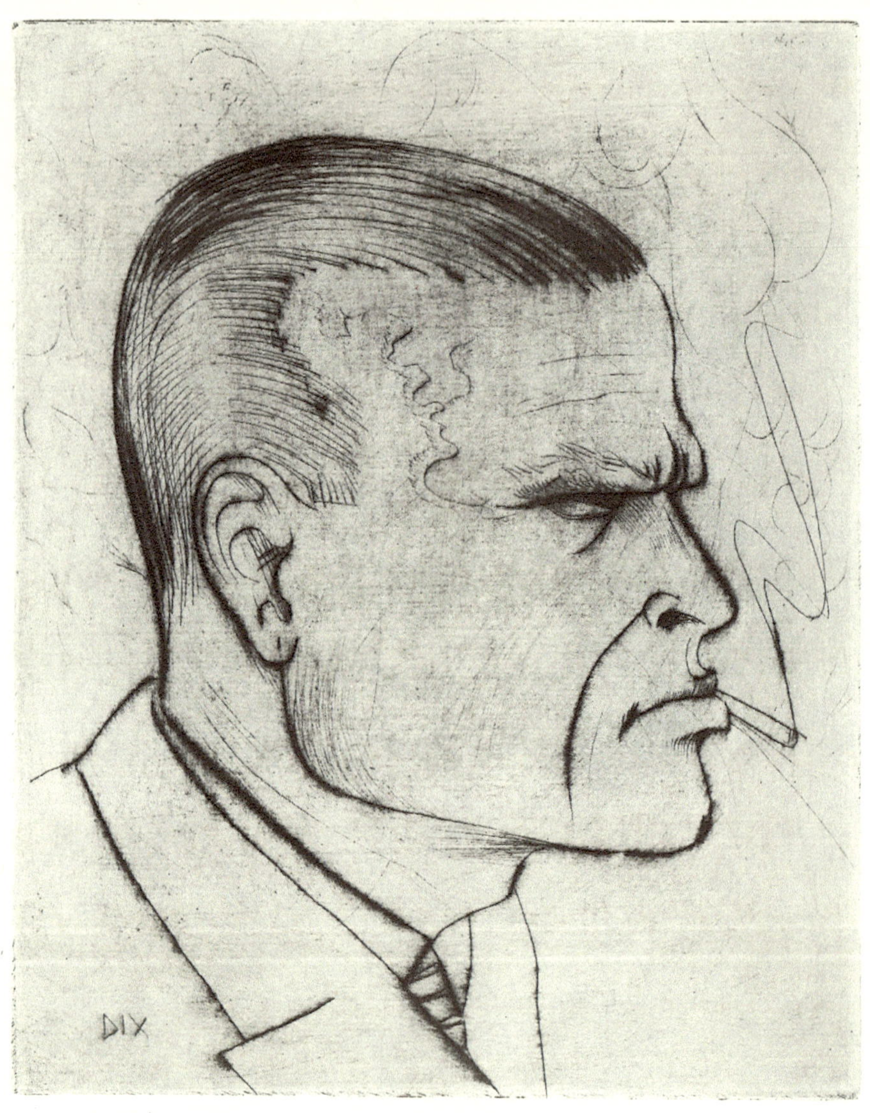

Selbstbildnis (mit Zigarette) [Self-portrait (with cigarette)], etching, 1922

To Martha [1923 | Dusseldorf]

My dearest, sweet love I've just come up from Kaufmann's; I was invited for lunch and in the evening we moved the stove into the studio and then had dinner. We should invite Kaufmann sometime, when you're here. Don't fret because of money, sweetie, let Koch keep his 1500 Mk; we absolutely don't need it. The thing with the 150,000 from Ndf. [Nierendorf] is crap. Ndf. already croaked when he paid me the 10,000 I wrote to you about. Therefore, don't cry, not because of these jerks, neither about money nor any of this nonsense. — I live very frugally, but it will also work out when you are here; at any rate we will find a way to get through it all, these others aren't starving like us and all the whining about money is meaningless, anyway. Leave all that to me, sometimes — I don't mean it so seriously when I whine — but you shouldn't turn into a 2nd Frau Direktor B. Lindner over it all. — *You should always stay beautiful & funny, & even then, unaffected by such things when they go sour on us. You shall always be lighter than I am* [arrow] That's the ideal, Mutzlein, that I always imagine.
I love you, even if I am disgusting & only striving to improve, like today.
Many kisses Jim

The letter was addressed to Martha at St. Goar, the home of the Lindner family, Martha's parents.

To Martha [1923 | Dusseldorf]

My child, my dear, do not be sad!
I'm sending you caresses and much warmth and love, do not be discouraged! Most beautiful one! I love you with all my heart. And I am very fond of the baby, very very fond. —
Be good and kind.
Could I not infer, because you always write that I do not love you anymore, that you in fact no longer love me? But I will not do so.
I have just returned from Dresden and received your despondent note. — You'll see, it will still turn out nicely for us, I'll be happy if you come on the 15th.
I'll try to arrange everything in the apartment beforehand. Hopefully, we'll be able to get coal.
My feet are cold to the knees; I have to go to bed.
Many Many kisses on all sweet, nice, soft things
Your Jim

To Johanna Ey [1923 | Dusseldorf]

To the gallery "Mother Ey," Dusseldorf
[drawing]
You are a guardian angel!
Mutzli was sick for some days —
Rheumatism, but things have improved again,
Regards
Your Dix.

Remmert and Barth Gallery Archives, Dusseldorf
Drawing: Lorenz EDV 13.1.30

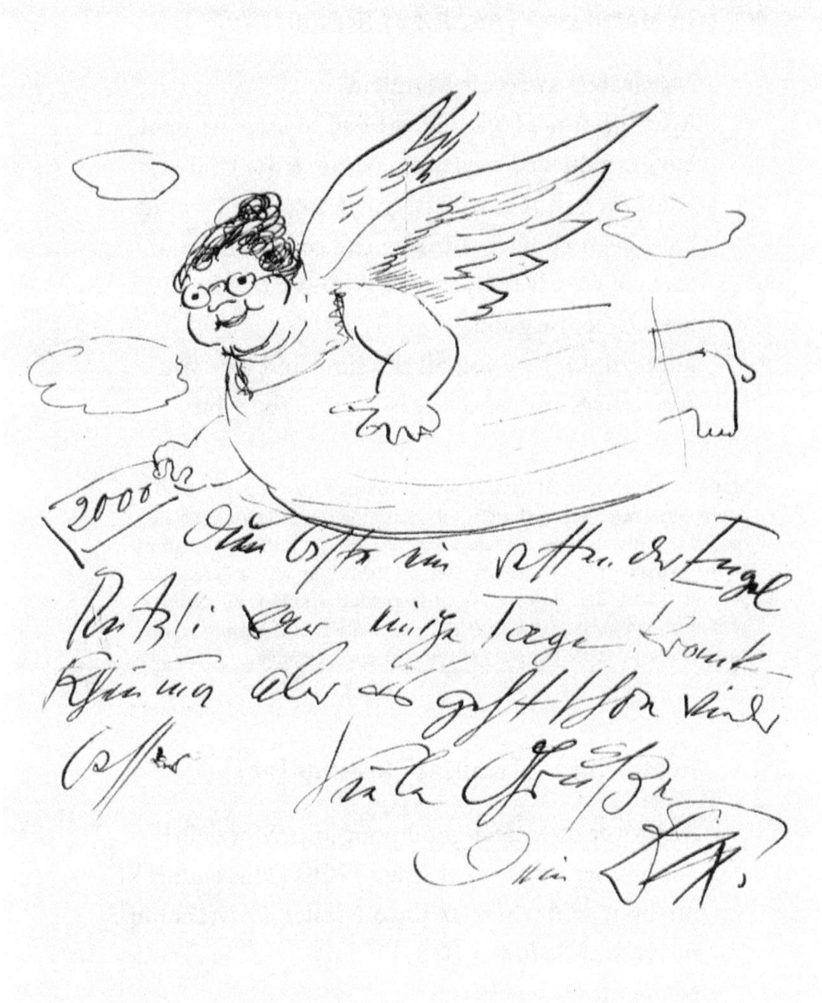

Letter to Johanna Ey with drawing, *Quittung über vom Himmel gefallene 2000 Mark* [Receipt for 2000 marks fallen from heaven], 1923

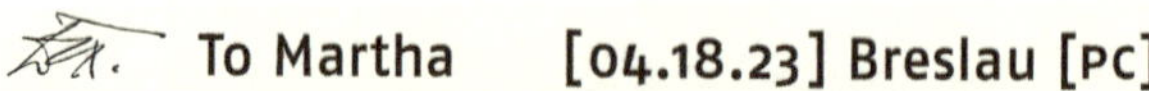

To Martha [04.18.23] Breslau [PC]

My dearest sweetest Mutzlein!
After 4 hours of waiting, we had to leave without having achieved anything, because the trial was adjourned. But maybe it's good, because I would have been convicted under the composition of this court. I'll tell you everything later. In the meantime, be good.
I am thinking of you all the time and love you very much, 100,000 kisses Your Jim

On 04.17.1923, the trial against Dix for obscenity was opened by the public prosecutor before the District Court of Berlin following the confiscation of his painting *Mädchen vor dem Spiegel* [Girl at the Mirror], Löffler 1921/8, at the Great Jury Free Art Exhibition at the Berlin Glaspalast (10.30.1922). However, Dix's Dusseldorf attorney, Obuch, was able to file an objection against the composition of the court on the basis of bias, so that the start of the trial was postponed.

To Martha [4.18.23] Breslau [PC]

My sweet little dear good poor lone Mutzlein!
Tonight we want to celebrate NDfs [Nierendorf's] birthday with them & Otto Müller. O.M. is [an] interesting fellow.
Many nice warm kisses
Jim
[verso:] Athens via Breslau [drawing]

Otto Müller (1874–1930) was a painter and a graphic artist. From 1919, he was a professor at the Academy in Breslau. Karl Nierendorf was very devoted to him and his work.

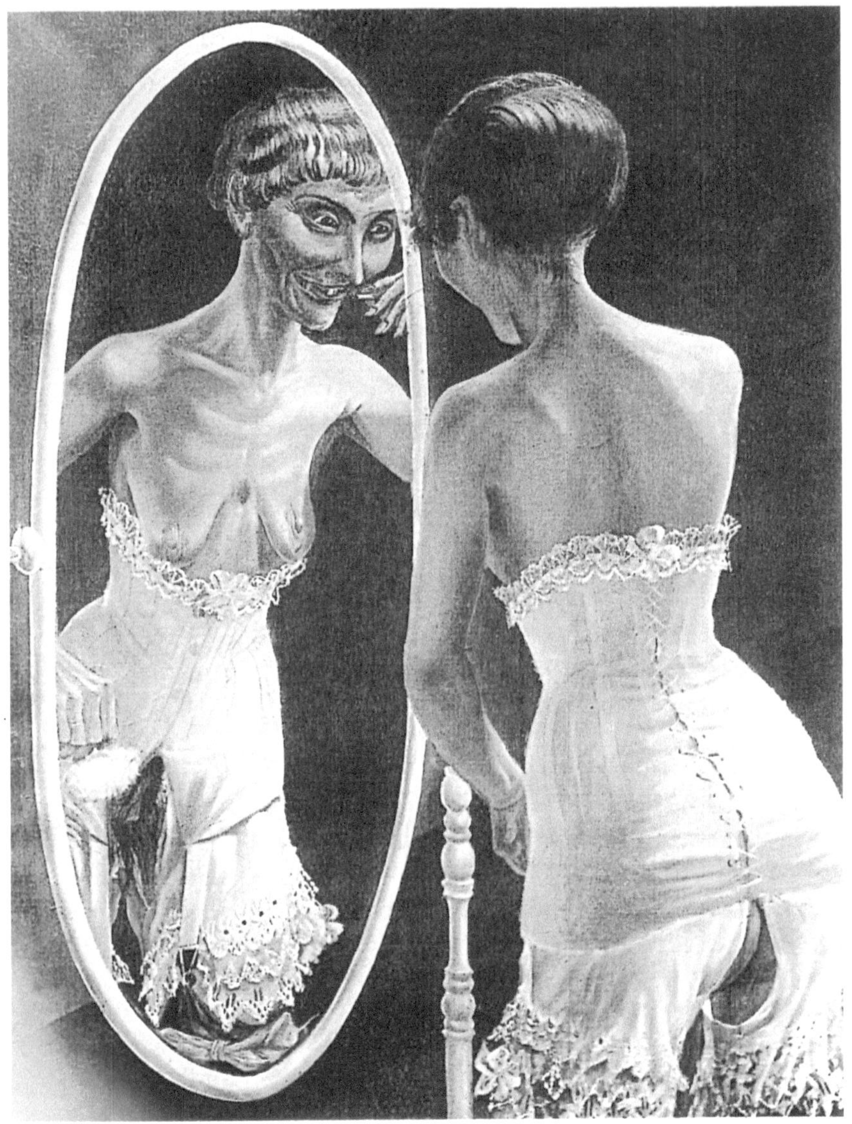

Mädchen vor dem Spiegel [Girl at the Mirror], 1921, painting Drawing: Lorenz EDV 01.13.31

To Martha [1923] Münster

dear Mutzlein It is getting more and more barren here; things are also closed till the 15th of September. Bredt posted 12,000,000 to you on Friday. Hopefully you still have money. I work out of desperation, draw & produce watercolors, but nothing worthwhile comes of it. Are you angry because of my last awful letter? — I wrote to young Nierendorf that he is to arrange a passport [*illegible*]. Maybe you could even give notice of departure & register in Cologne, Mozart Straße 15, so you can get a safe-conveyance document. Although I do not know how long the permit is valid, it may be that it only applies for travel on a one-time basis. When Fuhrmann is no longer [*illegible*] with you, then please ask Kaufmann to send an English permit [to me], so I'll get in. But I don't know yet whether he will or not. Please send Frau Fuhrmann to the registration office with my apartment registration form. You should sign off in Dusseldorf and say that I am moving to Cologne. Then send your notice of departure to Nierendorf, who is then to register me there, & a safe-conveyance document [*illegible*]. I was also considering whether or not I should go home and paint a portrait, but I have so much to do in Du [Dusseldorf]. How are the two of you? Is little Nelly back in good health? I kiss you warmly
Jimmy

Dix stayed in Münster in order to portray John Bredt: *Bildnis Johannes Bredt mit Hund* [Portrait of Johannes Bredt, with Dog] (Löffler 1923/11;

Pfäffle 1923/137). Bredt was a collector & advised Dix to let himself be represented by an art dealer, Nierendorf (GNM, DKA, NL Dix, Otto, I, C 94). – The occupation of the Rhineland by Allied troops had been determined after the end of WWI by the Treaty of Versailles. Since German reparation payments had not been complied with to the amount requested, the Ruhr region was also occupied by French & Belgian troops in January 1923. They stayed until August 1925. This letter provides a small glimpse into the bureaucratic impact that these measures had on everyday life for the population. Beyond inflation, which reached a high point in November 1923, it presented a considerable daily burden for those who had to travel in the occupied regions.

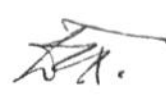

To Arthur & Elisabeth Kaufmann VI.14.23 [Dusseldorf]

dear Kaufmann & dear Frau Kaufmann.
We have this morning received a beautiful young lady [drawing] and therefore, unfortunately, cannot attend your fete on Saturday. We wish you all much enjoyment. Visits are provisionally not allowed.
VI.14.23
sincere greetings Dix
with wife & daughter

Remmert and Barth Gallery Archive, Dusseldorf
Drawings: Lorenz EDV 01.13.32

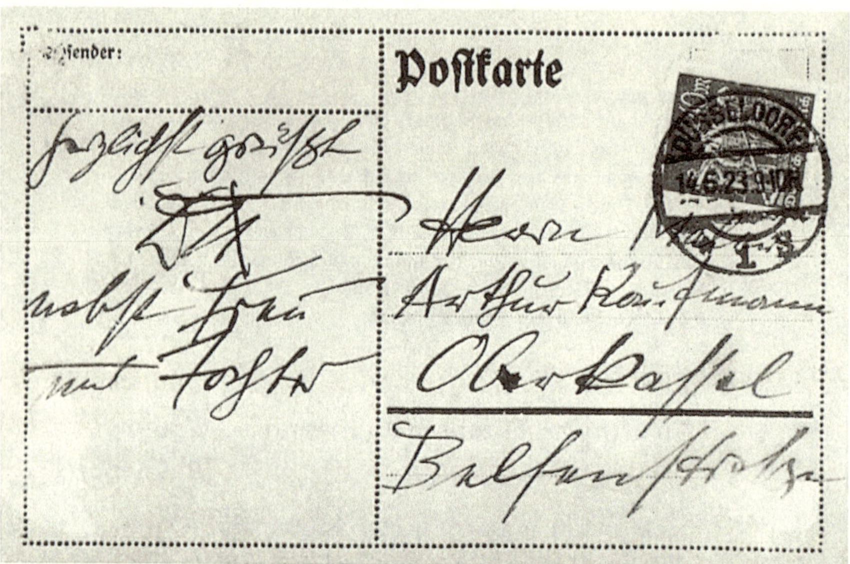

Postcard to Adolf Kaufmann, with drawing, *Neugeborene Nelly* [Newborn Nelly], 6.14.1923

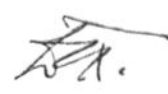 To Max Grünbaum June 28, 1923 [Dusseldorf]

Dear Herr Grünbaum!
You have probably read that my trial in Berlin went well. Unfortunately, I had only one day in B., otherwise I would much liked to have visited you & discussed the following matter.

The exhibition at the Academy of Arts in Berlin recently closed and moved to Nuremberg and is being shown there at the Albrecht Dürer Bund. Since I really should like to have the picture *Tod und Auferstehung* shown there & Max Lieberman also asked me to see to it, I ask you sincerely to lend me the picture for the duration of this exhibition. The images will be packed by the Academy of Arts and brought to N. Make sure to list the insurance sum specifically in gold marks. The insurance is paid by the Academy.

With that, the thing is set. I have instructed the Academy to send you the exhibition papers, which I kindly ask you to fill out. In the hope that you will grant my request, I send cordial greetings
Your Dix.

AdK, Berlin, Visual Arts Autograph Collection № 43
Painting: *Tod und Auferstehung* [Death and Resurrection], Löffler 1922/4 – There were two trials in 1923, the above-mentioned one on obscenity, and a second after Dix's brothel painting *Salon II* (which was owned by Hans Koch) was confiscated from the Exhibition of German Art in Darmstadt. At the first trial in October 1923, Dix argued that the painting's grotesqueries were necessary to convey the spiritual death and physical depravity of prostitution. The judge ruled in Dix's favor, yet due to the newspaper coverage of both trials, Dix attained a reputation as a grotesque painter of prostitutes. Cf. Dennis Crockett, *German Post Expressionism: The Art of the Great Disorder* (1999).

To Martha [probably October 1923] [Berlin]

My dear sweet Mutzlein The weather here has been most glorious, both yesterday & today. Maybe you've gone out with Wusti [di Nelly] Taita (Nelly). You & the [sausage-drawing, without Lorenz Nr.] Best wishes & good Matzkisses. So, I arrived early in B. in the morning around 10h and went to Nierendorf's. Thanks to the colossal price increases, the portrait commission came to nothing. On the side, I am painting a picture for the Graphische Kabinett. In spite of it all, Nierendorf has paid my apartment, food, & 5 dollars per day. I asked Hübner to coffee on Saturday, but he didn't show. I haven't gone to duty-free yet, but I am going today. Yesterday morning, Bredt arrived. He was outraged that Hans had sold his portrait. — Night before last we visited the American dancer Henry & went to the Lustspielhaus where a Hamsun play was performed. Mertens was also part of the cast.[7] Today, Dr. Schmidt is coming from Dresden. Nierendorf will exhibit him at the Graphische Kabinett. Schmidt wants to give up his Dresden Museum. The latest hit is "Yes, we have no bananas." This letter looks like Berlin; everything twists up over & back through itself. Mutzlein, change M [pounds] if you have no money left. I'll get more money from [Nierendorf]. I accidentally

7 The play Dix most likely saw was *Dronning Tamara* (Queen Tamara). It is listed as being performed in 1923 in Ruth Freydank's *Der Fall Berliner Theatermuseum* (Berlin: 2011) 69 & 103. Gerda Mueller portrayed Queen Tamara.

kept a 10 shilling note, so don't think it's lost. The day before yesterday I met Davringhausen; he's a true gent, squinting slightly & looking around like a camel or llama, but otherwise looks very chic. Then, of course, I spoke to Flechtheim and the painter Levi. I sometimes feel impoverished because my shoes are too tight and I have cold feet. Otherwise, Berlin is still the old Talmi and the distances are unpleasant. Actually, it's already become unappealing to me. It's all very expensive & no one has money. A lunch costs 15 billion, the streetcar 1½ M., a coffee 8 billion, not even Bredt has enough money.

Dearest, sweet Herzensmutzlein, I've written you a nice bit of tripe! I love you very much and I'll be very happy when I can get back to my two Wurstis

Your Jim

Greetings from Ndf.

Write: Dix Graf. Kab. I.B.N. / Kurfürstendamm 232

Ulrich Hübner (1872–1932) was a painter, graphic artist, member of the Prussian Academy of Arts from 1919, and head of an academic master studio. In this case, he is probably serving as the exhibition representative of the Academy.
– The Dancer Henri [Henry] was the future husband of Anita Berber.
– Group portrait: *Günther Franke, Paul Ferdinand Schmidt, und Karl Nierendorf*, Löffler 1923/7. *Portrait der Dr. Hans Koch*, Löffler 1921/13.

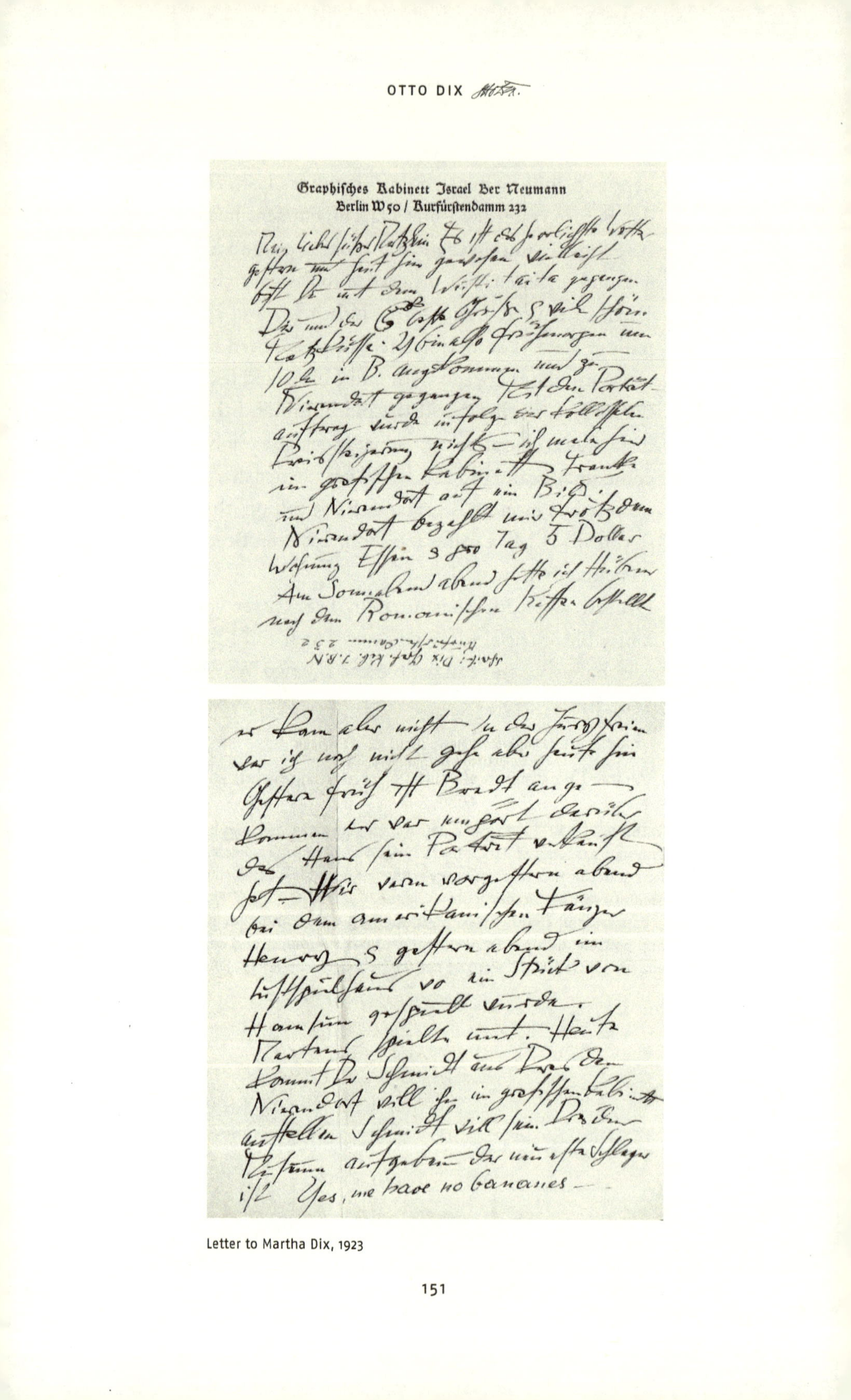

Graphisches Kabinett Israel Ber Neumann
Berlin W 50 / Kurfürstendamm 232

Yes, we have no bananas—

Letter to Martha Dix, 1923

To Martha October 23 | Berlin

My beloved Mutzlein! The big shock had happened. The Wallraf-Richartz-Museum has bought the war painting. Secker telegraphed yesterday. Sicily is secured. — Dear little heart, do not hold money back, under no circumstances, change M. noodle Nelly properly. Bredt's gone again. Tonight I'm invited to dine with Grosz, tomorrow night with a writer, Angermaier, who has a lot of connections in Paris & wants to promote me there. The man is completely thrilled by my work. Guess what else is new? Kokoschka has left Dresden by night and fog with his studio in tow (meaning the paints & brushes) and has gone to Switzerland, where no one knows he has abandoned his professorship. Hübner, with whom I spoke yesterday, has invited me for the next Academy exhibition. I will get the hall, no idea where I am supposed to get enough pictures for it. — My Süßlein I always think of you & love you very much. One soon tires of Berlin; there's nowhere to really call home. I have to get on with it now & start painting, have slept too long anyway. Dearest, be cheerful and good and kiss that little frog Nelly for me. I am yours forever
Haksch

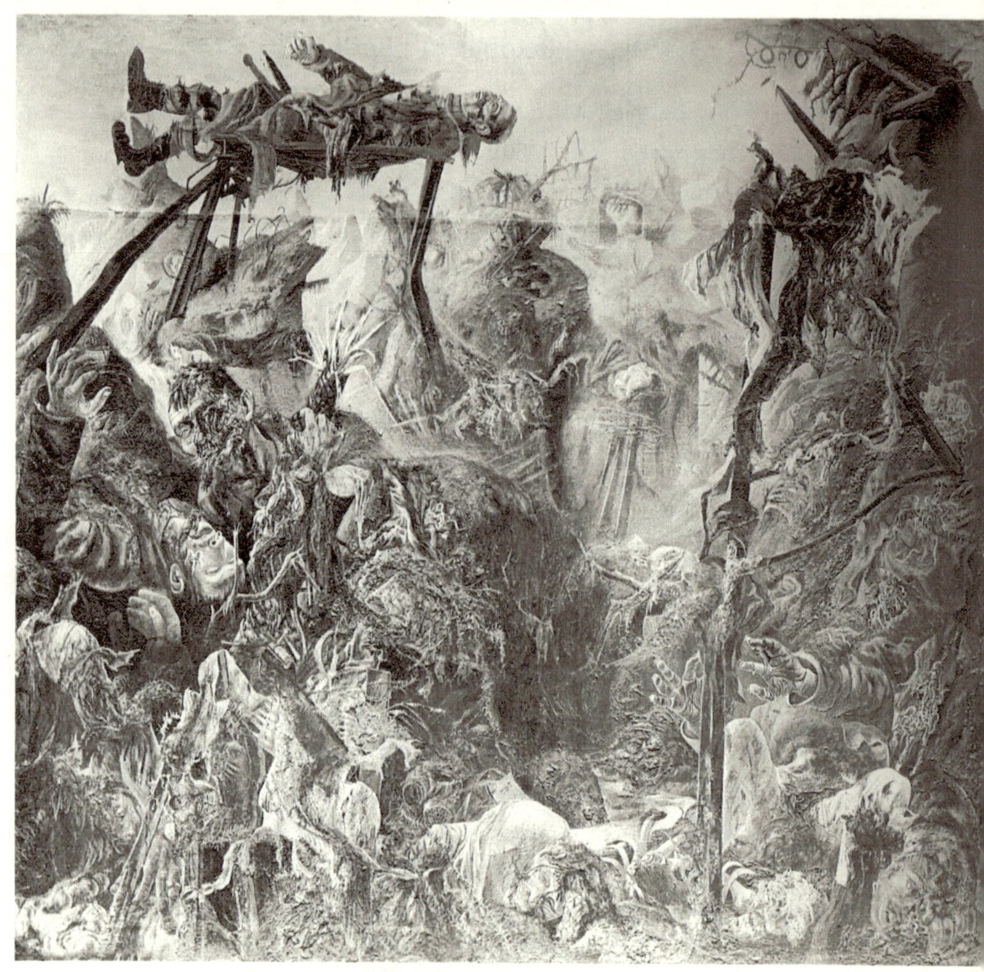

Der Schützengraben [The Trench], 1923

The war painting Dix is referring to is *Der Schützengraben* [The Trench], Löffler 1923/2; it was destroyed. In a letter dated 10.31.1923, Secker writes Dix: "It took no little amount of hand-wringing and haranguing to get the Wallraf to take the picture. I think congratulations are in order, and not only for you, but even more so myself [...]. The reopening of our gallery will probably take place on December 1. Your painting will well-be the greatest of sensations. It would be lovely if you could come to the small opening celebration [...]" (GNM, DKA, NL Dix, Otto, I, B 12 r). In spite of all, however, the sale was canceled due to the intervention of certain politicians who were against it, and the painting had to be

returned to Karl Nierendorf. Later, in the spring of 1924, the painting was the centerpiece of the Prussian Akademie der Künste show in Berlin and incited a great deal of discussion and controversy. Max Liebermann openly defended it (see Roland März/Rosemarie Radeke, 1991), & in reaction to all this, Nierendorf finally sent it to the "Internationale Kunstaustellung" in Zurich in 1925, where it was universally praised as a masterpiece. The publicity generated by the painting even later prompted A.W. Lunatscharski, the Commisar of Education in the USSR, to extend Dix an invitation to attend an exhibition in Moscow (GNM, DKA, NL Dix, Otto, I, B 12t).
– In writing "Sicily is secured," Dix was referring to a planned trip to Italy that the family did in fact take in 1924, in spite of the sale with Kaufmann falling through. Seeing the mummies in the catacombs in Palermo had a profound effect on Dix, and influenced his 1923/1924 war drawings.
– Oskar Kokoschka served as a professor at the Academy in Dresden but left under controversial circumstances.
– Ulrich Hübner (1872–1932) was a painter & graphic artist, member of the Prussian Academy of Arts, & director of the 1924 Spring Exhibition.
– The writer Dix refers to in the letter was named Fred Antoine Angermayer (1889–1951), who Dix painted in 1923 as well (Karsch 70–119).
– In September of that year, he asked the Saxon Ministry of the Interior for exemption for two years, but did not return afterwards.

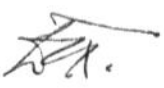

To Martha   Thursday morning [1923] [Berlin]

You dearest, sweet Mutzlein, many long, warm Matzkisses [drawing] — I love you.
I'm leaving here early Saturday morning & coming to Cologne in the evening. If I can be reached (via Vohwinkel [?]) before 8h in Dusseldorf, I'll be coming Saturday night, if not, Sunday morning. In Berlin, nothing gets done. I'm going to be filmed tomorrow, that is, if the weather is nice, *"Die Hand des Meisters bei der Arbeit"* [The Hand of the Master at Work]. A documentary film company is doing it. I'll be happy when I can get back to my two girls! With my sweet little Speckchen! Dearest, you needn't save D. [dollars] — change them! Kiss the little Nelly for me, tell her I'll be

coming back soon. My mother wrote me that she knitted ſtockings for little Nelly, & a dress, and complains that... I don't *write at all.*
Nierendorf is talented and does a good job, and sends his beſt greetings. In 14 days, Segall is sailing to Brazil for 3–4 years.

Greetings, Kisses
Jim

Drawing: Lorenz EDV 13.1.48
The film mentioned was part of the 1926 series, *Schaffende Hände* [Hands at Work]. "Painter I" was filmed by Hans Cürlis and shows the painting *Drei Weiber* [Three Women] (Löffler 1926/1) and the watercolor *Marianne* [Pfäffle A] 1927/24). In the booklet (actually a brochure) for *Schaffende Hände* (Berlin: 1926), Cürlis emphasizes Dix's brilliance based on a watercolor, *Weiblicher Halbakt* [Female Semi-Nude] (Fig. 16/17). This part was probably filmed in 1923, but does not seem to have been included in the final version. Hans Cürlis wrote to Dix on 05.10.1968, saying he had given all the films produced by his company to the London Film Society for copying. After 1945, this was then the only source left, because "on Goebbels' orders in 1943, I had to turn over all of my films because I had filmed so many non-Aryan & 'degenerate' artists listed, and no longer have them. One of the five films in London also includes your film, which we recorded in 1923. You are sketching the big picture with the three whores in the room, plus a detailed study of one of the heads. The running time is about 9 minutes. I have already given a copy to the Federal Archives." Cürlis offered Dix a copy of the movie (GNM, DKA, NL Dix, Otto, I, B 18a).

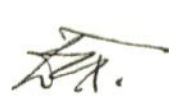

To Karl Nierendorf [November 1923] [Dusseldorf?]

dear Ndf. It's a goddamned disgrace that you, in ſpite of having promised to, [ſtill] have not arranged the credit. I tell you herewith that I have no desire to conſtantly write my fingers to the bone until you ſpare me a few marks. The sale of the painting in Cologne is done, and I don't want to wait any longer, I want my money. I don't give a shit what private agreements you have made with Secker. I am at my wit's ends with all your fucking around & blind confidence! I haven't even money enough to give my parents something for Christmas this year. I have to give Kaufmann the 100 guilders again, and you can only imagine the money I've lost on this sale and purchase of foreign currency.

I think it's better if you transfer me the money for the war picture as soon as possible so I can hire a local bank with the credit letter for Italy, for I definitely cannot rely on you. According to the contract I am due a monthly payment; I've had nothing from you for 3 months. This must be sent to me immediately.

What good to me are all your Proverbs! Who was it that said to write if I need money, yet in return I get a few paltry dollars. — It's very surprising that Kaufmann, who is not a well-known painter and has sold less than me, lives better than I do. But this man, his wife & children have wonderful ski equipment & have fun all day long, but I, I work. I'm just starting to notice that you yourself are slowly developing into what one refers to as a capitalist art dealer. You've sure as hell got no goddamned reason to be outraged if I turn a bit crass with you. Yet you seem to have been turned into such an art dealer that you no longer understand. — I have to work on my etchings. The Munakate picture won't be done before August next year.

I am fed up!

With greetings Dix

Nierendorf Gallery Archives, Berlin (copy in GNM, DKA, NL Dix, Otto, I, C 524). – Karl Nierendorf had sent an enthusiastic, soliciting letter to Dix on 02.14.1922 and since then had suggested projects with verve (such as the "Circus" portfolio) and had represented and sold works by Dix. This led to the first contract. A friendly relationship developed between Nierendorf and the Dix couple. Nierendorf urged Dix to complete the portfolio of etchings, *Der Krieg* [War] (Karsch 70–119), which was published by Nierendorf Verlag in 1924 (with an essay by Henri Barbusse in the print edition). Tensions between the partners varied alternately – due to Dix's volatile temperament – ranging from close friendship to angry exchanges.

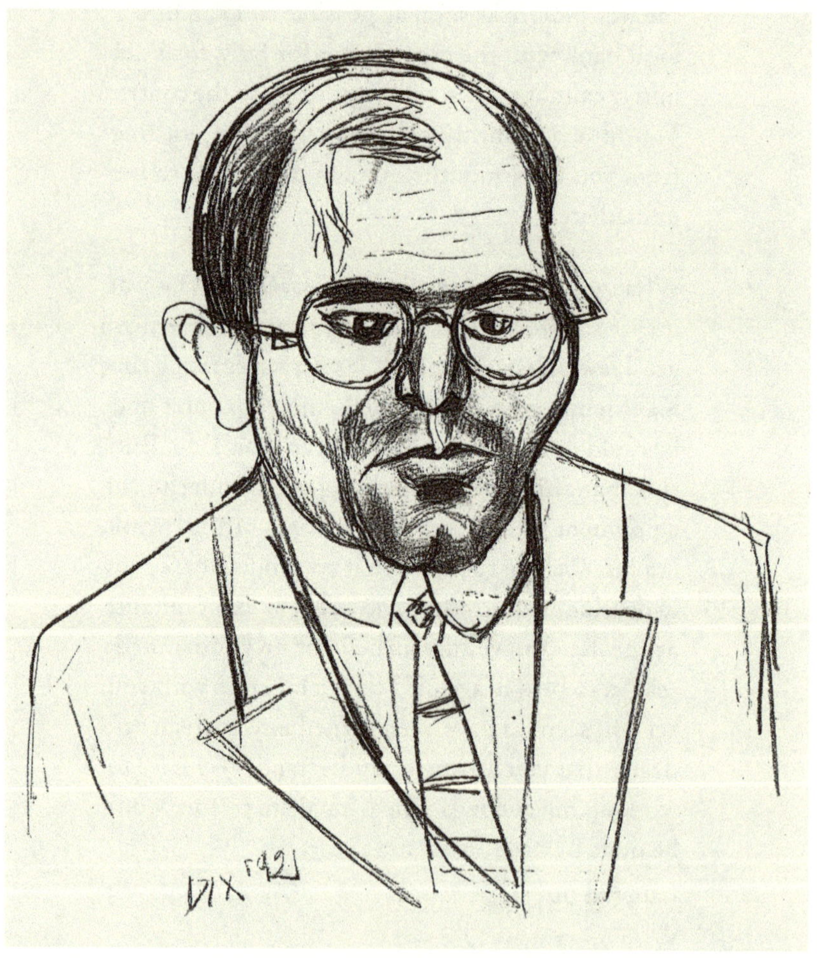

Bildnis Karl Nierendorf, 1921, drawing

– On 12.17.1924, Nierendorf responded to a similar complaint from Dix with a detailed letter: "Dear Jim! [...] You really can't complain – during this difficult summer I've always given you as much as you wanted and I'll send you more money in the next few days, though not a single thing has been sold in recent weeks. [...] You always write about Kaufmann, how much money he earned, but never about the real artists who in some cases are doing very poorly. From me alone you have received over 10,000 Mk, and from Frau Ey & Gottschalk as well. Given the bad year, the result is really not unfavorable [...]" (GNM, DKA, NL Dix, Otto, I, C 524).
– Regarding the sale of the *Schützengraben* [Trench] painting (Löffler 1923/2) to the Wallraf-Richartz Museum in Cologne, see the 1.10.1923 letter to Martha.
– Dix's complaining letters increased in number and were repeated, in a similar tone, so that Nierendorf again explained on 4.10.1925: "Dear Jim! [...] I have so long become accustomed to this berating and have come to know that everything I do for you, even attending to your artistic and material interests right down to the slightest detail, goes unacknowledged. You see in me only the dealer who exploits you [...]. Through the years, I've proven that I appreciate you as a person and artist, have stayed true to you when I was still ridiculed by everyone & was then brusquely rejected by the whole art market [...]. The fact that they call me here, as in Cologne, Nierendix, says it all and is significant enough. [...] I certainly wouldn't attend to all these things in such detail if that mattered to me at all, and somehow hoped that you'd treat me as respectably as I treat you. You can't dare impose upon me in this way, extending myself to the limits of my own existence on your behalf when you yourself treat me like an exploiter and idiot. That simply cannot be, it's impossible! How can I work for a man to this extent who, at any opportunity, treats me like a dog." But in spite of the antagonistic letters, Nierendorf always stood by Dix, even in the darkest of times, for example when Dix was being pushed by the Nazis out of his Chair at the Academy. On May 3, 1933: "[...] I hear you're on leave. It is important to me that you know that I will continue to stand by you" (GNM, DKA, NL Dix, Otto, I, C 524).
– Dr. H. Munakata of Berlin had angrily written Nierendorf regarding a watercolor Dix had done of him. A corresponding painting remains unknown.
– As a cycle of prints *Der Krieg* is consciously modeled on Goya's (1746–1828) equally famous, & equally devastating, *Los Desastres de la Guerra* [The disasters of war]. *Los Desastres* detailed Goya's own account of the horrors of the Napoleonic invasion & the Spanish War of Independence from 1808 to 1814. Goya's cycle of 82 etchings, which he worked on for a decade after the Spanish War of Independence, were not, however, published until 1863, long after his death.

1924

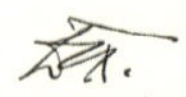

To Anneliese Lenk [1924 | Dresden]

Dear Frau Lenk They're cute! I thank you warmly. I have to paint a double portrait by Christmas. I think I'll be moving to Berlin in early March or April. Dimensions c. 7x6 mtrs with a side room. If possible, central heating. Telephone, unnecessary. Cost, about 60–70 M. monthly. Location Kurfürstendamm to Potsdamer Platz. My wife is coming to Dresden in early December; maybe we will come once together to Bln. [Berlin] and look forward to seeing you again
Many greetings Your Otto Dix

GNM, DKA, Franz Lenk Estate

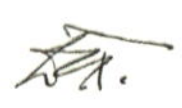

To Ludwig Justi [1924 | Dusseldorf?]

Dear Herr Councilor
With reference to the meeting with Nierendorf, regarding the request to stage a watercolor exhibition of my work in the Kronprinzenpalais.
Yours sincerely Otto Dix
Presently at Gera-Untermhaus
Uferstr. 4

Berlin State Museums, Central Archives, Otto Dix, Nr. 1.
The exhibition took place on 11.28.1924, with watercolors & drawings, mostly from private collections. Nierendorf made Dix aware of the steady, significant – and thus useful – reception in the press for the exhibitions at the National Gallery; the response was not completely positive. The National Gallery acquired works from the exhibition; Nierendorf to Dix: "J. [Justi] is a special friend of your portraits" (GNM, DKA, NL Dix, Otto, I, C 525).

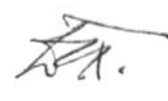

To Max Roesberg [06.01.1924 | Dusseldorf]

dear Herr Roesberg! I received your letter & send you the best of thanks for it. Since I was just drawing the War cycle, I could not write you sooner. — I hope that in the course of this summer I can come to Dresden for several days, so I can visit you then.

I find it very interesting that VOLL has not yet finished the sculpture and I'm looking forward to seeing this at your residence. But since I have no sense of "possessions" of any kind & never intend to stay in one place for good, such a block of bronze would prove more of a burden than a joy, and I'm sorry to have to refuse your kind offer.

I am currently painting a picture of my daughter Nelly. I send you & your wife warm greetings Your Dix

Max Roesberg was a manufacturer of industrial tools and collected works by young Dresden artists.
Paintings: *Der Geschäftsmann Max Roesberg* [The Businessman Max Roesberg], Löffler 1922/9; *Kriegszyklus* [refers to *Der Krieg*, (War)], etchings 1923/1924 (Karsch 70–119); and *Nelly mit Spielzeug* [Nelly with Toy], Löffler 1925/12.
– Dresden sculptor Christoph Voll (1897–1939) had done a portrait of Dix.

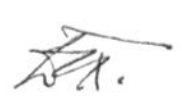

To Martha [June 1924] [Berlin]

You, my sweet, dear heart!
We've pulled out the final stops on the studio and have turned to the cultural ministry. I've been summoned on Monday afternoon to appear before Councilor Wætzoldt. Hopefully, things will work out. Consequently, I'm going there Monday night and will be there Tuesday. Last night I attended the "Sturm Ball." "Dreadful" sluts in glasses and

sandals, reform dresses, the often-effeminate Jewish Mœler, a dreadful group. Decadent to the bone. The new dance they're all doing, well, you know them from Italy. Very boring to dance with. I'll soon be back with my two sweet girls and am looking forward to it.

Many beautiful kisses to you & the Wurstkind

Jimm

Greeting to grandmother, Uncle Bernd, & Aunt

This letter concerns the move from Dusseldorf to Berlin; see the letter to Karl Hofer from 06.25.1924.
– The "Sturm Ball" refers to the Galerie Der Sturm, Berlin.

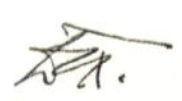

To Martha [June 1924 | Berlin]

My soft, sweet Mutzlein. I kiss all your beautiful things, I love you. What are the cherished little mollusks [axolotls] doing all day long? Drinking, eating, going wah-wah?

Today, I printed etchings at Felsing — Panpresse. The man is an artist by profession, but I'm not quite satisfied because some of the sheets turned out very dark — that's my fault — & anyway — I hope I can still redo [the] best quality sheets of the lot. I then had dinner with Heckel & his wife. I've met little Paulie Schmidt; he intends to divorce his wife. Griebel is also divorced from Elis. Angermayer ran into me in the Romanian coffeehouse. I've received a commission to do the sets for Angermayer's *Komödie in Rosa*, something that will pay well (as Grosz had assured me back in the day). The idea is that we'll do the thing together. You've got to help me. Not much is going on in fashion currently. People are running around dressed in a very banal way. I see a lot of slit skirts (it is possible that I perhaps do not quite have the eye for finer variations on the theme). Imagine, I've already thought up 26 new war etchings. Regarding the studio & apartment, we'll do whatever we can to make it happen. Heckel also wants to help. It's easier to get a studio than an apartment. There are fabulous Fräuleins in Berlin. Probably by now you have received the fashion magazines. Many beautiful kisses & extra kisses to the birthday girl.

For decades, the printer Felsing in Berlin was considered the best for gravure printing. See the October 1923 letter to Martha.
– Dix was getting etchings of the *Kriegszyklus* [War cycle] (Karsch 70–119) printed on behalf of the gallerist Karl Nierendorf, who published these in 1924.
– On the efforts at finding a Berlin apartment and studio, see the letters starting from 06.25.1924.

To Martha [06.22.1924 | Berlin] [PC]

My Dearest! I send you and Nelly the loveliest greetings & kisses. Tuesday afternoon, I'll be there. Grandmother also sends cordial greetings
Jim
[On the front, from Nierendorf:]
Dear Mutzlein
We are avidly hunting for a giant flat-studio and will definitely find something good. You definitely must come to Berlin; things are terribly boring here and it would be excellent if you were to come. "Otto" has his snout full to the brim and pines only about his Mutz! Affectionately yours Karle Ndf

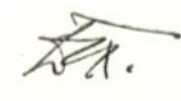

To Martha June 24th | Berlin

My dearest, sweetest!
Many beautiful kisses for your letter & the Imblon letters. The people are really nice. What did this little [sausage-drawing without Lorenz number] say on her birthday? What should I bring for the child? Send me a quick drawing of your feet because of the shoes and the height of the arch. The brocade jackets with fur trim are very modern, but need to be customized. — I long for you both. Be good & loving. — For the time being, nothing has been arranged with housing. Today, we placed an ad. —
Many sweet kisses Jimmy
Greetings to Grandmother.

Dix's sister Toni had married into the Imblon family.

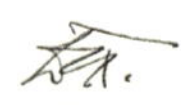

To Karl Hofer June 25, 1924 [Dusseldorf?]

To Prof. Karl Hofer, Akademie der Künste Berlin on June 25, 1924

Dear Master!
Given that I intend to move to Berlin soon, a few days ago I discussed the possibility of obtaining a studio in Berlin with Prof. Wætzoldt. Councilor Wætzoldt told me that it would be best if I were a student of the Academy. Since I am also a student of the Academy in Dusseldorf currently, being approved will probably prove no difficulty in this respect.

I therefore ask you sincerely to accept me as a master student in your studio. If possible, will you please indicate to me whether you do in principle agree. I'd then begin the necessary formalities with the Academy Registrar. — Councilor Wætzoldt even told me that if you should not have a space right now, he would do his utmost to make one.
I look forward to a positive answer and send best wishes
Otto Dix
Dusseldorf Art Academy

Universität der Künste Berlin, Archiv

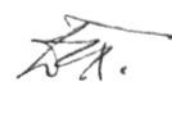

To the Prussian Cultural Ministry Berlin
St. Goar, July 3, 1924

To the Prussian Cultural Ministry Berlin
Application of the artist, Otto Dix, for admission to the Academy of Fine Arts. I hereby ask the High Culture Ministry to accept my application as a student at the Academy of Fine Arts from Autumn 1924. I have consulted with Herr Professor Hofer; he has consented to accept me as his student.
In expectance of a favorable decision from the most distinguished High Ministry of Culture, your most obedient Otto Dix

Universität der Künste Berlin, Archiv
Dix wrote from the property of Martha's family at Villa Rheinfels in St. Goar, where he was working on the etchings of the war cycle (Karsch 70–119). On the back page of the letter is a draft from a ministry employee to a letter of Dix's from July 18: "He may arrive at the beginning of the 1924/25 semester in early October, presenting research projects and curriculum vitae, along with a police clearance certificate."

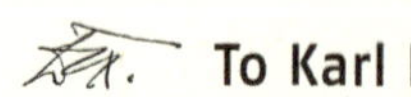

To Karl Hofer July 3, '24 | St. Goar

Very dear Herr Professor!
I offer my sincere thanks for your letter and for your friendly willingness and efforts on my behalf. I have today sent a petition to the Ministry of Culture & sought to be accepted into the Academy, with reference to our conversation. I hope that something suitable will be found for me by fall.
Again many thanks
Yours sincerely Otto Dix.

AdK, Berlin, Historical Archive, PrAdK

1925

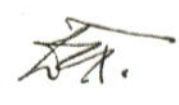

To Karl Hofer 3.17.1925 [PM] [Dusseldorf?]

Very dear Herr Professor!
I'd asked you for inclusion in your master class in the previous year and you had also kindly promised me acceptance. Unfortunately, I was later compelled to retract my request because I was unable to secure an apartment in Berlin. I was completely remiss and failed to inform you and cordially ask you to excuse me this impertinence. Today Nierendorf wrote me that it would be possible, on a rental basis, to obtain a studio on the premises of the School of Applied Arts. If this were possible & you could be of any help to me, I would be very

grateful. Along with this letter, I am also sending a request to the Secretariat of the Staatlichen Kunstschulen. Again, the best of thanks for everything, and cordial greetings to you, Yours,
Otto Dix
Presently at Lanzkirch, Schwarzwald

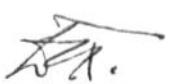

To Karl Hofer [1925 | Dusseldorf]

Very dear Herr Professor!
Nierendorf told me that I will be able to get a studio in Prinz Albrechtstr. As I still have as of yet received no definite decision, I would be very grateful if you could tell me whether the matter is finally settled. When I could move into the studio, etc. I am extremely grateful to you for your efforts on my behalf. Sincerely Yours, faithfully,
Otto Dix
Aachenerstr 114, Dusseldorf

The search for a studio took until late 1925. On 4.30.1925 Hofer advised Dix that he should register as a student with him, and that he, Hofer, could offer him one: "I would be delighted to welcome you here [...]." Hofer further wrote to Dix on 05.16.1925: "It was my pleasure to be able to be helpful as a sign of my appreciation [...]." "Up in the Museum of Decorative Arts is a large, high room, cool in the summer. The thing is as good as settled" (GNM, DKA, NL Dix, Otto, I, C 347). The Staatlichen Kunstschulen (National Art Schools, later Hochschule der Künste, University of the Arts) had studio spaces in the Prinz-Albrecht-Straße 7-8 in Berlin for students and alumni.

– With Hofer's intervention on his behalf, Dix eventually moved into a studio in a building formerly owned by the School of Applied Arts at Prinz-Albrecht-Straße 7-8, but in 1926 had already moved again, this time to Kurfürstendamm 190, at the corner of Schlüterstraße.

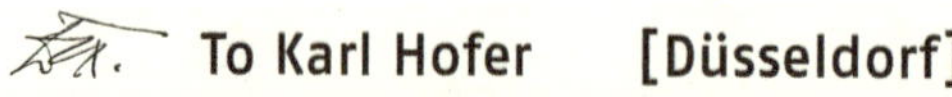

To Karl Hofer [Düsseldorf]

dear Master!
Many thanks for your kind letter. I will, as soon as I receive a message, move into the studio. I would prefer the larger one. From Berlin I have heard, though not officially, that my picture, which I had [brought] to the Academy exhibition, was not hung or not shown at all. I would feel very sorry if this proved to be true, because it would then be impossible for me to continue sending pictures to the Academy. —
Thank you again for your efforts. With best regards
Otto Dix.

– Shown in the catalog of the spring exhibition of the Prussian Academy of Arts in 1925 was *Altes Liebespaar* [Old Couple], Löffler 1923/6.

To Will Grohmann 5.10.25 [PM] St. Goar [PC]

dear Herr Dr. [Grohmann] Since I am showing a large collection of paintings in December or later in Dresden, it is unfortunately not possible to send any to the Secession, or the Kunstverein, either. The paintings you mentioned on your card were shown in Zurich & go from there to Berlin. If you or the Kunstverein must necessarily have something, take pictures from private collections, e.g., the portrait of Heinar Schilling, Rœsberg (ask Glaser for the address) (Klotzsche). Unfortunately, I'll not be able to come to Berlin in early October, I'm sick.
With warm regards
Your Dix

Staatsgalerie Stuttgart, Will Grohmann Archive
For 1925 and 1926, no Dix exhibitions are listed in Dresden; however, he did participate in the Sächsischen Kunstverein exhibition in Dresden in 1925. Dix's work was shown in Zurich at the International Art Exhibition.

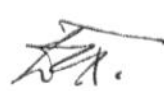

To Hugo Simons [December 1925 | Berlin]

Dear Herr Dr.
We arrived safely in Berlin & have settled in temporarily. Since I still have much to do and need money, I would be very grateful if you could send me something. How are your wife and your children? Greet them warmly from me, from my wife & Nelly, cordial greetings
Your Dix
I have spoken with Nierendorf about the money thing. Since he has no claims on you, send money directly to me.

The Montreal Museum of Fine Arts, Montreal, Canada, Hugo Simons Estate

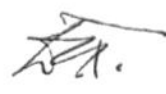

To Carl Krall [beginning of December 1925 | Berlin]

Dear Krall For the past 14 days we have been living in Charlottenburg Kaiser Damm 20. Visit us when you come to Berlin. This summer, in Idar, we bought some beautiful semi-precious stones, 2 opals and 1 aquamarine, which we would like to have made into rings and ask you to take care of this for us. Mutzli is doing well. Nelly is increasing both in age and impudence.
[verso:] We wish you a New Year full of HAPPINESS
Sincerely Your Dix, including wife & child

GNM, DKA, NL Dix, Otto, II, C 10
The family had moved to Kaiserdamm at the corner of Saldernstraße in November. Martha's father, Dr. Lindner, had paid the rent for seven years in advance.

Letter to Carl Krall, 1925

To Hugo Simons [12.31.1925] [Berlin]

dear Herr Dr. Thanks for sending the money. You must excuse my constant tapping for money, but I simply do not understand how Nierendorf

can claim we don't "necessarily need it." We had
Chriſtmas and enough to eat for the next days but
not nearly enough. All the far-flung ſpeeches N.
gives about how much I earn, etc., everything is
idiotic blabbering —
I wish you a happy 1926
& thank you
Your Dix.

The Montreal Museum of Fine Arts, Montreal, Canada, Hugo Simons Estate

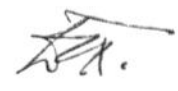

To the Hans Koch family [12.31.1925 | Berlin]

dear palace residents of Hohen Randen!
We have celebrated Chriſtmas with a fat goose
& a Chriſtmas tree. After the holidays, however,
we made due with the dry leftovers [goose].
Things are going somewhat better in the meantime,
more or less.
[diverse drawings]
We thank you for the beautiful gifts. We're sorry,
but could not send you & Hans anything because
we did not have enough money. Little Nelly got a
[drawings — doll pram and Chriſtmas gifts]
Happy New Year to all
Jim Mutz Nelly

Remmert and Barth Gallery Archives, Dusseldorf
Drawings: Lorenz NSK 8.7.1 and 8.7.2
"Hohen Randen" refers to the acquisition of Schloß Randegg (a villa) by Hans Koch in 1923.

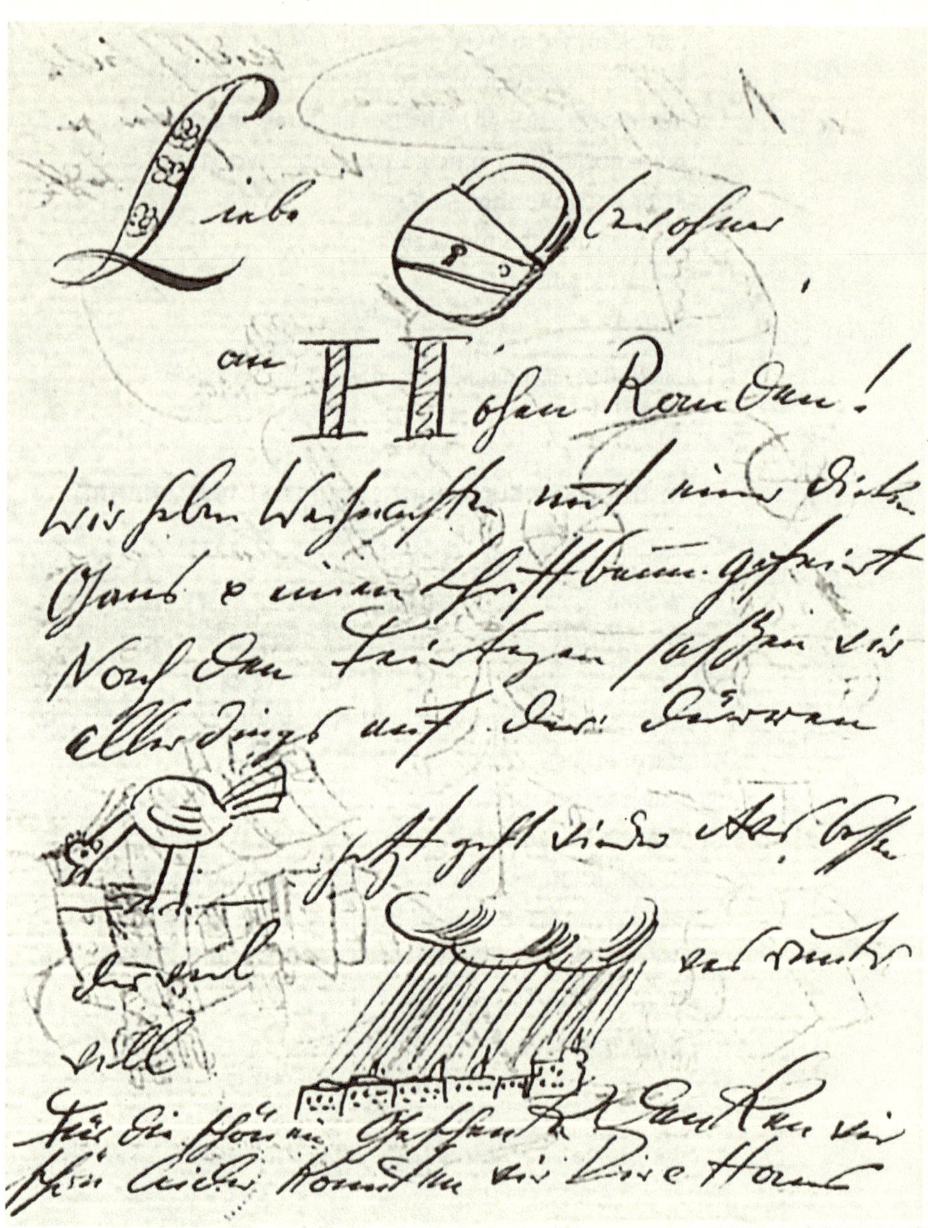

Letter to Hans and Maria Koch, with drawings *An die Schlossbewohner von Hohen Randen* [To the Castle Residents at Hohen Randen] and *Nelly und ihre Weihnachtsgeschenke* [Nelly and Her Christmas Gifts], 12.31.1925

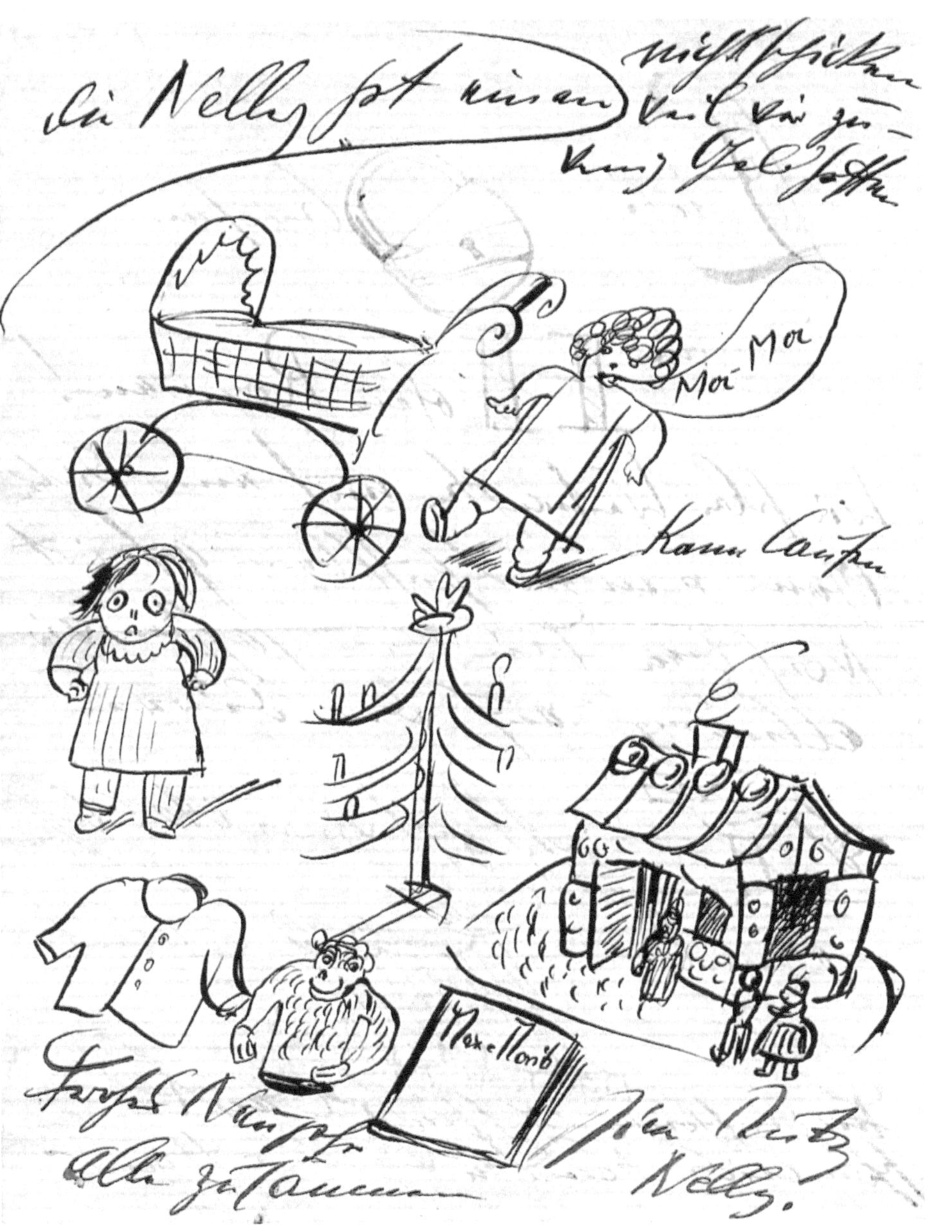
Moi Moi

1926

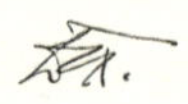

To Hugo Simons [1926 | Berlin]

Dear Herr Dr.
800 M. received, thank you. A letter to Dr. Hesse is going out by the same post. Hopefully the contract will be concluded. Your painting will be varnished in the next few days & then go to Dresden, from where it will then go out again. If this Dr. Oppenheimer, of whom you write, is thinking about a portrait, he should get in touch with me personally. I have just written to Herr Hesse, because you repeatedly asked me to. When I go to Dusseldorf, I will gladly do watercolors of your children.
Many greetings Your Dix & wife

The Montreal Museum of Fine Arts, Montreal, Canada, Hugo Simons Estate Paintings: *Bildnis des Fabrikanten Dr. Julius Hesse mit Farbprobe* [Portrait of the Factory Owner Dr. Julius Hesse with color sample], Löffler 1926/7, and *Bildnis Rechtsanwalt Dr. Hugo Simons* [Portrait of Dr. Hugo Simons, Lawyer], Löffler 1925/11, was loaned to the 1926 International Art Exhibition in Dresden. See the letter to Hans Posse from the beginning of 1926.

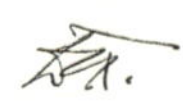

To Arthur Kaufmann [1926 | Berlin]

dear Arthur I ask for the following details: How significant are the damages, & to what extent, length, & width. II. I beg you to determine which substance was used for impregnation, and please specify this exactly. I ask that [you] get in touch with the restorer Gerhard (Pempelforterstr. I think) and ask him for his opinion.

He can undertake the restoration at the expense of the architect (mending only the points), maybe the thing can be removed by a gentle rinsing. Linseed oil was used in painting it. Otherwise, the matter proves once again the contempt shown to artistic work, which is also evident in how paintings are packed, which is simply lousy these days. It's good that you wrote immediately, because we have to close ranks when it comes to such matters.

Best regards Your Dix

Under the 3rd Reich, are you going to move to Palestine or Switzerland? As for me, I'm going to Switzerland until the dawn of the IV. Reich.

To Hugo Simons [1926 | Berlin or Dresden]

dear Herr Dr. Sorry that I haven't written sooner, but I'm too lazy to write. So: I. best of thanks for winning the court hearing. I got the money! And II. If you please, will you tell your father-in-law or mother-in-law that the portraits are going to take a bit because I've important work to get done here. As for the exact time, I'll let you know

Best regards Your Dix

The Montreal Museum of Fine Arts, Montreal, Canada, Hugo Simons Estate. Simons represented Dix in Dusseldorf in civil litigation (GNM, DKA, NL Dix, Otto, I, B 26), i.e., against the client Grünthal, who didn't like the portrait of his daughter (Löffler 1926/15, whereabouts unknown). Painting: *Bildnis Frau Anna Grünebaum-Wahl* [Portrait of Frau Anna Grünbaum-Wahl], Löffler 1926/11.

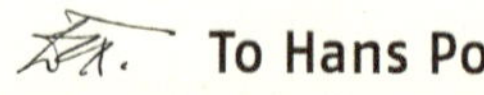

To Hans Posse Kunstsammlungen Dresden [beginning of 1926 | Berlin]

Dear Director!
Many thanks for your letter of 12.31.25 & for the invitation to the International Art Exhibition. I am happy to take part in the exhibition & to send you 3 or 4 paintings, provided that I am not subject to any jury. I will of course send my best paintings & also your request for the portrait of my daughter. You previously obtained photos of the pictures I intend to exhibit.
Yours faithfully
Yours sincerely
Otto Dix
Charlottenburg Kaiserdamm № 20

Dresden, Archiv der Staatlichen Kunstsammlungen, Altregister der SKD, 01/GG 16, Bd. Six paintings were exhibited, seven were included in the catalog, including Kat.-Nr. 462 *Bildnis Herbert Eulenberg* [Portrait of Herbert Eulenberg], Löffler 1925/9; *Bildnis des Fotografen Hugo Erfurth mit Objektiv* [Portrait of the Photographer Hugo Erfurth with Lens], Löffler 1925/10; Kat.-Nr. 464 *Bildnis des Laryngologen Meyer-Hermann* [Portrait of the Laryngologist Dr. Meyer-Hermann], Löffler 1926/5; Kat. -Nr. 465 *Bildnis der Tochter des Künstlers* [Portrait of the Artist's Daughter], Löffler 1924/5; Kat.-Nr. 466 *Der Maler und sein Modell* [The Artist and his Model], no Löffler number; *Künstler-Selbstbildnis und Muse* [Self-portrait of the Artist with Muse], Löffler 1924/3; Kat.-Nr. 467 *Stilleben mit Maske* [Still Life with Mask], Löffler 1925/13. Will Grohmann was part of the jury of the International Art Exhibition in Dresden, June-September 1926; Hans Posse was artistic director. Karl Nierendorf wrote to Dix (6.26.1926): "Your paintings are hanging quite nicely in Dresden" (GNM, DKA, NL Dix, Otto, I, C 524).

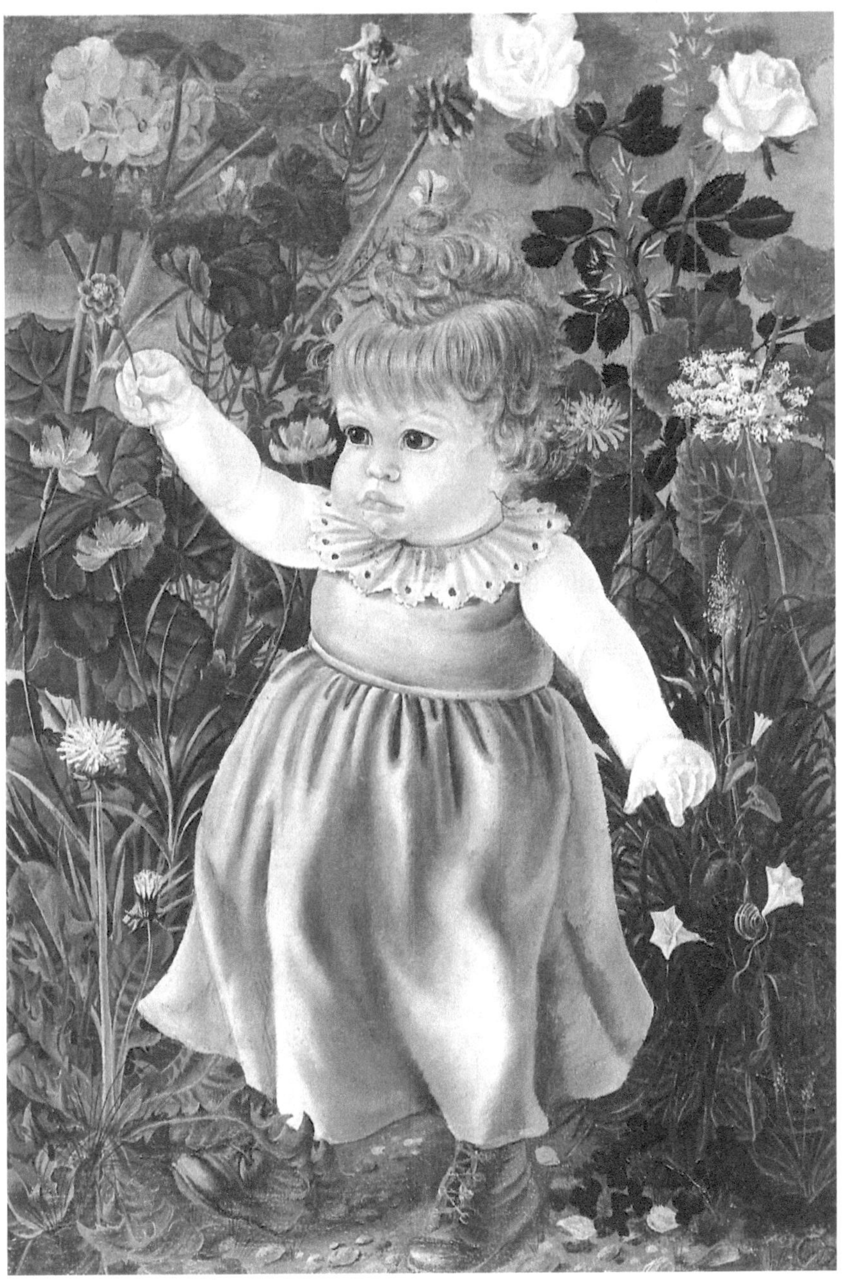

Nelly in Blumen [Nelly in Flowers], 1924

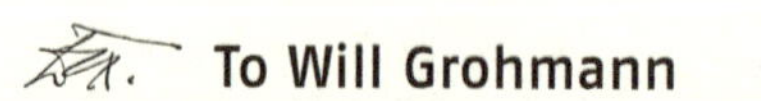

To Will Grohmann [1926 | Berlin]

dear Dr. [Grohmann] Thank you so much for the Kirchner book. It's very interesting for me because of the composition problems that Kirchner always deals with over & over again, and he always finds new solutions. A very rich nature. Please do notify me why Griebel, Hoffmann, etc. withdrew from the Secession. Griebel urged me to quit, but I didn't heed his written advice and can't really discern the reason for their withdrawal anywhere in it either. Another thing [worth considering] is whether or not the Secession is really of any use in terms of ideas & practice anymore these days. I can't really decide from here, either, because I don't know the situation there well enough with respect to the politics surrounding the art. Ultimately, a man's words are not a speech and I would much like to hear the reasons for those colleagues' exit, from their points of view.

I await your response & send sincere regards

Your Dix

Staatsgalerie Stuttgart, Will Grohmann Archive

Dix had been invited to participate in the 1925/26 Dresden Secession exhibition in which Grohmann had played an important role. By 1926, the group had already disbanded again. Griebel had written to Dix: "Rather, I just wanted to inform you that Eugen Hoffmann, Lachnit, Skade, Grundig, I, Busyn, Tröger, so in general all the softer lads, have left the Secession [...]. Those of us that have left do not want to start any new Verein [group], but do hope that you won't help prop up the old one, because it really has nothing much to say for us [anymore]" (GNM, DKA, NL Dix, Otto, I, C 278).

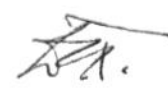 To Martha and Nelly [1926 | Erfurt?]

My two dear hearts
I send you Sunday greetings. I think I'll be leaving here on Tuesday, then I'll have to go again for just one day & will come right back to you, and I'm looking forward to it. — Please don't be even more upset because I was naughty in D. Has Nierendorf sent you the new calculation? I've ordered various materials from Klimsch-Frankfurt, it is coming cash on delivery. Be so kind as to accept it. —
I'll be happy when it's spring again & I can have the good, happy courage to do some work. I've never been so chronically discouraged in my life as I am now. Is it possible that my strength is already gone? Perhaps this negative trend will only continue for a little while. Why am I simply unable to bear these things on my own, so you mustn't suffer through them as well?
Keep me in your heart and receive my warm kisses
From Jimmy & Papp

Dix went "home" to Gera from Erfurt.

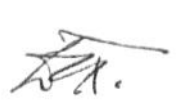 To Martha [1926 | Erfurt]

My dearest I am still an old grumpy face & sad sack, work, and the picture too, is becoming a pain in the neck. As a painting, good. I have written to Nierendorf, as we discussed; afterwards I remembered something. Ndf. already received 250 Mk from Henes &, according to the bill, is still demanding another 1000 Mk. In fact, he is only due the third part of the sum delivered today from Henes, minus Mk 250. — I love you very much & often think of you and the baby. Keep me in your heart too, always; things will go better for us that way.

I'm looking forward to being with you again. — I'm having money from Rudnicki paid to me entirely, since I am still getting money from Ndf anyway (the Mutzli drawing is also missing in the bill), 50 Mk. The Neue Sachlichkeit exhibition is here at the moment and will open on Sunday. I've met the local museum director and got him to buy something from me. It seems, however, he is a fool and only buys old furniture, china, etc.

May things go well for you, rejoice and keep me in your hearts
Your Pappiche

Staying in Erfurt was necessary for the commissioned *Bildnis Frau Rudnicki* [Portrait of Frau Rudnicki], Löffler 1926/12. *The Bildnis des Chirurgen Dr. Carl Henes* [Portrait of the Surgeon Dr. Carl Henes] in Leverkusen was a Nierendorf-mediated contract (Löffler 1925/14; however, the picture is dated "1926" by Dix).
– Neue Sachlichkeit [New Objectivity] Exhibition: The exhibition was conceived by the Kunsthalle Mannheim and shown there first, then in different cities across Germany.

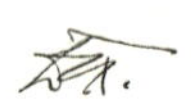

To Martha and Nelly [01.19.1926 (PM)] [Erfurt]

dear Mutzlein & [snail drawing]
I'm staying here in the Erfurter Hof, which is the best hotel. The bed is good; I sleep too long every day. I've ripped up the portrait, already for the third time; it's a godawful headache. Hopefully it will get done yet. Erfurt's quite a nice little town (Rudnicki asserts it's a big city) and has many

beautiful gothic houses and churches. — On Sunday, I went to a few dance halls, on Sunday afternoon we went through the snowy woods. The area resembles Gera. The language is exactly the same. — The boy here is 8 or 9 years old, handsome, looks like a Roman boy, slightly melancholic & feminine. The girl, 3 years old, is very funny, but not nearly as smart as Nelly. Even her language is much more primitive and childish than Nelly's. On the whole it's boring here & I'll be happy when I'm with you again. Excuse me, dear heart, that I write so little; I'm disgruntled because the work is not coming along. Many thanks for your letter. I am coming on Saturday.

Many Matzkisses to you both Jim

GNM, DKA, NL Dix, Otto, II, C2
Drawing: Lorenz NSK 8.7.4
The working visit was in connection with the commission for a child's portrait (not named).

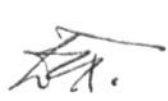

To Martha and Nelly February 1926 [Gera]

dear Mutzlein & little Nelly-CHILD!

I arrived in Gera yesterday evening and drank a good deal of wine. Rudnicki paid me the whole amount. I hope that Nierendorf gets none of it. In Erfurt, I made an application to the museum fools to act on my behalf & get me a commission to paint the mayor of E. Here, I have something else in store. The hereditary prince of Reuss is supposed to allow himself to be painted by me — that is, if he wants me to and if he pays. Did you get the 300M? Be good, & don't be grumpy. I'm looking forward to being [home] with you again. Did you get the cacti from Ms. Rudnicki?

I'm bringing a beautiful doll for Nelly with me. I've given R.'s [Rudnicki's] girl two dolls and the boy a pocketknife.

If I knew Segall's address, I would've long since sent the money.

When I come back, we'll want to toaſt our reunion and the painting with a bottle of champagne. Please get a [*illegible*]. I'll telegraph you a message as to when I'm coming, probably Saturday night. Muſt take a closer look at the timetables firſt.
I love you, always Your Jim.
All send you & Nelly heartfelt greetings

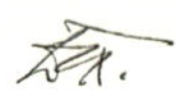

To Martha and Nelly [1926 | Berlin]

My deareſt & little [little snail drawing]
I groaned my way to Berlin on Monday. Emmy was ſtrangely dismayed when I arrived. Yeſterday was the niceſt weather, but here it was cold. Of course, I worked hard yeſterday. Unfortunately, Däubler has fallen ill & has taken to the countryside. So I muſt wait with the painting. Felixmüller has been here, but Emmy was not here, & wanted watercolors for Dresden. Now it's too late; I won't be able to send any more. I am going to do the thing with Reissner Verlag; do you think I should, too? P.F. [Schmidt?] writes from Abazzia that the roses are blooming everywhere and that it's beautiful. It is incredibly calm here; I miss my Mutz and little snail. What are you all up to?

Are the flowers growing in our garden? Here there is cress, in boxes, growing straight skyward. Nierenkarl [Nierendorf] immediately tried to give me another job as a substitute for Däubler and offered me his sweet face as a replacement [of] equal value, which I declined. It seems in my letter, everything [cabbage & turnip-drawing, Lorenz NSK 3.3.19] is growing into a confused mess.
I kiss you & the little snail warmly & love you as ever
Jim
The furniture is not there yet.

Drawing: Lorenz NSK 3.3.18
Theodor Däubler (1876–1934) was a writer and art critic.
The *Bildnis des Dichters Theodor Däubler* [Portrait of the Poet Theodor Däubler] is dated 1927 and originated in Dresden (Löffler 1927/9).

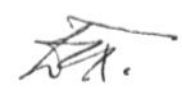

To Martha [1926 | Berlin]

My Herzensmutz Thank you so much for your letter. The Nele [Nelly] anecdotes are quite typical. The paintings that are currently being exhibited in New York were selected last year. The critique in the *Cicerone* was certainly shortened by Biermann, as Wolfradt told me today. Biermann has received several letters because of the Dix-book (immorality), and Biermann "now has something against me." There are unfortunately too many beermen in the world! Yesterday I thought of the two of you continuously when working & was very cheerful. Last night I took a trip to my beloved north. There is an amusement park there; even the fortuneteller from the car hall is again [there?]. He again told me exactly the same, including that I don't have much of an imagination; things are always moving in the realm of the possible (possibilities). Segall's exhibition opening was today. Frau Segall is thin & well again. Tonight I'm going with Karl [Nierendorf] to see the film *Battleship Potemkin*, which according to Wolfradt is supposed to be the most fabulous movie that he has ever seen (Russian). Deals with the Revolution. The fortuneteller told me outright that I am always under intense pressure, i.e., feeling is suppressed by the will, & that's true. Given the strict nature of my work, including emotion and exuberance, perhaps I ought to work less intensely. The Segalls send their regards, Rubin also [*following missing*]

Dr. Georg Biermann Klinkhardt & Biermann published the fortnightly magazine *The Cicerone*. The critique refers to an article by Willi Wolfradt (1892–1988) – a writer, journalist, editor, and editor-in-chief from 1951–1963 at Rowohlt Verlag – in Vol. 41 of the journal *Junge Kunst* (1924) in which Dix's work was favorably reviewed.

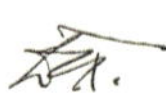

To Martha [1926 | Dusseldorf]

My ever ever dearest sweet Mutzlein
I've worked so much yesterday afternoon; today I start painting. I even started drawing Dr. Henes today & then I was with Josef [Nierendorf] yesterday evening in K.P. and also danced. Next week I have to go to Hagen and finish the painting there. Then, I hope, however, to remain in Sangewar [St. Goar] 'til the fall. Nierendorf has a Dix graphics exhibition running here. Wadler arrived yesterday with a canvas, wants to paint me. — My heart, Darling, I love you, don't feel too down & come to Dusseldorf if you want.

The Berbers are driving to Wiesbaden on Saturday & Anita would be pleased to be with you once again. 1000 kisses, for the little snail, too
Your Jim

Painting: *Bildnis des Chirurgen Dr. Carl Henes* [Portrait of the Surgeon Dr. Carl Henes], Löffler 1925/14 (dated "1926" by Dix).
The reference to "the Berbers" is to the married dance couple that Dix followed to Wiesbaden, Anita Berber and Henry Martens.

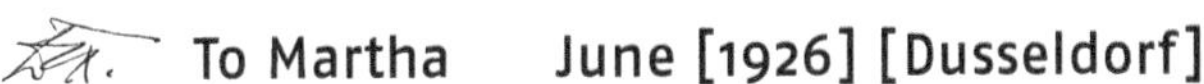

To Martha June [1926] [Dusseldorf]

dear [heart drawing] Mutz
The day before yesterday I was with Hans [Koch]. He inquired why you're not coming to Randegg. He's also given me something against nicotine weakness, a kind of gypsum, which tastes sweet and actually helps. I met Anne Wolf at Hans's; she is being treated by him, and in the evening I went with her to the exhibition. Yesterday the "little negro" called, he had come in from Paris. I wanted to go with him to the exhibition in the evening, but he didn't come on time and since I ran into Niehaus & Breker, I went with them instead. I was at Dr. Simons', who's managed to find a job for me, a grain merchant at the Hindenburgwall; that is, he has to ask his wife first (who is out of town) before the thing can be settled. On Saturday, Hans wants to come along to St. Goar. We're invited to spend summer solstice on the 21st O.T.M. in Eulenberg. We have to see where we can stay in Dusseldorf, because we want to attend the exhibition. I don't think staying at Dr. H. [Henes?] will work out; these people are colossal philistines. I would like to bring something, but don't know what.

I laughed 'til my sides hurt at Nelly's Skaldengesänge [singsongs], the second one, eſpecially, is wonderful.
Many kisses for Popöle Jim

Drawing: Lorenz NSK 07.08.22
Painting: *Bildnis des Dichters Herbert Eulenberg* [Portrait of the Poet Herbert Eulenberg], Löffler 1925/9.
Hans Breker (1906–1993), a sculptor and draftsman who studied with Karl Albiker from 1925–27. He worked after 1945 under the pseudonym Hans van Breek. In 1954, he attained a Professorship in Dusseldorf.

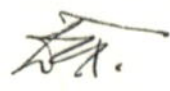

To Martha & Nelly June [1926 | Dusseldorf]

Mutzschatz & little Naivlein Nelly!
I am sitting in the ſtudio in Nauen writing with the maſter's charaƈteriſtic, full script, replete with errors. I have today already drawn Herr May; afterwards it'll be the young lady's turn. I'm ſtaying in a crummy place, Hotel Henk, in a room without any light, coſts 8 Mk plus 10%. Breakfaſt you have to pay no matter what, even if you don't eat, and a meal at the hotel is ſtill 10% more otherwise. Starting next week, I'll be ſtaying at the druggiſt Brück's place, who offered me a room for 3 Mk, not much worse than in Henkhotel. Laſt night I went with the Hesses to the Rheinpalaſt. Büller was there and your little [drawing — owl]
Many Matzkisses
Your Jimmy

Drawing: Lorenz NSK 07.08.21
In 1922, Dix had been a master student at the Düsseldorf Akademie under Heinrich Nauen (1880–1940), the most important representative of Rhenish Expressionism. In this connection, the situation described above arose during the absence of Heinrich Nauen.

– Painting: *Bildnis Josef May* [Portrait of Joseph May], Löffler 1926/13. The sitter was the brother of Dr. Hugo Simons, a lawyer and art collector in Dusseldorf, whom Dix had befriended and procured portrait commissions from, including of family members, among others.
– See also *Bildnis Frau Anna Grünebaum-Wahl* [Portrait of Mrs. Anna Grünebaum-Wahl], Löffler 1926/11, Simons' former mother-in-law. Simons' wife died while giving birth to their son Georg.
– A possible reference to Dr. Julius Hesse, whom Dix had also painted in Dusseldorf (Löffler 1926/7).

To Martha [1926 | Dusseldorf]

My dear Mutzlein I will be very bored on Sunday if you don't show up here. Hans is coming back again early on Tuesday.
I think you are coming on Monday; I'll pick you up at one o'clock from such-&-such train.
Mars [*illegible*] have been invited on Monday for lunch. And will you also come, what should I say? — It's not so bad, a little brother will come! Be calm, Mummy! In the meanwhile, be comforted by Nelly. So, come on Monday. I don't know what to give you for your birthday. Many kisses Jim

To Martha [1926 | Dusseldorf]

dear Mutzi It's good that the package has arrived; I was already quite grumpy about it. Hopefully the suit will be there on Sunday. The little dresses have come. I'm a hopeless grouch, Matz, but what I'm painting is a load of crap, too. And I have a continuous pain in my chest. Hans examined me. The I. heartbeat is irregular, nothing to be done there. — The models I'm painting are not uninteresting,

all the sadder is what I'm painting. 2 years ago I would have made great portraits of the same people; to-day it gets a weak going over [?]
Many Matzküsse
Jimmy
Please write to Kesser

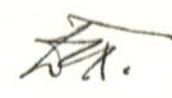

To Martha [1926 | Dusseldorf]

My dearest What is the little brother up to that is no brother at all, but a little sister?
I am a walking drugstore. Today Hans has given me a thing for gargling and a thing to stick in the ass, both to stop the heavy vomiting. Last night I threw up half of dinner on the Königsallee. I am hardly smoking at all, and do not booze either. Krachel is traveling to Randegg on Friday night. I gave the pharmacy your prescription to process and send. I work a lot and badly, even technically lousy; it's bad. I have a painting of Anita Berber in the *Frankfurter Illustrierte*. Nauen is back. He warmly recommends Marseille. Warmest Lenze! You have to see the painting of the Frl. on Friday; the background still needs to be painted.
Many many kisses. Jim

Painting: *Bildnis der Tänzerin Anita Berber* [Portrait of the Dancer Anita Berber], Löffler 1925/6.
– Anita Berber (1899–1928) took 1920s Berlin by storm – and reflected the abandon of the city at the time. Berber drank excessively, appeared in soft-porn silent films, was a drug addict and generally loudmouthed hellraiser wherever she went. Dix used vivid reds, to stunning effect, for her portrait. If not for the Dix portrait, Berber most likely would have remained an obscure footnote in history.
– Anita Berber to Dix: "My dearest Otto! Did you see the picture in the *Illustrierten Blatt*, I was so happy about it. What are you up to, and Muschi & little Nelly? Things are misera… no commitments, no money.

I wanted to therefore ask if you can possibly lend me 200 M. In mid-August we will be in Leipzig, then I can give it back to you. Please don't be angry, anyway, you're an artist and you can understand when people are down on their luck. Others always think you are swimming in money" (GNM, DKA, NL Dix, Otto, I, C 64).

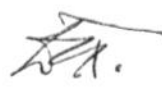

To Martha [summer of 1926 | Dusseldorf]

Herzlein Today I bought a "Motaitel" [suit] at Hamsät [?], I hope it will come Sunday. — I believe that such Galli Matti food impresses father, who has a weak spot for such things. — I'll definitely be coming on Wednesday & look forward to seeing all of you. We'll then take a walking tour of the Eifel. The Flechtheim painting is going well. Yesterday our little negro was here. But I had no desire to talk to him & went to the Mays for dinner. I don't enjoy talking about boring things like that. One can't help but turn into a sucker with a typewriter & writing. Grünthal wants his daughter's mouth, which "he considers more than just a figura," set higher, which I energetically rejected. Simons made the great joke about it that there are "a few other things on the girl he would like to "raise."

Many kisses Jim

Painting: *Bildnis des Kunsthändlers Alfred Flechtheim* [Portrait of the Art Dealer Alfred Flechtheim], Löffler 1926/10, and *Bildnis Josef May* [Portrait of Joseph May], Löffler 1926/13.
Due to disagreements about the quality of the portrait of the daughter of Moritz Grünthal (Löffler 1926/15 – whereabouts unknown) litigation ensued, which the lawyer friend of Hugo Simons was able to have turned aside in Dix's favor. The suggestion to Dix that he change the girl's appearance in the painting was firmly rejected by the latter. Technically, that would have been impossible given the use of tempera technology. Dix himself reacted adamantly & demanded the agreed-upon remuneration amounting to 3000 M., giving Flechtheim an ultimatum that it be paid by Wednesday, August 5, 1926 (7.31.1926, Ms. Dix Grünthal, Archives of Galerie Remmert and Barth, Dusseldorf).

To Martha [1926 | Dusseldorf]

My dear Herzensmutz!
I have moved into a cruddy room in the Wittelsbacher Hof district. Since everything was full in the back, I got a "tube" in the front with no running water, noise from cars and the electrics 'til 2 in the morning, costing 5.75 M. An improvement in matters is absolutely nowhere in sight. If I don't get a better room today, I'm moving out. — Breakfast costs 1.35 Mk, everything is bad & cheap; it's also a filthy room with no elevator. I might as well stay in the homeless shelter for 50 p. Flechtheim never has any time. Today he was gone again the whole day because Mr. Renoir was visiting him.
Lots of kisses Jim
Today I am going out with Dr. Simons.

Painting: *Bildnis des Kunsthändlers Alfred Flechtheim* [Portrait of the Art Dealer Alfred Flechtheim], Löffler 1926/10.

To Martha [1926 | Elberfeld]

[*Beginning missing*] not Dusseldorf perhaps, because here every night there is something going on. Either the Grün(e)baums [sic.] have invited someone or [the] Kralls have something going on. The Rudnickis are an insolent gang that haggle for cheap prices, but I think we'll still give them the stuff anyhow. I've been working diligently every day and even at night by light, that's why things have gone so fast. I've also learned a lot. Almost everything painted on the undercoat turned out very nicely. What is the source of our little snail's pains?

[Drawing]
I received a long letter from Fritz about family research.
Stay well.

Drawing: Lorenz NSK 8.7.5
Grün(e)baums: Hugo Simons' in-laws.

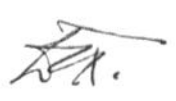

To Martha [1926 | Dusseldorf]

My dear Mutzlein!
I have started painting; Dr. Hesse is a cross between [Kaiser] Wilhelm and [Otto von] Bismarck. But that's already saying too much. Actually: nose typical, mouth typical, forehead typical. Only his eyes are set wide. I was with Jankel [Adler] & Bottig [?] last night in the [*illegible*], which is so large that you can wear yourself out just walking it. I received the letter & the things. I think we're not going to Dresden; my black suit is in Berlin; it's too complicated.
The most interesting things in the exhibition are the airplanes. You will certainly find some things here; there are also clothes shops here. I'll bring a nice toy along for Nele. This afternoon I have to do the Jankel [Adler] painting (for the suit), the Hesse I'll paint with paint making machines in the background.
Tomorrow I'll write more.
Many kisses
Your Jim.

Lorenz NSK 3.3.5: Letter drawing, portrait study of Dr. Hesse. Paintings: *Bildnis des Malers Jankel Adler* [Portrait of the Painter Jankel Adler], Löffler 1926/3, and *Bildnis des Fabrikanten Dr. Julius Hesse mit Farbprobe* [Portrait of the Factory Owner Dr. Julius Hesse with Color Sample], Löffler 1926/7.

To Martha [1926 | Erfurt]

My dearest Received 2 letters from you today! Today, after the umpteenth attempt, I finally progressed somewhat, even if the thing is not all that great. Anyway, I'm starting now with painting; the color make[s] so much difference. Sometimes I'm directly shocked by my lack of talent and often do not understand the simplest things, but I do know the forms of the head so precisely that I could model them, when drawing they simply flow [from my hands]. Nothing more distinctive is left to do.
I am pleased that you are "lippy."
[Drawing]
At the beginning I colored the Matzkisses. I'm looking forward to being together again.
Pappiche!

Drawing: Lorenz NSK 3.3.13
Painting: *Bildnis Frau Rudnicki* [Portrait of Frau Rudnicki], Löffler 1926/12.

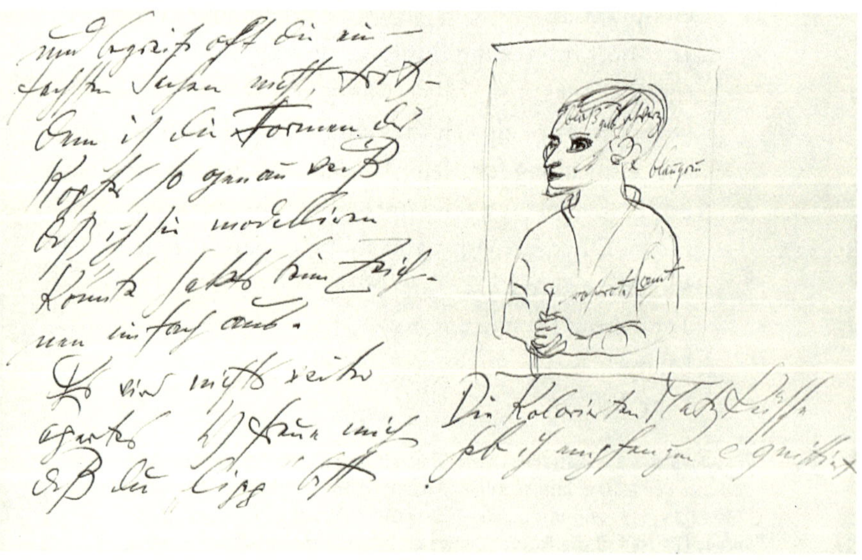

Letter to Martha Dix, with portrait sketch *Damenporträt (Frau Rudnicki)* [Portrait (Frau Rudnicki)], 1926.

To Martha [1926 | Erfurt]

My sweet Mutzlein Yesterday morning I gave Herr Rudnicki the letter to you, but he didn't put it in the box until the evening. I am still struggling horribly with the portrait, have already made 5 drawings and none are good. It's dismal. Most of all, I just want to give up. Tell the sweet children that I'm also bringing along a picture book. Here, in the room where I'm working, there's a collection box with a Magen David [star drawing] for the Zionists. I asked Rudniki about it; it turns out that they are Jews. Isn't that funny? At first I couldn't believe it, but it seems to be the case. The man looks like a Protestant minister. Due to his almost swastika-like appearance, the most embarrassing things must happen to the man, of course, so much so that he wants a proper [nose drawing] — Heartfelt kisses for you both. Not playing
Jimmy
Bored as ever now

Drawing: Lorenz NSK 3.3.14
Painting: *Bildnis Frau Rudnicki* [Portrait of Frau Rudnicki], Löffler 1926/12.

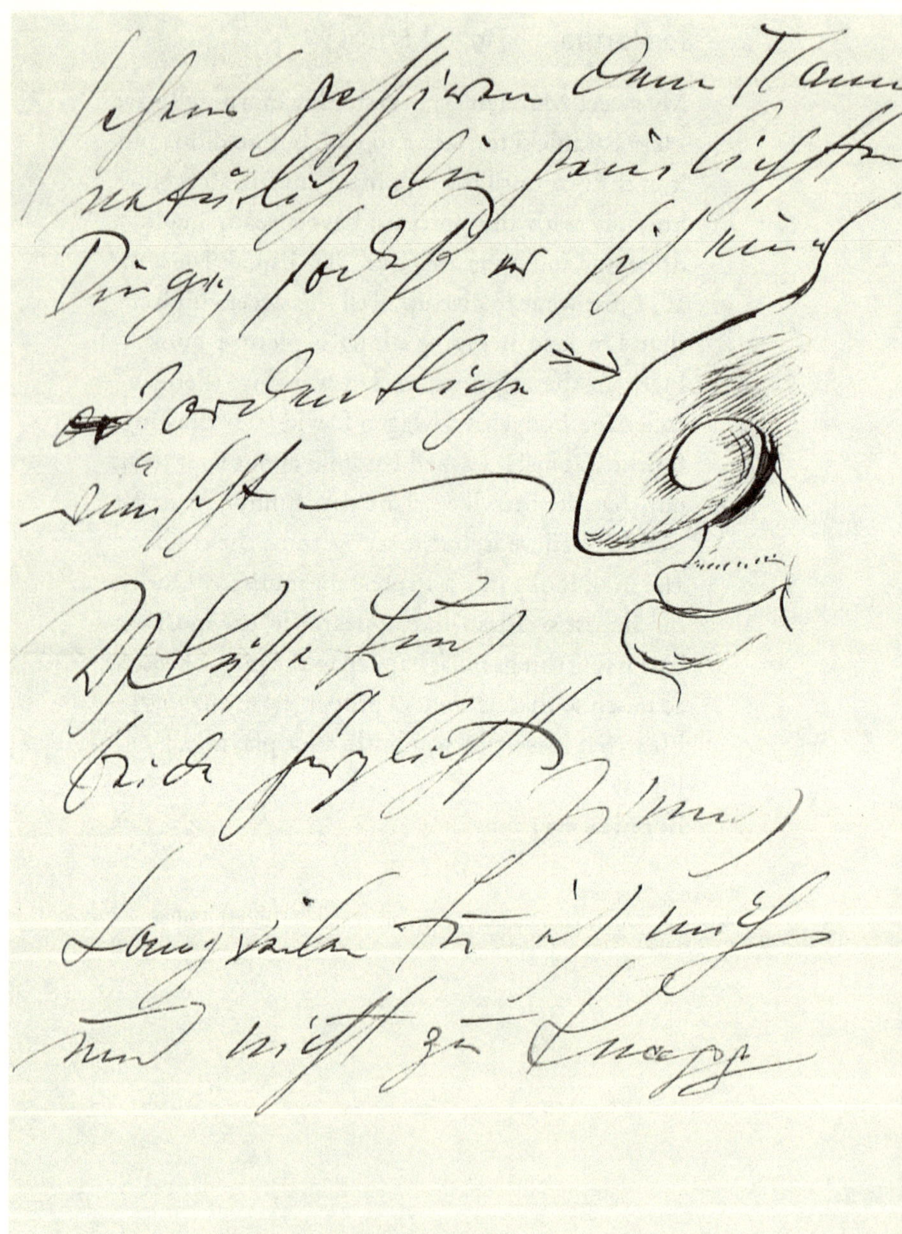

Letter to Martha Dix, with *Idealnase* drawing [Ideal nose], 1926.

To Martha [1926 | Dresden]

My dearest Mutzlein & little one How are you? You've surely received the money. Have you heard anything from Segall? Did you send erasers & rollers? I am still drawing on the [surface of the] picture, hopefully the wooden panel will come soon from Ddorf. Last night I spent some time with the sculptors Kind & Eugen Hoffmann. Kind wants to come to Berlin this week or next and spend a night in my studio, give him the keys. Today, my court hearing was held in Dusseldorf. If a message comes, let me know right away. Don't forget to set the frames around the paintings. — Be cheerful and not grim!
I love you Your Jim

Kind & Eugen Hoffmann were Dresdner sculptors & painters.

To Martha [1926 | Dresden]

My dear Mutzheart!
Why do I hear nothing from you? Are you in good health? Or are things not going well? How is the snail? Are you happy? Has Segall checked in? Yesterday we were in the Sächsische Schweiz (Saxon Switzerland) to visit Cassel; today I went to the boarding school with Griebel. Exhibition. The latest: My painting boards have not yet arrived; the idiots, they sent it via express freight rather than by mail, so I telegraphed and received news that they went out on the 18th from Ddorf, they should arrive here tomorrow. Dr. Gurlitt was here (I went with him to Glaser's who's lent him a picture for

the Zwickauer exhibition. Glaser seems completely glum to me.) —
On Saturday, I'll be coming home to you.
Many beautiful Matzkisses
Your Jim
I'm pretty grim, as is befitting this ugly autumn weather!
The Erfurths are also terrible sourpusses

Dr. Hildebrand Gurlitt (1895–1956) was director of the museum in Zwickau beginning in 1925. He consistently built a collection of contemporary art and staged important exhibitions, and in 1927 a show with works from newer Dresden artists.

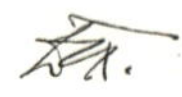

To Martha [1926?] Berlin W 50 Kurfürstendamm 232

dear little heart!

I. Passport is enclosed

II. Karin Dargas is in America, Söndlin followed a few days ago. They want to stay over there. Old Dargas inquired about "Nell"-Dix. Yesterday, we went with an actor, George, and a Frl. Herzfelde to Lunapark, the Frl. knows Meta very well & has heard much about you, what a charming & talented woman you are. The girl is very nice, has a beautiful head, maybe a little too clever. I'll probably come to St. G. [Goar] on Sunday or Monday & look forward to seeing you both.

I also ran into George Grosz, he is & remains one of the friendliest people that I know. —
I send you a lot of nice little kisses & the child as well
Jimmy

Frl. Herzfelde likely refers to one of the sisters of Wieland Herzfelde & John Heartfield, with whom Dix was well acquainted.
– Meta: most likely, Meta Karsch.

To Hugo Erfurth 8.6.1926 | St. Goar

dear Herr Erfurth!
I received your letter of the 25th of VII. I would like to paint the picture in mid-September; I'll let you know exactly when. I assume that I can reside with you as usual during the period of work.
Yours sincerely,
Dix.
Presently in St. Goar. Villa Rheinfels

Painting: *Bildnis Fotograf Hugo Erfurth mit Hund* [Portrait of Photographer Hugo Erfurth with Dog], Löffler 1926/14.

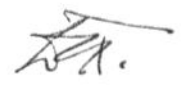

To Hugo Simons [1926 | Berlin]

dear Herr Dr. I haven't heard from you in quite some time. How do you like the portrait of Frau Grünebaum? Try to convince old man Grünebaum to have his portrait done, too. Frau May, too, to whom I spoke about the matter personally, should also have her portrait done by me. Incidentally, I haven't forgotten that you have received I. a 10 Mk credit from me, II. acted as intermediary in getting a commission for the watercolor of Frau Grünebaum. Frau Ey has watercolors there; pick one out for yourself; if you like none, I will send you a selection. I send you warmest greetings.
Please pass along cordial greetings to your wife as well.
Your Dix.
My wife sends her best greetings

The Montreal Museum of Fine Arts, Montreal, Canada, Hugo Simons Estate
Painting: *Bildnis Frau Anna Grünebaum-Wahl* [Portrait of Frau Anna Grünebaum-Wahl], Löffler 1926/11. Hugo Simons was able to transport

the portrait of the mother of his deceased first wife, Hedwig, and his own (Löffler 1925 / 11), to Montreal, past emigration controls; cf. Olaf Peters (ed.), *Otto Dix* (The Montreal Museum of Fine Arts / Neue Galerie, New York 2010 / 2011; Munich 2010).

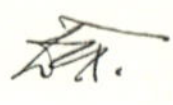

To Ferdinand Dorsch Sept. 6, '26 | St. Goar

Dear Herr Professor
I received your letter of 2nd Spt. This week I'm not in Berlin, but probably will be in the near future. Once I'm there, I'll send you further news.
With kind regards Your
devoted Dix
St. Goar Villa Rheinfels

HfBK Dresden, Archives, Dix letters, № 18
The background is Dorsch's requested visit to Berlin on September 2, 1926 to deliver the news of his appointment to the Dresden Academy and receive his answer. The contract dated October 1, 1926 (see Dix's March 18, 1953 letter to the university). Dix actually began his activity in the summer semester of 1927, reported in the press as being due to the fulfillment of large orders and a trip to Italy. As a professor, Dorsch had previously asked his colleagues for their consent to begin negotiations with Dix: "Dix should take the place of Kokoschka." Ludwig von Hofmann wrote on September 9, 1926: "I hasten to inform you that I have no objections to the proposal" (Dresden Academy of Fine Arts, Archives).

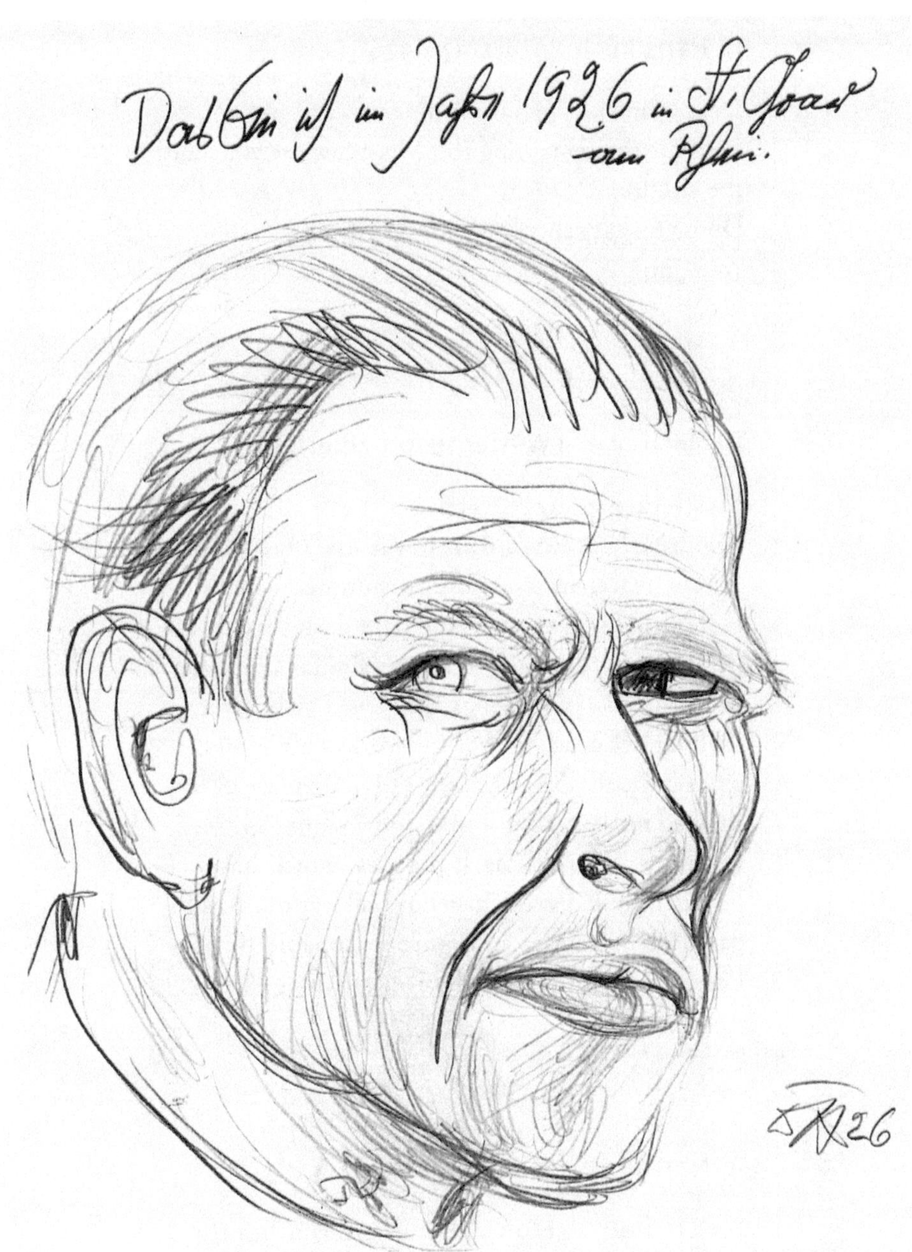

Das bin ich im Jahre 1926 in St. Goar am Rhein [This is me in St. Goar am Rhein in 1926] drawing, 1926

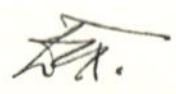

To Hans Koch Oct. 17, 1926 [Berlin]

Dear Hans We haven't a penny, & I beg you to send me the remaining 100 Mk. How are you, and the children?
Doing fine at school? Kind regards
Your Jim

Archives of Galerie Remmert and Barth, Dusseldorf

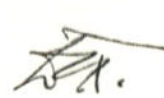

To Martha [Winter 1926 | Elberfeld]

My Herzensmutz!
The drive here was a pain in the ass. One simply cannot travel in winter on a summer schedule. Here it is foggy & ugly and gets dark very early. I drew yesterday and today, so similar does the woman look. [*Drawing*] She has a tick, always shaking her head, so that the work is made all the more difficult. I was already at Krall's place & he showed me beautiful stones, tourmalines as green as the dark forest, black topazes, which have a peculiar, dulled greyish-yellow coloration. Krall has become calmer and more reasonable; is no longer as fat and not so hysterically high-strung.

Drawing: Lorenz NSK 3.3.12

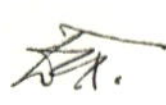

To Martha [1926 | Elberfeld]

My Dearest How are you, are you healthy. Or do you feel glum-glum. I also worked today & have painted part of the clothes black. Tomorrow

I paint the face and hands, hopefully for good. Whether the picture is similar, I don't know. Last night I was with Krall in the theater. Asta Nielsen performed in a very moral American piece, but seemed very sympathetic. Krall sent her flowers & invited them for Sunday lunch, for dinner. But she wasn't able because she was sick, but wrote Krall a nice letter. Carlie was blissful and would have hugged me on the street (almost), if I hadn't prevented it. Because of the letter, basically. Then I got to enjoy the whole evening with Krall's swarm. — Today at noon we ate the venison alone, Gebhardt and Krall's brothers were also there. This is all crap I'm writing you, but I haven't much more to report. There are lovely Marèes in the museum here. I'm going to bed. Many many kisses,
Jim
Kiss little Nelly.

Dix was working on a portrait of *Frau Anna Grünebaum-Wahl* [Frau Anna Grünebaum-Wahl], Löffler 1926/11

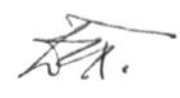

To Hugo Simons [autumn of 1926 | Berlin]

dear Herr Dr. Enclosed is a letter from the lawyer, and one from Barmen. The matter is the following: Mr. Moritz Adler gave me a suit [two years ago] in 1925 under the condition that in exchange, I provide him a small oil sketch. This summer, Jankel Adler assured me in front of witnesses that his brother had ceded the claim against him. I believed this & painted Herr Jankel Adler a portrait sketch for it. This he sold, to my knowledge, to Frau Ey, for 700 Mk.

I now sent a registered letter to the painter Arthur Kaufmann in Ddorf because I don't know Adler's address, & enclosed a letter to J. Adler. I informed him herein that he should pay the 192 Mk to his brother, or immediately send the portrait sketch back to me. Adler has not yet reacted to this and I also have no acknowledgment of receipt from Kaufmann. I ask you sincerely to request on my behalf that J. Adler immediately send the money to his brother or the picture back to me. If he does neither of these, I will make a criminal complaint of fraud against him. I ask you to get in touch with M. Adler's lawyers in conjunction with this. I look forward to your speedy response & send my regards. Your Dix.
Kaiserdamm 20 Charlottenburg

The Montreal Museum of Fine Arts, Montreal, Canada, Hugo Simons Estate
Jankel Adler ended the dispute himself with the letter: "Dusseldorf, the 15th of XI. '26 Dr. Weyl and Dr. Simons, Attorneys-at-Law, Dusseldorf / After receipt of your letter dated XI.13, I wish to inform you that more than a week ago I responded to a letter of Prof. Dix in which I wrote to him that I wanted to clarify the whole thing with my printer, Moritz Adler Barmen. Today I have already received a letter from my printer in which he tells me that he (Dix) has given his lawyer instructions to withdraw his demands, thus the entire matter is settled. / Sincerely Jankel Adler" (The Montreal Museum of Fine Arts, Montreal, Canada, Hugo Simons Estate).

To Martha [November? 1926] [Elberfeld]

[*The beginning of the letter is missing*] tonight I am at [the Kralls] for dinner. We cannot agree on the versions of the ring, he claims I've got horrible taste in jewelry and makes fun of me when I show him snake rings and other beautiful things. Eating & living is good here. 800 Mk will be transferred to you today. What is Feller up to? [*Drawing*]

Say hello to the [*snail drawing*],
many many kisses
Jim

Drawing: Lorenz NSK 8.7.3
On stationery of Emil Grünebaum, Elberfeld. Most likely in relation to the *Bildnis Frau Anna Grünebaum-Wahl* [Portrait of Frau Anna Grünebaum-Wahl] (Löffler 1926/11)

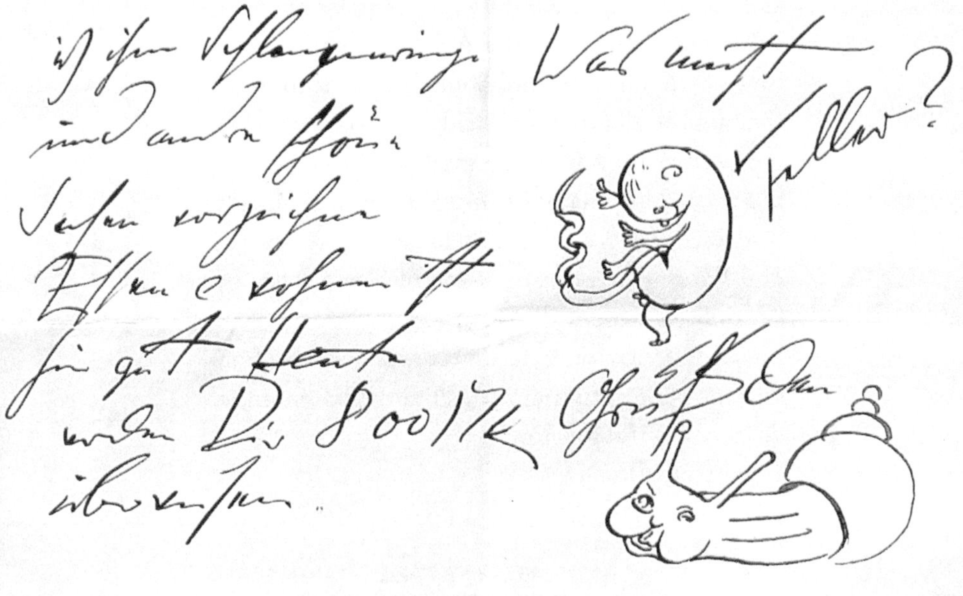

Letter to Martha Dix, with drawings *Embryo* and *Schnecke* [Snail], Nov. [?] 1926

To Martha [November? 1926 | Elberfeld]

My Sweet
So, the picture. It's almost finished & looks very elegant, almost too genteel. Tomorrow I'll still get some more done and then come home. Maybe I'll go again tomorrow afternoon again to
[*The beginning of the letter is missing*]
[*Drawing on separate sheet*]

Drawing: Lorenz NSK 3.3.11

1927

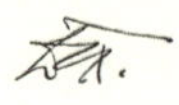

To Ferdinand Dorsch [January 1927 | Berlin]

dear Herr Dorsch! I again return to our discussion concerning the studio and request that you submit my wishes to the Academic committee. Since your small ground floor studios & those of the same size on the other side are not suitable for me because they are I. too small II. the sidelight is too weak, I ask that it be decided that I, as already discussed, can receive 2 student-studios on the second floor, which can be made into one space by breaking out the wall.
I would otherwise prefer to request a second holiday and wait until there is a suitable space for me.
With respectful greetings
Yours truly Otto Dix

HfBK Dresden, Archives, Dix letters, № 19
On 2.2.1927 Dorsch sent his consent to Dix's proposal and also offered assistance with a letter from the Academy to the housing office for help in finding an apartment.

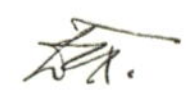

To Karl Nierendorf January 30, 1927 | Charlottenburg [Berlin]

To Herr Karl Nierendorf
Berlin W. Lützowstr. 32
I hereby terminate the contract concluded on May 21, 1926, expiring on May 21, 1927.
Yours faithfully
Otto Dix.

Galerie Nierendorf Archives, Berlin
Contract: Dix refers here to the termination of the third contract with Galerie Nierendorf. The first was concluded by both parties for a period of three years in Dresden on September 4, 1922, the second also for three years in Cologne on April 1, 1923. The contract Dix was terminating had been for general representation through the gallery and had been concluded for a period of one year. Thanks to the professorship in Dresden, Dix considered himself in a safe financial position and no longer so dependent on commercial ventures.

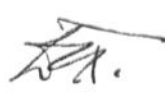

To Ferdinand Dorsch February 18, 1927 [PM] [Berlin]

dear Herr Dorsch, dear Colleague!
I received your letter dated the 12th of this month. It would be very nice if the Academy were to undertake something for me concerning an apartment. I need 5–6 rooms with accessories, if possible the use of the garden in a nice convenient location (Swiss quarter, Großer Garten).
I thank you very much for your efforts & send you best regards sincerely your
devoted Dix
My wife sends warm greetings.

HfBK, Archives, Dix letters, № 21
Apt: In fact, Dix lived with his family in Dresden in a spacious apartment with a large garden, at Bayreuther Straße 32, in a southern suburb.

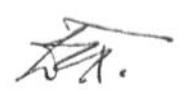

To Nelly [around March 11, 1927] [Berlin]

dear Nelly We've got a little brother, he looks like this [drawing]. He does nothing but eat, sleep, & cry. Once he's fed, he is re-wrapped, then he's happy and laughing. [*Drawing*] Then he is placed in his little pram. Mummy is still in bed [*drawing*],

the axe [axolotl] is healthy. I'll send you stamps, so you can write to me sometimes.
Your Pappi
[Insert from Martha:] I've received beautiful little flowers, many tulips, are they also blooming there in the garden? Matzkisses from Mammi

Drawings: Lorenz NSK 8.7.6 and 8.7.7

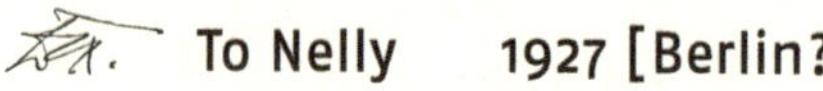

To Nelly 1927 [Berlin?]

dear Nelly
the
[*Easter bunny drawing*]
is coming soon
and will be bringing you beautiful eggs. Watch the bunny-garden carefully in the morning; maybe the bunnies will already be painting their eggs out there
[*Continued by Martha Dix*]
.... + Pappische

Drawing: Lorenz NSK 8.7.9

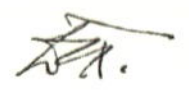

To Karl Nierendorf April 3, 1927 [Dresden]

dear Karl On 21 May this year our contract expires & I would ask you to deliver all my paintings, watercolors, drawings, and prints to my studio at Kurfürstendamm 190 on or before June 1, 1927. Any exhibitions need to have concluded by June 1, 1927. Enclosed is an invitation to an exhibition in Holland. I request your return reply, if it is convenient to exhibit some pictures there, and

I also ask you to confirm receipt of my letter in writing. with best regards
Dix

Galerie Nierendorf Archives, Berlin

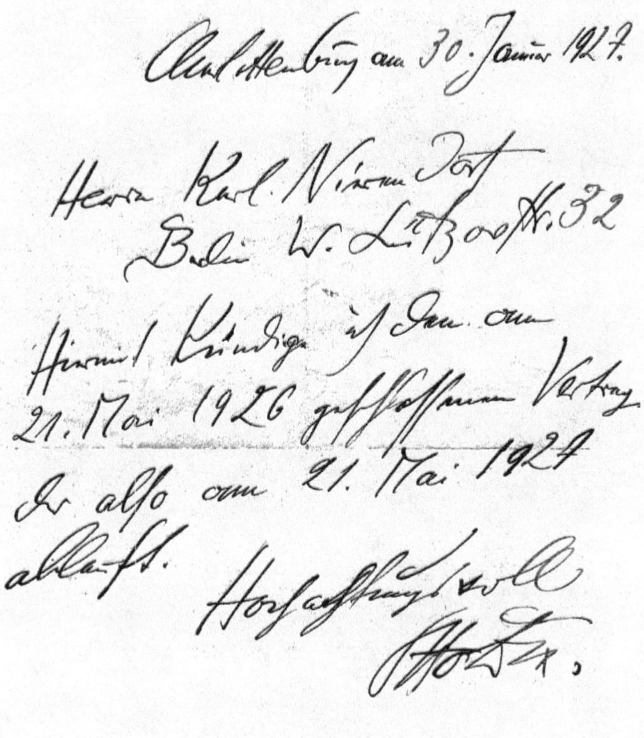

[illegible] am 30. Januar 1927.

Herrn Karl Nierendorf
Berlin W. Lützowstr. 32

Hiermit kündige ich den am 21. Mai 1926 geschlossenen Vertrag der also am 21. Mai 1927 abläuft.

Hochachtungsvoll
Otto Dix.

Contract termination letter to Galerie Nierendorf, 1.30.1927

To Nelly & Martha [May 1, 1927 | Dresden]

dear Nelly! Tend nicely to your garden, so that it's nice when I come. The peaches and dandelions are blooming near the little wolf in the garden. Sleep tight & be kind to

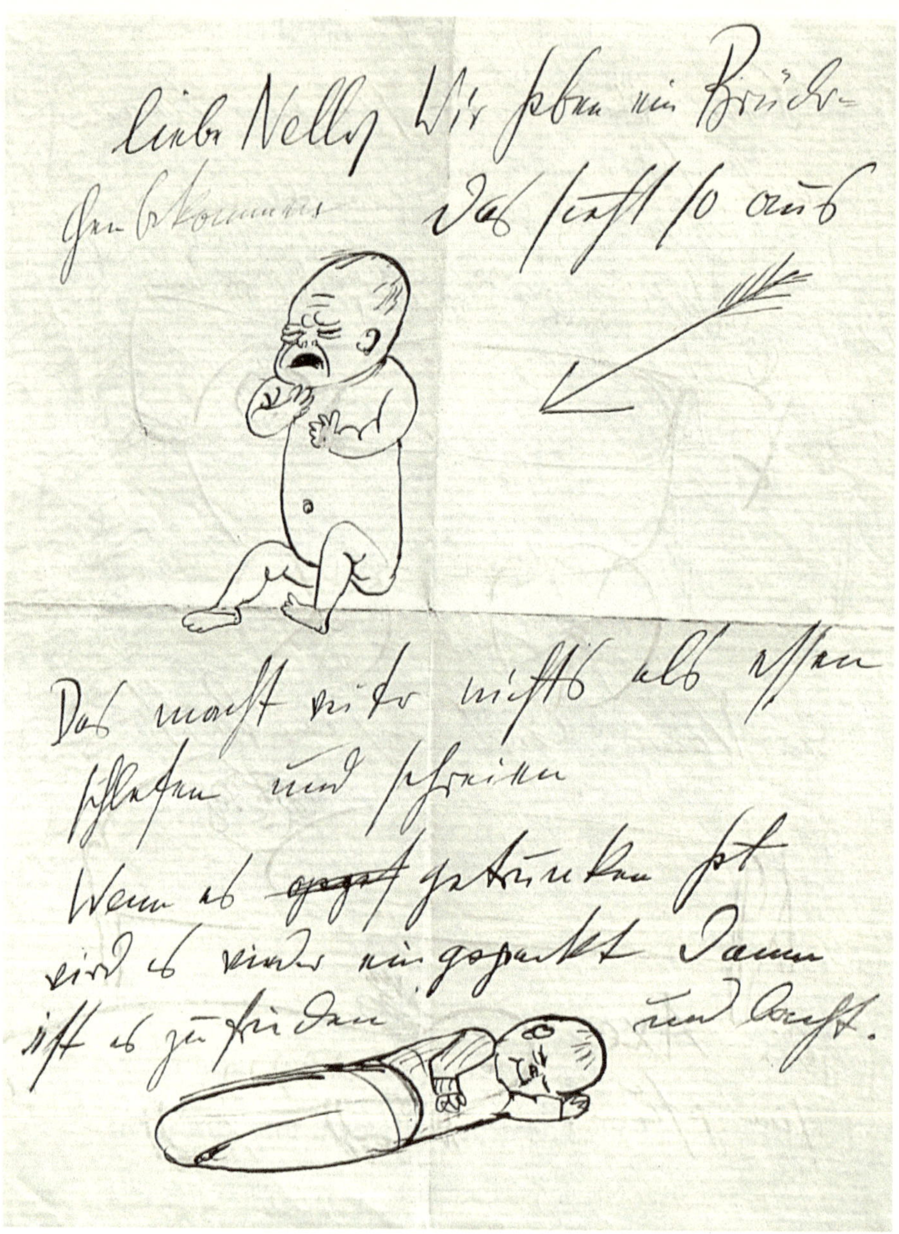

Liebe Nelly Wir haben ein Brüderchen bekommen Das sieht so aus

Das macht weiter nichts als essen schlafen und schreien

Wenn es ~~[illegible]~~ getrunken hat wird es wieder eingepackt Dann ist es zufrieden und lacht.

Letter to Nelly Dix, with drawings "We've got a new little brother," around November 3, 1927.

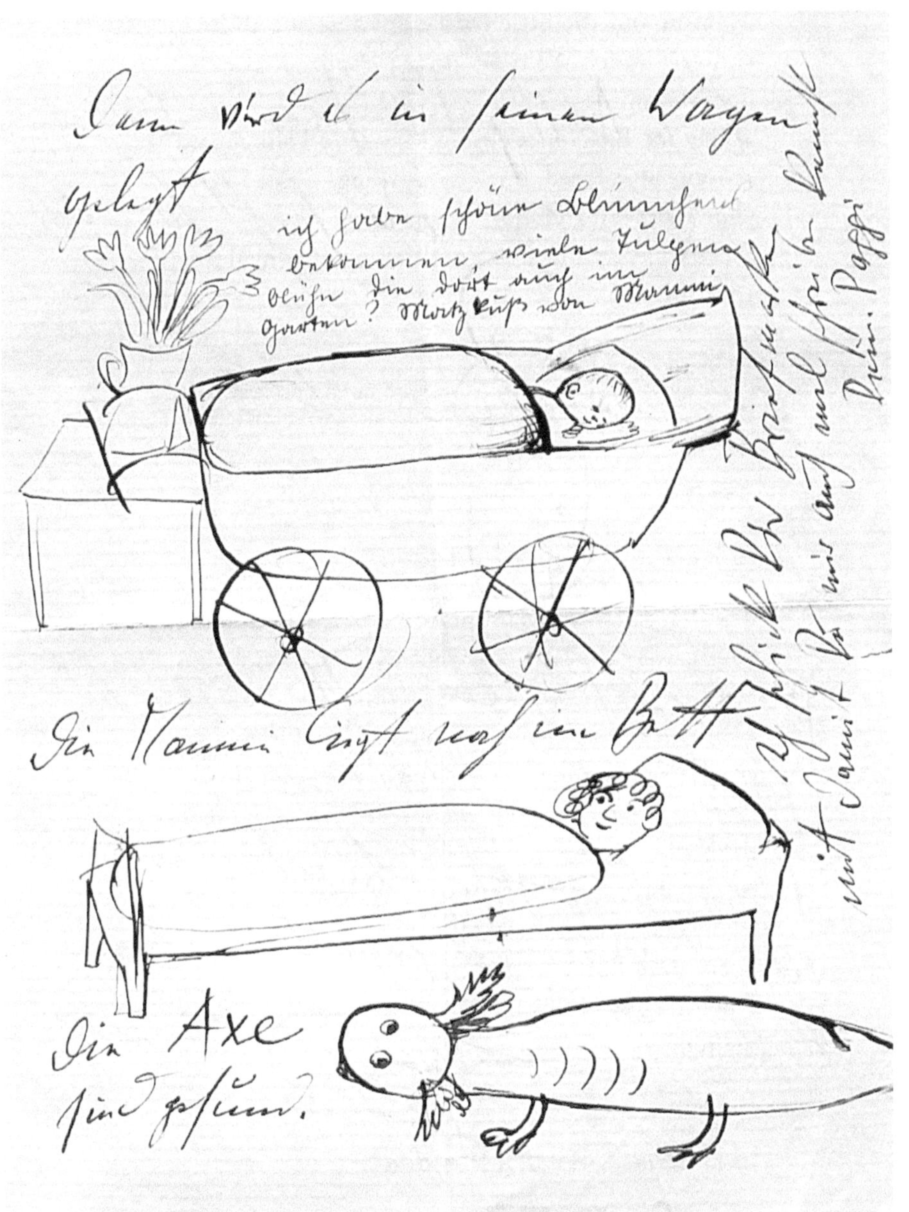

Dann wird es in seinen Wagen gelegt

ich habe schöne Blumen und bekommen, einen Tulpen
blühen die dort auch im Garten? Moritz kuss von Mammi

Die Mammi liegt noch im Bett

Die Axe sind gesund.

Ich schick Dir Briefmarken
und damit Du mir auch mal schreiben
Dein Pappi

Mammi and the little laddie, because we all love you very much. Your [*drawing*] Pappi
For Mammi
Today the Saxons celebrate May 1st, all shops and schools are closed, but I'm working. Shall I send your swimsuit to Ddorf [Dusseldorf]?
I love you very much & am thinking of you all the time
Your Jim

Drawing: Lorenz NSK 8.7.19
Mailed by Dix to St. Goar, where Nelly was with the grandparents when Ursus was born in Dresden. Apparently, Martha also then traveled there to recuperate.

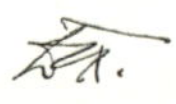

To Martha [1927 | Dresden]

dear Mutzlein & Mammische Enclosed are your cards. The lad's day went well, except for the fact that the lad did not want to fall asleep at night, I kept after him until about 8:30. Then Griebel arrived, & we drank wine and the boy kept an eye on us 'til 9 o'clock. Be well, recuperate nicely, & greet the Kaufmanns. Yesterday aftern. I didn't get around to drawing, the mouse is too much work for me.
Many Matzkisses
Ever yours Jim
The little guy is sitting next to me, rocking, & says "mam mam"

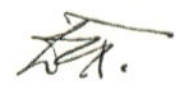

To Martha [1927 | Dresden]

My dearest Darling it's naughty of you that you have not even written me whether and how you arrived. Everything's all right here at home.

The boy is chubby and healthy, caca beautifully golden to stone ocher, shshsh available in sufficient quantities. I came home unexpectedly yesterday afternoon at 2 o'clock & everything was fine. Last night I was at the Grohmanns; they send best wishes. Reichel, the artist, was still there and a Frl. Hoihen [*illegible*]. I didn't go to the premiere — too worn out. On another day we visited Spiro and Leo von König, who had come down especially from Bln [Berlin] for the premiere. This morning I didn't weigh the lad because Hulda only woke me at 10:30. Today, it's very dark and snowing. I'll weigh him tomorrow. The boy is a little bit [*illegible*] & drools a lot, probably the teeth. Just imagine, I've bought a new pair of shoes. Rubber.

Had the gilding done on my picture, *Maldoror*. Not very nice, but it's going to get painted over again anyhow. It's very boring without you, and sleeping alone isn't nice, either. Say hello to the Kaufmanns & Kochs and have fun and recoup well. The beautiful tourmaline (Pragerstr.) costs 600 Mk, is set in platinum. Unfortunately, a little too expensive for me. Many beautiful kisses Ever Your Jim

Hans Reichel (1892–1958) was a painter and draftsman.

To Martha [1927 | Dresden]

My Dearest I thank you for your beautiful letter and for the medical advice. I nevertheless went to Dr. Steiner & was given a thorough examination. He ran a long tube into my stomach. After that

I had to suck down a big glassful of thick bolus mash [?] & was x-rayed. From tomorrow on, I need to live on a strict vegetarian diet for three weeks [?] and will be examined again on Saturday. The lad is a funny little guy; he constantly wants to stand up and gets upset when one keeps him from doing so. Since he had some grey caca on Sunday, I have prepared a grits diet for yesterday; he's also taken castor oil. Today he's eaten properly again. Imagine, he no longer wants to be swung (head down) through the air. He cries and has the greatest expression of horror when I simply touch him on the legs. I had to give up this exercise as a result. On Sunday there was a big gathering at Grohmann's; the painters Reichel, Griebel, & my student Hopta [?]. Yesterday evening we were invited to the Albikers. The [*illegible*] (dancer) gave a lecture on dance at the Academy & afterwards Albiker invited guests. There was good wine, soup, fish and cheese. Frau Albiker would be delighted if we came to see them again. I am slowly but surely working on my big picture. My studio stuff from Berlin has arrived. Freight and packaging costs were 184 Mk. Aside from getting rid of your doctors, hopefully you're still feeling cheerful & fun & drinking some good wine. If I just spend one day taking care of the boy, I soon realize how stressful it is and how capable you are given that you can still get other things done along the way. I'm certainly not getting much done in terms of painting, but rather constantly have to find some way to entertain the boy. I've also written a letter to Nelly. My Dearest, I always think of you; write me whether or not the living is good there & whatever you are doing. I keep you in my heart   Your Jim

The "big picture" that Dix was working on was the *Großstadt* [Metropolis] triptych (Löffler 1928/1).

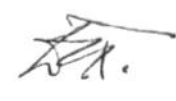

To Martha [1927 | Dresden]

My dear heart! I sent you a *long* letter on Tuesday, but you must have received it on Thursday at the latest. Meanwhile, a lad-chasing-Wednesday is over. In the evening Griebel, Johannson, Lachnit were here to visit me & we drank some very good wine that Johansson had brought along. A basket of apples from St. Goar arrived, which I put in the small room. Otherwise everything is going quite well, somewhat whiny. Incidentally, he's not quite as patient as before and sometimes expresses that he wants something else with wild screaming, or by tearing up a book, for instance. Yesterday he whistled; that was so funny.

Tonight I'm going to Grohmann's and on Saturday to Fritz Bienert's — take good care & send regards to the Koch's, the children, and the Kaufmann's. Maybe you ought to give Dr. Hesse a call.
Many greetings & kisses
Otto

Dr. Julius Hesse, factory owner from Dusseldorf. See also letters to Martha from 1926.

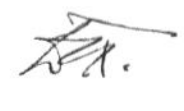

To the Academy of Fine Arts Dresden April 26, 1927 [Berlin] [T]

taking work as a result move not before third may
= dix

HfBK, Archives, Dix letters, № 23

To Herr Henninger July 5, 1927 [PM Gera] [Dresden]

Dear Stadtverwaltungsdirektor
[City Administrative Director],
acknowledging your letter of June 27, '27, I inform you that I am willing to send, under the conditions you mention, a collection of my pictures for the autumn exhibition. I'm thinking roughly 10 paintings & 10 watercolors.
Yours faithfully
I remain Yours sincerely Otto Dix
Academy of Applied Arts
Dresden

City Archives, Gera
Autumn Exhibition of the Artists' Association Thuringia.
The acquisition of work was cited as a "condition."

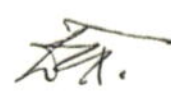

To Herr Henninger Spt. 15, '27 | Dresden

Dear Sir
In your letter of 27 June of t.y., you assured me, inter alia, a purchase of 400–500 Mk. Meanwhile, my exhibition as I hear, has already opened. Since a part of the works exhibited there no longer belongs to me, but to the art dealer, I ask you kindly to wait a few more days before the actual purchase. I'll be coming to Gera on Friday this week & bring with me a number of recent works that were intended for the exhibition. I trust that I'll have the pleasure of meeting you on the above-mentioned days in Gera.
Yours faithfully
respectfully Otto Dix

City Archives, Gera
The very next day, Dix arrived in Gera. The city made an acquisition of three watercolors for 700 Mk (City Archives, Gera).

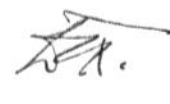

To Maud Grosz, attached to a letter from Martha Dix to Frau Grosz [09.28.1927 | Dresden]

I heard you no longer will be coming to Germany and George is already a Cavalier de Légion de Honneur. On this end, we're hard at work moving things about [?] with or without success. Salus & au revoir Otto
We look forward to seeing you in the fall. We'll take some romantic trips to Saxon Switzerland & [will] drink wonderfully delicious Meissen wine.

AdK, Berlin, George Grosz Archives № 410

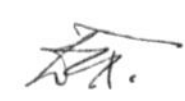

To the Lord Mayor of Gera 11.26.1927 [Dresden]

Dear Herr Dr.!
I have heard, much to my amazement, that my former art dealer Nierendorf recently visited you to negotiate on the matter of my parents' portrait with you.
I should just like to inform you that Mr. Nierendorf has not received any such order from me whatsoever. You will recall that we had already negotiated the matter. I had promised you the picture as a loan under the condition that the city ablates the amount (3000 Mk) with annual installments.

I ask you kindly to state if and when I can send the picture there. Yours faithfully, Yours sincerely
Otto Dix
Prof a.t. Art Academy Dresden

City Archives, Gera
Dix had cancelled the contract with the Galerie Nierendorf in April 1927. He had been told of the possibility of the acquisition of the *Elternbildnis II* [Portrait of Parents II] (Löffler 1924/4) by the city of Gera. On November 30, the mayor informed him that there was no agreement with the art dealer and that money for the purchase was lacking. Only works by local artists were being exclusively purchased.

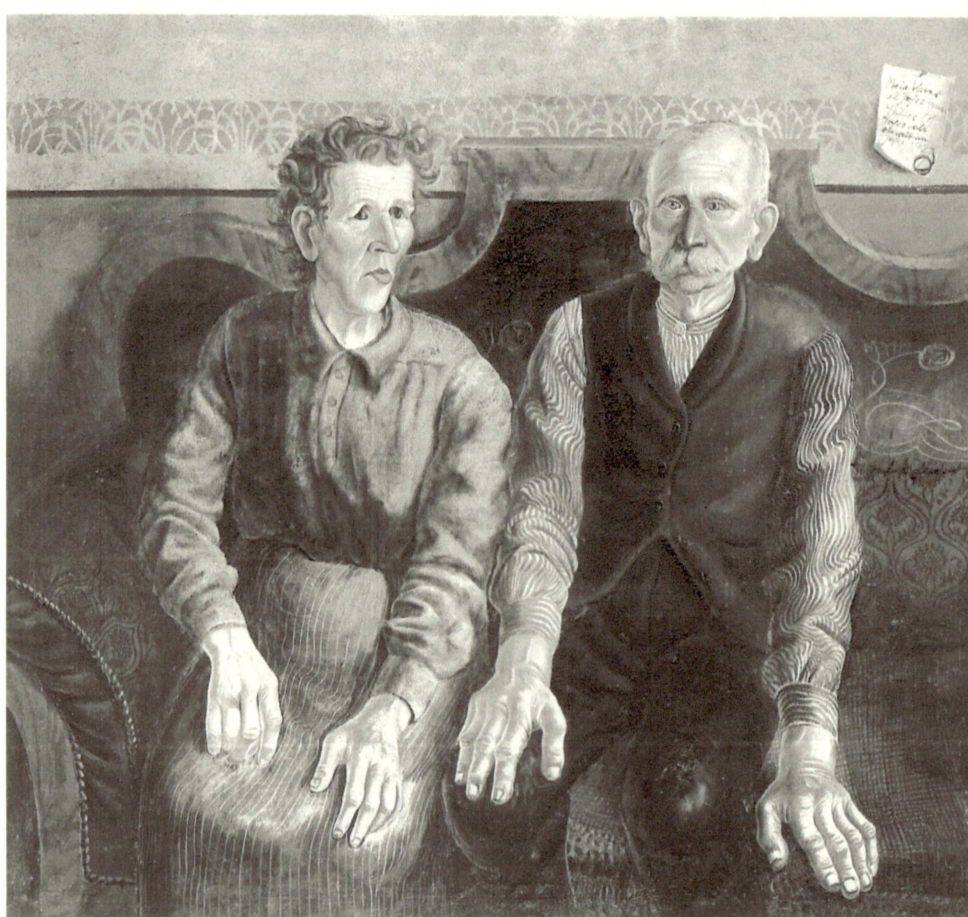

Elternbildnis II [Portrait of Parents II], 1924, painting

Object Shapes Form[1]

By Otto Dix, the well-known expressionist painter

In recent years, a certain slogan has moved through the ranks of a generation of creative artists. "Create new forms of expression!" it goes. Whether this is at all possible seems extremely doubtful to me. Standing before the paintings of the old masters, or immersing oneself in the study of their creations, may certainly lead some to agree with me.

Anyway, what's new for me in painting lies in the broader use of materials, in an intensification of those forms of expression that existed precisely with the old masters in their forms of expression. For me, at any rate, the object remains primary, & form is first given shape by the object. And that is why I've always been keenly interested to know whether I can get as close as possible to the thing that I see, because the What is much more important to me than the How! It is from the *What* that the *How* first develops!

Creating new forms of expression is the prerogative of every artist, regardless of his medium. Yet the question remains whether what he considers new is truly new. As evidence, one might take the example of the paintings that were unearthed in Egypt in the mummy excavations and which bear a striking resemblance to what is often referred to in painting as a new form of expression.

But be that as it may, true art will always strive to find possibilities of expression that go beyond the level of everyday life. What was new millennia ago, is old today, & yet in spite of that, new again. How should one decide where the old ends and the new begins — how can one say whether the new forms of expression will be overtaken by even newer ones?

1 Originally published in the *Berliner Nachtausgabe* (December 3, 1927).

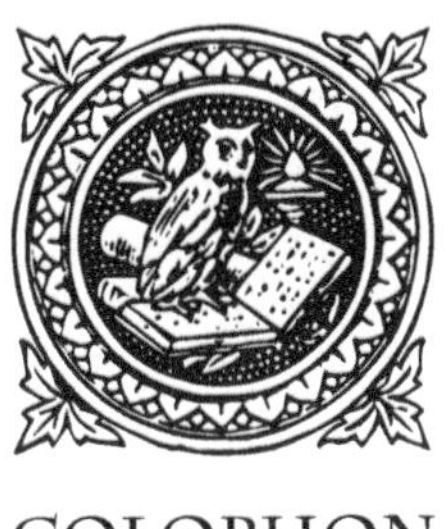

COLOPHON

LETTERS
was typeset in InDesign CC.

The text is set in *Adobe Jenson Pro.*
The titles, captions & page numbers are set in *FF Jago*
The commentaries are set in *FF Jago Office Serif*

Book design & typesetting: Alessandro Segalini
Cover design: Contra Mundum Press

LETTERS
is published by Contra Mundum Press.
Its printer has received Chain of Custody certification from:
The Forest Stewardship Council,
The Programme for the Endorsement of Forest Certification,
& The Sustainable Forestry Initiative.

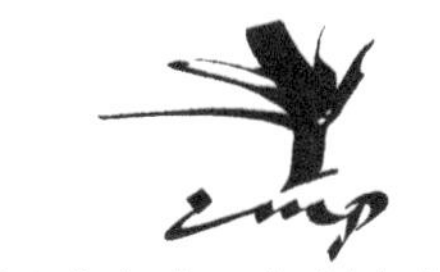

Contra Mundum Press New York · London · Melbourne

CONTRA MUNDUM PRESS

Dedicated to the value & the indispensable importance of the individual voice, to works that test the boundaries of thought & experience.

The primary aim of Contra Mundum is to publish translations of writers who in their use of form and style are *à rebours*, or who deviate significantly from more programmatic & spurious forms of experimentation. Such writing attests to the volatile nature of modernism. Our preference is for works that have not yet been translated into English, are out of print, or are poorly translated, for writers whose thinking & æsthetics are in opposition to timely or mainstream currents of thought, value systems, or moralities. We also reprint obscure and out-of-print works we consider significant but which have been forgotten, neglected, or overshadowed.

There are many works of fundamental significance to *Weltliteratur* (& *Weltkultur*) that still remain in relative oblivion, works that alter and disrupt standard circuits of thought — these warrant being encountered by the world at large. It is our aim to render them more visible.

For the complete list of forthcoming publications, please visit our website. To be added to our mailing list, send your name and email address to: info@contramundum.net

Contra Mundum Press
P.O. Box 1326
New York, NY 10276
USA

OTHER CONTRA MUNDUM PRESS TITLES

Gilgamesh
Ghérasim Luca, *Self-Shadowing Prey*
Rainer J. Hanshe, *The Abdication*
Walter Jackson Bate, *Negative Capability*
Miklós Szentkuthy, *Marginalia on Casanova*
Fernando Pessoa, *Philosophical Essays*
Elio Petri, *Writings on Cinema & Life*
Friedrich Nietzsche, *The Greek Music Drama*
Richard Foreman, *Plays with Films*
Louis-Auguste Blanqui, *Eternity by the Stars*
Miklós Szentkuthy, *Towards the One & Only Metaphor*
Josef Winkler, *When the Time Comes*
William Wordsworth, *Fragments*
Josef Winkler, *Natura Morta*
Fernando Pessoa, *The Transformation Book*
Emilio Villa, *The Selected Poetry of Emilio Villa*
Robert Kelly, *A Voice Full of Cities*
Pier Paolo Pasolini, *The Divine Mimesis*
Miklós Szentkuthy, *Prae, Vol. 1*
Federico Fellini, *Making a Film*
Robert Musil, *Thought Flights*
Sándor Tar, *Our Street*
Lorand Gaspar, *Earth Absolute*
Josef Winkler, *The Graveyard of Bitter Oranges*
Ferit Edgü, *Noone*
Jean-Jacques Rousseau, *Narcissus*
Ahmad Shamlu, *Born Upon the Dark Spear*
Jean-Luc Godard, *Phrases*

SOME FORTHCOMING TITLES

Pierre Senges, *The Major Refutation*
Maura Del Serra, *Ladder of Oaths*
Hugo Ball, *Letters*

www.ingramcontent.com/pod-product-compliance
Lightning Source LLC
LaVergne TN
LVHW091637100826
845152LV00005B/80

* 9 7 8 1 9 4 0 6 2 5 1 8 8 *